ACCOUNTING:
The Language of Business
Second Edition

Sidney Davidson, Ph.D., CPA
Arthur Young Professor of Accounting
The University of Chicago

James S. Schindler, Ph.D., CPA
Professor of Accounting
The State University of New York at Buffalo

Clyde P. Stickney, D.B.A., CPA
Associate Professor of Accounting
The University of North Carolina at Chapel Hill

Roman L. Weil, Ph.D., CPA, CMA
Professor of Accounting
University of Chicago

Thomas Horton and Daughters, Inc. / 22 Appleton Place / Glen Ridge, New Jersey 07028

For Our Children

ISBN 0-913878-08-1

Library of Congress Cataloging in Publication Data

Davidson, Sidney 1919-
   Accounting: the language of business, second edition

1. Accounting—Terminology. 2. Accounting.

I. Schindler, James Schwartz, 1917-   joint author.
II. Stickney, Clyde P., 1944-   joint author.
III. Weil, Roman Lee, 1940-   joint author.
IV. Title.

HF5621.D28   657.03   75-5974

Typography by Kathryn Bailey Composition Service
Atlanta, Georgia

Printed by R. R. Donnelley & Sons
Crawfordsville, Indiana, U.S.A.
Robert Ewing, Sales Representative
Ken Loerzel, Operator

Preface

The study of accounting is both difficult and rewarding. Part of the difficulty stems from accounting's use of a specialized vocabulary. Unlike many technical areas, however, accounting's vocabulary consists of many words that have other meanings in ordinary usage. Understanding the concepts and using accounting reports requires that the reader know how to interpret the words used and their special meaning. The student of accounting and the reader of accounting reports will find the tasks easier the sooner he or she learns, for example, the difference between the meanings of *revenue* and *receipt,* between *expense* and *expenditure,* and between *fund* and *reserve.* The purpose of the glossary is to define just how these and some 1,300 other terms (30 percent more than in the first edition) are used or should be used, when describing an accounting event or reporting the results of that event. Because understanding the process of accounting is so essential to the understanding of business, the glossary should prove useful to other functional areas of business as well.

A glossary is not a dictionary so that we have given definitions of terms only as they are, or should be, used in accounting.

Students and readers of financial reports will not encounter all the terms in the glossary. We have tried to include, however, all the terms that are used in a wide range of textbooks, problems, financial reports, financial periodicals and newspapers. Many textbook writers, not excluding ourselves, often include terms in problems that have not been carefully explained in the text preceding the problem. We suspect that students will find the glossary particularly useful in understanding what the problems in a textbook are attempting to ask.

Many words and phrases in the glossary are defined in terms of other entries in the glossary. Terms in a given definition that are themselves explained elsewhere are *italicized.* Many of the entries in the glossary are multiple-word phrases because much of the specialized terminology of accounting depends upon such phrases. We have tried to anticipate the most likely phrase that will occur to the reader and have used that phrase in the glossary. Nevertheless, we probably have failed in some cases to put the explanation by the word or phrase that occurs to you. Words and phrases are alphabetized using the letter-by-letter principle, not the word-by-word principle. Thus, the following terms are defined in the order shown: *fund, fund balance, funded, funding, funds, funds provided by operations, funds statement.*

WE ARE PROFIT-ORIENTED and are eager to learn from you how we can make the book more successful. We will pay the first person who makes a given suggestion incorporated in subsequent editions. Such suggestions might include typographical errors ($.50), additional cross references ($.50), errors of fact or substance ($1), and additional terms requiring explanation ($1).

There are a few words in accounting, most notably *cost* and *expense,* that mean different things to different people. Our own notions of learning lead us to the conclusion that the more precise the meaning of the words used, the easier is the understanding of accounting. Consequently, we give the restricted definition of, for example, *cost* that we think enhances the user's ability to understand but we also give the variants in meaning often used in practice. Further, certain terms used widely in the accounting profession, for example, *prepaid expenses,* seem to us to be self-contradictory given our preference for restricted and unambiguous definitions. We point out these contradictions knowing that many people, nevertheless, use these terms.

In addition, this book contains the following sections which we think useful for learning accounting and interpreting accounting statements.

1. Accounting Magic. This example shows how generally accepted accounting principles allow a range of accounting treatments so that two firms, exactly alike in all respects except for their accounting methods, can report drastically different incomes.

2. General Electric Company's annual report. GE's annual report is consistently among the best published. We reproduce GE's annual report issued in 1975 along with our own comments and notes which should help in understanding it and, we hope, other financial statements as well.

3. Inflation Accounting. In 1975 the Financial Accounting Standards Board proposed requiring that excerpts from general price level adjusted accounting statements be included in all annual reports issued in the near future. These new statements attempt to show the effects of inflation on the conventional statements. We explain the nature of these statements, show our estimates of general price level adjusted statements for the General Electric Company, and highlights from estimated general price level adjusted statements for 64 other companies. See also **6** below.

4. Penn Central Transportation Company's annual report just before its bankruptcy. One of the most widely known bankruptcies, and one of the largest, was that of the Penn Central. We reproduce excerpts from that report so that the reader can see the limitations of analyzing the stockholders' equity section of the balance sheet in forecasting bankruptcy. The annual report shows retained earnings of almost half a billion dollars and stockholders' equity of almost $2 billion. Yet soon after the report was issued, the company petitioned for bankruptcy because it could not meet its obligations.

5. An annual report for the U.S. Government. The government does not account for its operations in the same way that a corporation does. *Fortune* magazine compiled financial statements for the government based on the accounting that corporations use. We reproduce, with permission, modified versions of those statements along with our own comments and explanations so that the reader can learn about the fiscal operations of the federal government.

6. Supplementary Price Level Adjusted Financial Information for the Shell Oil Company. During 1975 Shell Oil Company published supplementary general price level adjusted financial information. This is the kind of information that the Financial Accounting Standards Board proposes to require. Shell's disclosure is typical, although somewhat more comprehensive, than is required to meet the FASB proposal.

7. Excerpts from the Annual Report of Sears, Roebuck and Co. We include the income statement, balance sheet, and some of the notes to financial statements from the Sears annual report issued in 1975. These excerpts are particularly interesting because of Sears' enormous amount of current liability for deferred taxes arising out of sales accounted for on the sales basis for financial statements but on the cash collection (installment) basis for tax returns. This "current liability" for $782 million is likely never to be paid. We think this item should be considered to be a part of shareholders' equity; including it in shareholders' equity, contrary to generally accepted accounting principles, would increase shareholders' equity by about 15 percent.

8. Balance Sheet and Statement of Changes in Stockholders' Equity for Caterpillar Tractor Co. Caterpillar is the only major company we know of which discloses all causes of changes in stockholders' equity since incorporation (more than 50 years ago). This interesting statement is reproduced, along with the balance sheet, to emphasize that the amount stockholders' equity, which Caterpillar calls *ownership,* is independently derived in double-entry record keeping; it is not merely a residual or plug.

We also include a list of pronouncements governing generally accepted accounting principles and their dates of issuance. We also list the presidents and directors of research of the American Accounting Association.

We gratefully acknowledge the permission of The Dryden Press to reproduce material from our *Fundamentals of Accounting,* and *Financial Accounting: An Introduction to Concepts, Methods, and Uses,* published by them. We thank the General Electric Company, Penn Central Company, Shell Oil, Sears, Caterpillar, and *Fortune* magazine for their material. Kathryn Bailey and Eli Worman designed the book and planned the layout. We thank them for their help.

TABLE OF CONTENTS

Glossary

A

AAA. *American Accounting Association.*

Abacus. A scholarly journal containing articles on theoretical aspects of accounting. Published twice a year by the Sydney University Press, Sydney, Australia.

abnormal spoilage. Actual spoilage exceeding that expected to occur under normal operating efficiency. Spoilage that should not occur if operations are normally efficient. Usual practice treats this cost as an *expense* of the period rather than as a *product cost*. Contrast with *normal spoilage.*

absorption costing. The generally accepted method of *costing* which assigns *manufacturing costs,* both *fixed* and *variable,* to units produced. Sometimes called "full costing." Contrast with *direct costing.*

accelerated depreciation. Any method of calculating *depreciation* charges where the charges get progressively smaller. Examples are *double-declining-balance* and *sum-of-the-years'-digits* methods.

acceptance. A written promise to pay which is equivalent to a promissory *note.*

account. Any device for accumulating additions and subtractions relating to a single *asset, liability, owners' equity* item, *revenue, expense,* and so on.

accountancy. The British word for *accounting;* in the United States, it is used to mean the theory and practice of accounting.

Accountants' Index. A publication of the *AICPA* which indexes, in detail, the accounting literature of the period. Issued quarterly since 1974, but less frequently before then.

accountant's report. *Auditor's report.*

accounting. An *information system* conveying information about a specific *entity.* The information is in financial terms and is restricted to information that can be made reasonably precise. The *AICPA* defines accounting as a service activity whose "function is to provide quantitative information, primarily financial in nature, about economic entities that is intended to be useful in making economic decisions."

accounting changes. As defined by *APB Opinion* No. 20, a change in (a) an *accounting principle* (such as a switch from *FIFO* to *LIFO* or from *sum-of-the-years'-digits* to *straight-line deprecia-*

NOTE: Certain terms in the definitions are *italicized.* The *italicized* terms, or variants of them, are themselves explained in the glossary.

tion), (b) an accounting estimate (such as estimated useful lives or salvage value of depreciable assets and estimates of *warranty* costs or *uncollectible accounts*), and (c) the reporting *entity.* Changes of type (a) should be disclosed along with both the cumulative effect on *retained earnings* at the start of the period during which the change was made and the cumulative effect on the reported earnings for the period of change. Changes of type (b) should be treated as affecting only the period of change and, if necessary, future periods. The reasons for changes of type (c) should be disclosed and, in statements reporting on operations of the period of the change, the effect of the change on all other periods reported on for comparative purposes should also be shown. In some cases (such as a change from *LIFO* to other inventory *flow assumptions* or in the method of accounting for long-term construction contracts), changes of type (a) are treated like changes of type (c). That is, for these changes all statements shown for prior periods must be restated to show the effect of adopting the change for those periods as well.

accounting conventions. Methods or procedures used in accounting. This term tends to be used when the method or procedure has not been given official authoritative sanction by a pronouncement of a group such as the *APB, FASB,* or *SEC.* Contrast with *accounting principles.*

accounting cycle. The sequence of accounting procedures starting with *journal entries* for various transactions and events and ending with the *financial statements* or, perhaps, the *post-closing trial balance.*

accounting entity. See *entity.*

accounting equation. *Assets = Equities. Assets = Liabilities + Owners' Equity.*

accounting errors. Arithmetic errors and misapplications of *accounting principles* in previously published financial statements that are corrected with direct *debits* or *credits* to *retained earnings.* In this regard, they are treated like *prior-period adjustments,* but, technically, they are not classified by *APB Opinion* No. 9 as prior-period adjustments. See *accounting changes* and contrast with changes in accounting estimates as described there.

accounting event. Any occurrence that is recorded in the accounting records.

Accounting Magic. An illustration presented in another section of this book. Cross references to examples in *Accounting Magic* mean for you to look at that section for further illustration and explanation.

accounting methods. *Accounting principles.* Procedures for carrying out accounting principles.

accounting period. The time period for which *financial statements* which measure *flows,* such as the *income statement* and the *statement of changes in financial position,* are prepared. Should be clearly identified on the financial statements.

accounting policies. *Accounting principles.*

accounting principles. The concepts that determine the methods or procedures used in accounting for *transactions* or events reported in the *financial statements.* This term tends to be used when the method or procedure has been given official authoritative sanction by a pronouncement of a group such as the *APB, FASB,* or *SEC.* Contrast with *accounting conventions.*

Accounting Principles Board. See *APB.*

accounting procedures. See *accounting principles,* but usually this term refers to the methods prescribed by accounting principles.

accounting rate of return. Income for a period divided by average investment during the period. Based on income, rather than discounted cash flows and, hence, is a poor decision-making aid or tool.

Accounting Research Bulletin (ARB). The name of the official pronouncements of the former *Committee on Accounting Procedure* of the *AICPA.* Fifty-one bulletins were issued between 1939 and 1959. ARB No. 43 summarizes the first forty-two bulletins.

Accounting Research Study. One of a series of studies published by the Director of Research of the *AICPA* "designed to provide professional accountants and others interested in the development of accounting with a discussion and documentation of accounting problems." Fifteen such studies were published between 1961 and 1974.

The Accounting Review. Scholarly publication of the *American Accounting Association,* which appears four times a year.

Accounting Series Release. See *SEC.*

accounting standards. *Accounting principles.*

Accounting Trends and Techniques. An annual publication of the *AICPA* which surveys the reporting practices of 600 large corporations. It presents tabulations of specific practices, terminology, and disclosures along with illustrations taken from individual annual reports.

account payable. A *liability* representing an amount owed to a *creditor,* usually arising from purchase of *merchandise* or materials and supplies; not necessarily due or past due.

account receivable. A claim against a *debtor* usually arising from sales or services rendered; not necessarily due or past due.

accounts receivable turnover. *Net sales* on account for a period divided by the average balance of net accounts receivable. See *ratio.*

accretion. Increase in economic worth through physical change, usually said of a natural resource such as an orchard, caused by natural growth. Contrast with *appreciation.*

accrual. Recognition of an *expense* (or *revenue*) and the related *liability* (or *asset*) that is caused by an *accounting event,* frequently by the passage of time, and that is not signaled by an explicit cash transaction. For example, the recognition of interest expense or revenue at the end of a period even though no explicit cash transaction is made at that time.

accrual basis of accounting. The method of recognizing *revenues* as *goods* are sold (or delivered) and as *services* are rendered, independent of the time when cash is received. *Expenses* are recognized in the period when the related revenue is recognized independent of the time when cash is paid out. Contrast with the *cash basis of accounting.*

accrued. Said of a *revenue (expense)* that has been earned (recognized) even though the related *receivable (payable)* is not yet due. This adjective should not be used as part of an account title. Thus, we prefer to use Interest Receivable (Payable) as the account title, not Accrued Interest Receivable (Payable). See *matching convention.*

accrued depreciation. An inferior term for *accumulated depreciation.* See *accrued.*

accrued payable. A *payable* usually resulting from the passage of time. For example, *salaries* and *interest* accrue as time passes. See *accrued.*

accrued receivable. A *receivable* usually resulting from the passage of time. See *accrued.*

accumulated depreciation. A preferred title for the *contra-asset* account that shows the sum of *depreciation* charges on an asset since it was acquired. Other titles used are *allowance* for *depreciation* (acceptable term) or *reserve* for *depreciation* (poor term).

accurate presentation. The qualitative accounting objective suggesting that information reported in financial statements should correspond as precisely as possible with the economic effects underlying transactions and events. See *fair presentation* and *full disclosure.*

acid test ratio. Sum of *(cash, marketable securities, and receivables)* divided by *current liabilities.* Some non-liquid receivables may be excluded from the numerator. Often called the *quick ratio.* See *ratio.*

acquisition cost. Of an *asset,* the net *invoice* price plus all *expenditures* to get the asset in place for its intended use. The other expenditures might include legal fees, transportation charges, and installation costs.

activity accounting. *Responsibility accounting.*

activity-based depreciation. *Production method* of *depreciation.*

actual cost (basis). *Acquisition* or *historical cost.*

actuarial. Usually said of computations or analyses that involve both *compound interest* and *probabilities.* Sometimes the term is used if only one of the two is involved.

additional paid-in capital. An alternative acceptable title for *capital contributed in excess of par (or stated) value.*

adequate disclosure. *Fair presentation* of *financial statements* requires *disclosure* of *material items.* This *auditing standard* does not, however, require publicizing all information detrimental to a company. For example, the company may be threatened with a lawsuit and disclosure might seem to require a *debit* to a *loss* account and a *credit* to an *estimated liability*. But the mere making of this entry might adversely affect the actual outcome of the suit. Such impending suits need not be disclosed.

adjunct account. An *account* that accumulates additions to another account. For example, Premium on Bonds Payable is adjunct to the liability Bonds Payable; the effective liability is the sum of the two account balances at a given date. Contrast with *contra account*.

adjusted acquisition (historical) cost. Cost adjusted for *general* or *specific price level changes*. See also *book value*.

adjusted bank balance. The *balance* shown on the statement from the bank plus or minus appropriate adjustments, such as for outstanding checks or unrecorded deposits, to reconcile the bank's balance with the correct cash balance.

adjusted basis. The *basis* used to compute gain or loss on disposition of an *asset* for tax purposes. Also, see *book value*.

adjusted book balance of cash. The *balance* shown in the firm's account for cash in bank plus or minus appropriate adjustments, such as for *notes* collected by the bank or bank service charges, to reconcile the account balance with the correct cash balance.

adjusted trial balance. *Trial balance* taken after *adjusting entries* but before *closing entries*. Contrast with *pre-* and *post-closing trial balances*.

adjusting entry. An entry made at the end of an *accounting period* to record a *transaction* or other *accounting event,* which for some reason has not been recorded or has been improperly recorded during the accounting period.

adjustment. A change in an *account* produced by an *adjusting* entry. Sometimes the term is used to refer to the process of restating *financial statements* for *general price level changes*.

administrative expense. An *expense* related to the enterprise as a whole as contrasted to expenses related to more specific functions such as manufacturing or selling.

admission of partner. Legally, when a new partner joins a *partnership,* a new partnership comes into being. In practice, however, the old accounting records are kept in use and the accounting entries reflect the manner in which the new partner joined the firm. If the new partner merely purchases the interest of another partner, the only accounting is to change the name for one capital account. If the new partner contributes *assets* and *liabilities* to the partnership, then the new assets must be recognized with debits and the liabilities and other source of capital, with credits. See *bonus method*.

ADR. See *asset depreciation range*.

advances from (by) customers. A preferred term for the *liability* account representing *receipts* of *cash* in advance of delivering the *goods* or rendering the *service* (that will cause *revenue* to be recognized). Sometimes called "deferred revenue" or "deferred income."

advances to affiliates. *Loans* by a parent company to a *subsidiary*. Frequently combined with "investment in subsidiary" as "investments and advances to subsidiary" and shown as a *noncurrent asset* on the parent's *balance sheet*.

advances to suppliers. A preferred term for *disbursements* of cash in advance of receiving *assets* or *services*.

affiliated company. Said of a company controlling or controlled by another company.

after closing. *Post-closing;* said of a *trial balance*.

after cost. Said of *expenditures* to be made subsequent to *revenue* recognition. For example, *expenditures* for *repairs* under warranty are after costs. Proper recognition of after costs involves a debit to expense at the time of the sale and a credit to an *estimated liability*. When the liability is discharged, the debit is to the estimated liability and the credit is to the assets used up.

agent. One authorized to transact business, including executing contracts, for another.

aging accounts receivable. The process of classifying *accounts receivable* by the time elapsed since the claim came into existence for the purpose of estimating the amount of uncollectible accounts receivable as of a given date. See *sales, uncollectible accounts adjustment* and *allowance for uncollectibles*.

AICPA. American Institute of Certified Public Accountants. The national organization that represents *CPA*'s. It oversees the writing and grading of the Uniform CPA Examination. Each state, however, sets its own requirements for becoming a CPA in that state. See *certified public accountant*.

all capital earnings rate. Net *income* plus interest charges, net of tax effects, plus minority interest divided by average total assets. Perhaps the single most useful ratio for assessing management's performance. See *ratio*.

all financial resources. All *assets* less all *liabilities*. Sometimes the *statement of changes in financial position* explains the changes in all financial resources rather than the changes in *working capital*.

all-inclusive concept. Under this concept, no distinction is drawn between *operating* and *nonoperating revenues* and *expenses* and the only entries to retained earnings are for *net income* and *dividends*. Under this concept all income, *gains,* and *losses* are reported in the *income statement;* thus, events usually reported as *prior-period adjustments* and as *corrections of errors* are included in net income. This concept is not part of *GAAP*. (See *APB Opinions* Nos. 9 and 30.)

allocate. To spread a *cost* from one *account* to several accounts, to several products, or activities, or to several periods.

allocation of income taxes. See *deferred income tax*.

allowance. A balance sheet *contra account* generally used for *receivables* and depreciable assets. See *sales* (or *purchase) allowance* for another use of this term.

allowance for uncollectibles (accounts receivable). A *contra* to Accounts Receivable that shows the estimated amount of *accounts receivable* that will not be collected. When such an allowance is used, the actual *write-off* of specific accounts receivable (*debit* allowance, *credit* specific account) does not affect *revenue* or *expense* in the period of the write-off. The revenue reduction is recognized when the allowance is credited; the amount of the credit to the allowance may be based on a percentage of sales on account for a period or determined from *aging accounts receivable*. This contra account enables an estimate to be shown of the amount of receivables that will be collected without identifying specific uncollectible accounts. See *allowance method*.

allowance method. A method of attempting to *match* all *expenses* of a transaction with its associated *revenues*. Usually involves a debit to expense and credit to an *estimated liability*, such as for estimated warranty expenditures, or a debit to a revenue (*contra*) account and a credit to an asset (*contra*) account, such as for uncollectible accounts. See *allowance for uncollectibles* for further explanation. When the allowance method is used for *sales discounts,* sales are recorded at *gross invoice* prices (not reduced by the amounts of discounts made available). An estimate of the amount of discounts to be taken is debited to a *revenue contra account* and *credited* to an allowance account, shown contra to *accounts receivable*.

American Accounting Association. An organization primarily for academic accountants, but open to all interested in accounting.

American Institute of Certified Public Accountants. See *AICPA*.

American Stock Exchange. AMEX. ASE. A public market where various corporate *securities* are traded.

AMEX. *American Stock Exchange.*

amortization. The general process of *allocating acquisition cost* of assets to the periods of benefit as *expenses*. Called *depreciation* for *plant assets, depletion* for *wasting assets* (natural resources), and amortization for *intangibles*. Also used for the process of allocating *premium* or *discount* on *bonds* and other *liabilities* to the periods during which the liability is outstanding.

analysis of changes in working capital accounts. The *statement of changes in financial position* explains the causes of the changes in *working capital* during a period. This part of the statement, which may appear in footnotes, shows the actual changes in the working capital accounts which have been explained in the main section of the statement.

analysis of variances. See *variance analysis.*

annual report. A report for stockholders and other interested parties prepared once a year; includes a *balance sheet,* an *income statement,* a *statement of changes in financial position,* a reconciliation of changes in *owners' equity* accounts, a *summary of significant accounting principles*, other explanatory *notes,* the *auditor's report,* and, perhaps, comments from management about the year's events. See *10-K.*

annuitant. One who receives an *annuity.*

annuity. A series of payments, usually made at equally spaced time intervals.

annuity certain. An *annuity* payable for a definite number of periods; contrast with *contingent annuity.*

annuity due. An *annuity* where the first payment is made at the start of period one (or at the end of period zero). Contrast with *annuity in arrears.*

annuity in advance. An *annuity due.*

annuity in arrears. An *ordinary annuity* where the first payment occurs at the end of the first period.

annuity method of depreciation. See *compound interest depreciation.*

anti-dilutive. Said of a *potentially dilutive security* which will increase *earnings per share* if it is *exercised* or *converted* into common stock. In computing *primary* and *fully diluted earnings per share,* anti-dilutive securities may not be assumed to be exercised or converted and hence do not affect reported earnings per share.

APB. Accounting Principles Board of the *AICPA*. It set *accounting principles* from 1959 through 1973, issuing 31 *APB Opinions*. It was superseded by the *FASB.*

APB's. An abbreviation used for opinions of the *APB.*

APB Opinion. The name given to pronouncements of the APB that make up much of *generally accepted accounting principles;* there are thirty-one APB Opinions, issued from 1962 through 1973.

APB Statement. The *APB* issued four Statements between 1962 and 1970. The Statements were approved by at least two-thirds of the Board, but they are recommendations, not requirements. For example, Statement No. 3 (1969) suggested the publication of *general price level adjusted statements* but did not require them.

application of funds. Any transaction that reduces *working capital*. A *use of funds.*

applied cost. A *cost* that has been *allocated* to a product or activity; need not be based on actual costs incurred.

applied overhead. *Overhead costs* charged to jobs or departments.

appraisal. The process of obtaining an amount for an *asset* or *liability* that involves expert opinion rather than explicit market transactions.

appraisal method of depreciation. The periodic *depreciation* charge is the difference between the beginning and end-of-period appraised value of the *asset* if that difference is positive. If negative, there is no charge. Not generally accepted.

appreciation. An increase in economic worth caused by rising market prices for an *asset*. Contrast with *accretion.*

appropriated retained earnings. See *retained earnings, appropriated.*

appropriation. In governmental accounting, an *expenditure* authorized for a specified amount, purpose, and time.

appropriation account. In governmental accounting, an account set up to record specific authorizations to spend; it is credited with appropriation amounts and debited with *expenditures* during the period and *encumbrances* outstanding at the end of the period.

ARB. *Accounting Research Bulletin.*

arbitrage. Strictly speaking, the simultaneous purchase in one market and sale in another of a *security* or commodity in hope of making a *profit* on price differences in the different markets. Often this term is loosely used when the item sold is somewhat different from the item purchased; for example, the sale of shares of *common stock* and the simultaneous purchase of a *convertible bond* which is convertible into identical common shares.

arm's length. Said of a transaction negotiated by unrelated parties, each acting in his or her own self interest; the basis for a *fair market value* determination.

arrears. Said of *cumulative preferred stock dividends* that have not been declared on time. See *annuity in arrears* for another context.

ARS. *Accounting Research Study.*

articles of incorporation. Document filed with state authorities by persons forming a corporation. When the document is returned with a certificate of incorporation, it becomes the corporation's *charter.*

articulate. Said of the relationship between any operating statement (for example, *income statement* or *statement of changes in financial position*) and *comparative balance sheets,* where the operating statement explains (or reconciles) the change in some major balance sheet category (for example, *retained earnings or working capital*).

ASE. *American Stock Exchange;* AMEX.

assess. To value property for the purpose of property taxation; the assessment is determined by the taxing authority. To levy a charge on the owner of property for improvements thereto, such as for sewers or sidewalks.

asset. A future benefit or service potential, recognized in accounting only when a transaction has occurred. May be *tangible* or *intangible, shortterm* (current) or *long-term* (noncurrent).

asset depreciation range. ADR. The range of *depreciable lives* allowed by the *Internal Revenue Service* for a specific depreciable *asset.*

asset turnover. Ratio of net sales to average assets. See *ratio.*

at par. Said of a *bond* or *preferred stock* issued or selling at its *face amount.*

attachment. The laying claim to the *assets* of a borrower or debtor by a lender or creditor when the borrower has failed to pay debts on time.

attest. Rendering of an *opinion* by an auditor that the *financial statements* are fair. This procedure is called the "attest function" of the CPA. See *fair presentation.*

audit. Systematic inspection of accounting records involving analyses, tests, and *confirmations.* See *internal audit.*

audit committee. A committee of the board of directors of a *corporation* usually consisting of outside directors who nominate the independent auditors and discuss the auditors' work with them. If the auditors believe certain matters should be brought to the attention of stockholders, the auditors first bring these matters to the attention of the audit committee. See the GE annual report at note 84.

auditing standards. A set of ten standards promulgated by the *AICPA,* including three general standards, three standards of field work, and four standards of reporting. According to the AICPA, these standards "deal with the measures of the quality of the performance and the objectives to be attained," rather than with specific auditing procedures.

auditor. One who checks the accuracy, fairness, and general acceptability of accounting records and statements and then *attests* to them.

audit program. The procedures followed by the *auditor* in carrying out the *audit.*

auditor's opinion. *Auditor's report.*

auditor's report. The auditor's statement of the work done and an opinion of the *financial statements.* Opinions are usually unqualified ("clean"), but may be *qualified,* or the auditor may disclaim an opinion in the report. Often called the "accountant's report."

audit trail. A reference accompanying an *entry,* or *posting,* to an underlying source record or document. A good audit trail is essential for efficiently checking the accuracy of accounting entries. See *cross-reference.*

authorized capital stock. The number of *shares* of stock that can be issued by a corporation; specified by the *articles of incorporation.*

average. The arithmetic mean of a set of numbers; obtained by summing the items and dividing by the number of items.

average-cost flow assumption. An *inventory flow assumption* where the cost of units is the *weighted average* cost of the *beginning inventory* and purchases. See *inventory equation.*

avoidable cost. An *incremental* or *variable cost.*

B

bad debt. An *uncollectible account receivable;* see *sales, uncollectible accounts adjustment.*

bad debt expense. See *sales, uncollectible accounts adjustment.*

bad debt recovery. Collection, perhaps partial, of a specific account receivable previously written off as uncollectible. A *revenue,* or if the *allowance method* is used, a credit to the allowance account.

bailout period. In a *capital budgeting* context, the total time that must elapse before net accumulated cash inflows from a project including potential *salvage value* of assets at various times equal or exceed the accumulated cash outflows. Contrast with *payback period,* which assumes completion of the project and uses terminal salvage value. Bailout is superior to payback because bailout takes into account, at least to some degree, the *present value* of the cash flows after the termination date being considered. The potential salvage value at any time includes some estimate of the flows that can occur after that time.

balance. The difference between the sum of *debit* entries minus the sum of *credit* entries in an *account.* If positive, the difference is called a debit balance; if negative, a credit balance.

balance sheet. Statement of financial position

which shows *total assets = total liabilities + owner's equity.*

balance sheet account. An account that can appear on a balance sheet. A *permanent account;* contrast with *temporary account.*

bank balance. The amount of the balance in a checking account shown on the *bank statement.* Compare with *adjusted bank balance* and see *bank reconciliation statement.*

bank prime rate. See *prime rate.*

bank reconciliation schedule. A schedule that shows how the difference between the book balance of the cash in bank account and the bank's statement can be explained. Takes into account the amount of such items as checks issued that have not cleared or deposits that have not been recorded by the bank as well as errors made by the bank or the firm.

bankrupt. Said of a company whose *liabilities* exceed its *assets* where a legal petition has been filed and accepted under the bankruptcy law. A bankrupt firm is usually, but need not be, *insolvent.*

bank statement. A statement sent by the bank to a checking account customer showing deposits, checks cleared, and service charges for a period, usually one month.

base stock method. A method of inventory valuation that assumes that there is a minimum normal or base stock of goods that must be kept on hand at all times for effective continuity of operations. This base quantity is valued at *acquisition cost* of the earliest period. The method is not allowable for income tax purposes and is no longer used, but is generally considered to be the forerunner of the *LIFO* method.

basis. *Acquisition cost,* or some substitute therefor, of an asset used in computing gain or loss on disposition or retirement.

basket purchase. Purchase of a group of assets for a single price; *costs* must be assigned to each of the assets so that the individual items can be recorded in the *accounts.*

bear. One who believes that security prices will fall. Contrast with *bull.*

bearer bond. See *registered bond* for contrast and definition.

beginning inventory. Valuation of *inventory* on hand at the beginning of the accounting period.

betterment. An *improvement.*

bid. An offer to purchase; or the amount of the offer.

big bath. A *write off* of a substantial amount of costs previously treated as *assets.* Usually caused when a corporation drops a line of business that required a large investment but that proved to be unprofitable. Sometimes used to describe a situation where a corporation takes a large write off in one period in order to free later periods of gradual write offs of those amounts. In this sense it frequently occurs when there is a change in top management.

Big Eight. The eight largest *public accounting (CPA)* partnerships; in alphabetical order: Arthur Andersen & Co.; Coopers & Lybrand; Ernst & Ernst; Haskins & Sells; Peat, Marwick, Mitchell & Co.; Price Waterhouse & Co.; Touche Ross & Co.; and Arthur Young & Company.

bill. An *invoice* of charges and *terms of sale* for *goods and services.* Also, a piece of currency.

bill of materials. A specification of the quantities of *direct materials* expected to be used to produce a given job or quantity of output.

board of directors. The governing body of a corporation elected by the stockholders.

bond. A certificate to show evidence of debt. The *par value* is the *principal* or face amount of the bond payable at maturity. The *coupon rate* is the amount of interest payable in one year divided by the principal amount. Coupon bonds have attached to them coupons which can be redeemed at stated dates for interest payments. Normally, bonds are issued in $1,000 units and carry semiannual coupons.

bond conversion. The act of exchanging *convertible bonds* for *preferred* or *common stock.*

bond discount. From the standpoint of the issuer of a *bond* at the issue date, the excess of the *par value* of a bond over its initial sales price; at later dates the excess of par over the sum of (initial issue price plus the portion of discount already amortized). From the standpoint of a bondholder, the difference between par value and selling price when the bond sells below par.

bond indenture. The contract between an issuer of *bonds* and the bondholders.

bond premium. Exactly parallel to *bond discount* except that the issue price (or current selling price) is higher than *par value.*

bond redemption. Retirement of *bonds.*

bond refunding. To incur *debt,* usually through the issue of new *bonds,* intending to use the proceeds to retire an *outstanding* bond *issue.*

bond sinking fund. See *sinking fund.*

bond table. A table showing the current price of a *bond* as a function of the *coupon rate,* years to *maturity* and effective *yield to maturity* (or *effective rate*).

bonus. Premium over normal *wage* or *salary,* paid usually for meritorious performance.

bonus method. When a new partner is admitted to a *partnership* and the new partner is to be credited with *capital* in excess of the amount of *tangible* assets he or she contributes, two methods may be used to recognize this excess, say $10,000. First, $10,000 may be transferred from the old partners to the new one. This is the bonus method. Second, goodwill in the amount of $10,000 may be recognized as an asset with the credit to the new partner's capital account. This is the *goodwill method.* (Notice that the new partner's percentage of total ownership is *not* the same under the two methods.)

book. As a verb, to record a transaction. As a noun, usually plural, the *journals* and *ledgers.* As an adjective, see *book value.*

book inventory. An *inventory* amount that results, not from physical count, but from amount of initial inventory plus *invoice* amounts of purchases less invoice amounts of *requisitions* or withdrawals; implies a *perpetual method.*

bookkeeping. The process of analyzing and recording transactions in the accounting records.

book of original entry. A *journal.*

book value. The amount shown in the books or in the *accounts* for any *asset, liability,* or *owners' equity* item. Generally used to refer to the net amount of an *asset* or group of assets shown in the accounts which record the asset and reductions, such as for *amortization,* in its cost. Of a firm, the excess of total assets over total liabilities.

book value per (common) share. Common *stockholders' equity* divided by the number of shares of *common stock outstanding.*

boot. The additional money paid or received along with a used item in a trade-in or exchange transaction for another item. See *trade-in transaction.*

borrower. See *loan.*

branch. A sales office or other unit of an enterprise physically separated from the home office of the enterprise but not organized as a legally separate *subsidiary.* The term is not usually used to refer to manufacturing units.

branch accounting. An accounting procedure which enables the financial position and operations of each *branch* to be reported separately but later combined for published statements.

breakeven analysis. See *breakeven chart.*

breakeven chart. Two kinds of breakeven charts are shown on this page. The charts are based on the information for a month shown below. Revenue is $30 per unit.

Cost Classification	Variable Cost, Per Unit	Fixed Cost, Per Month
Manufacturing costs:		
Direct material	$ 4	—
Direct labor	9	—
Overhead	4	$3,060
Total manufacturing costs...	$17	$3,060
Selling, general, and administrative costs	5	1,740
Total costs.................	$22	$4,800

The cost-volume-profit graph presents the relationship of changes in volume to the amount of *profit,* or *income.* On such a graph, total-*revenue* and total *costs* for each volume level are indicated and profit or loss at any volume can be read directly from the chart. The profit volume graph does not show revenues and costs but more readily indicates profit (or loss) at various output levels.

Two caveats should be kept in mind about these graphs. Although the curve depicting *variable cost* and total cost is shown as being a straight line for its entire length, it is likely that at very low or very high levels of output, variable cost would probably be different from $22 per unit. The variable-cost figure was probably established by studies of operations at some broad central area of production, called the *relevant range.* For very low (or very high) levels of activity, the chart may not be applicable. For this reason, the total-cost

and profit-loss curves are sometimes shown as dotted lines at lower (or higher) volume levels. Second, this chart is simplified because it assumes a single-product firm. For a multi-product firm, the horizontal axis would have to be stated in dollars rather than in physical units of output. Breakeven charts for multi-product firms necessarily assume that constant proportions of the several products are sold and changes in this mixture as well as in costs or selling prices would invalidate such a chart.

breakeven point. The volume of sales required so that total *revenues* and total *costs* are equal. May be expressed in units *(fixed costs/contribution per unit)* or in sales dollars (selling price per unit × fixed costs/contribution per unit). See example at *breakeven chart.*

budget. A financial plan that is used to estimate the results of future operations. Frequently used to help control future operations.

budgetary accounts. In governmental accounting, the accounts that reflect estimated operations and financial condition, as affected by estimated

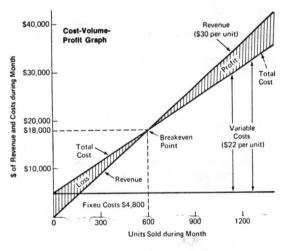

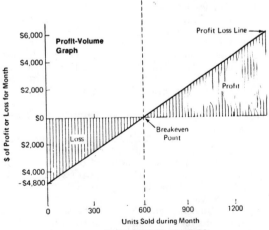

BREAKEVEN CHARTS
Cost-Volume-Profit and Profit-Volume Graphs

revenues, appropriations, and *encumbrances. Proprietary accounts* record the transactions.

budgetary control. Management of governmental (nongovernmental) unit in accordance with an official (approved) *budget* in order to keep total expenditures within authorized (planned) limits.

budgeted statements. *Pro forma* statements prepared before the event or period occurs.

bull. One who believes that security prices will rise. Contrast with *bear.*

burden. See *overhead costs.*

business combination. As defined by the *APB* in Opinion No. 16, the bringing together into a single accounting *entity* of two or more incorporated or unincorporated businesses. The *merger* will be accounted for either with the *purchase method* or the *pooling of interests method.*

business entity. *Entity. Accounting entity.*

bylaws. The rules adopted by the stockholders of a corporation that specify the general methods for carrying out the functions of the corporation.

byproduct. A *joint product* whose value is so small relative to the value of the other joint product(s) that it does not receive normal accounting treatment. The costs assigned to byproducts reduce the costs of the main product(s). Byproducts are allocated a share of joint costs such that the expected gain or loss upon their sale is zero. Thus, byproducts are shown in the *accounts* at *net realizable value.*

C

CA. *Chartered Accountant.*

callable bond. A *bond* for which the issuer reserves the right to pay a specific amount, the call price, to retire the obligation before *maturity* date. If the issuer agrees to pay more than the *face amount* of the bond when called, the excess of the payment over the face amount is the call premium.

call premium. See *callable bond.*

call price. See *callable bond.*

Canadian Institute of Chartered Accountants. The national organization that represents *Chartered Accountants* in Canada.

cancelable lease. See *lease.*

capacity. Stated in units of product, the amount that can be produced per unit of time. Stated in units of input, such as *direct labor* hours, the amount of input that can be used in production per unit of time. This measure of output or input is used in allocating *fixed costs* if the amounts producable are normal, rather than maximum, amounts.

capacity costs. *Fixed costs* in manufacturing context.

capacity variance. Standard fixed *overhead* rate per unit of normal *capacity* (or base activity) times (units of base activity budgeted or planned for a period minus actual units of base activity performed during the period). Often called a "volume variance."

capital. *Owners' equity* in a business. Often used, equally correctly, to mean the total assets of a business. Sometimes used to mean *capital assets.*

capital asset. Properly used, a designation for income tax purposes which describes property held by a taxpayer, except inventoriable *assets,* goods held primarily for sale, most depreciable property, *real estate, receivables,* certain *intangibles,* and a few other items. Sometimes this term is imprecisely used to describe *plant* and *equipment,* which are clearly not capital assets under the income tax definition. Often the term is used to refer to an *investment* in *securities.*

capital budget. Plan of proposed outlays for acquiring long-term *assets* and the means of *financing* the acquisition.

capital budgeting. The process of choosing *investment* projects for an enterprise by considering the *present value* of cash flows and deciding how to raise the funds required by the investment.

capital contributed in excess of par (or stated) value. A preferred title for the account that shows the amount received by the issuer for *capital stock* in excess of *par* (or *stated*) *value.*

capital expenditure (outlay). An *expenditure* to acquire long-term *assets.*

capital gain. The excess of proceeds over *cost,* or other *basis,* from the sale of a *capital asset* as defined by the Internal Revenue Code. If the capital asset is held more than six months before sale, then the tax on the gain is computed at a rate lower than is used for other gains and ordinary income.

capitalization of a corporation. A term used by investment analysts to indicate *stockholders' equity* plus *bonds outstanding.*

capitalization of earnings. The process of estimating the economic worth of a firm by computing the *net present value* of the predicted *net income* of the firm for the future.

capitalization rate. An *interest rate* used to convert a series of payments or receipts or earnings into a single *present value.*

capitalize. To record an *expenditure* that may benefit a future period as an *asset* rather than to treat the expenditure as an *expense* of the period of its occurrence. Whether or not expenditures for advertising or for research and development should be capitalized is controversial, but *FASB Statement* No. 2 requires expensing of *R & D* costs. We believe expenditures should be capitalized if they lead to future benefits and thus meet the criterion to be an asset.

capital loss. A negative capital gain; see *capital gain.*

capital rationing. In a *capital budgeting* context, the imposing of constraints on the amounts of total capital expenditures in each period.

capital stock. The ownership shares of a corporation. Consists of all classes of *common* and *preferred stock.*

capital structure. The composition of a corporation's equities; the relative proportions of *short-term debt, long-term debt,* and *owners' equity.*

capital surplus. An inferior term for *capital contributed in excess of par (or stated) value.*

carryback, carryforward, carryover. The use of losses or tax credits in one period to reduce income taxes payable in other periods. There are three common kinds of carrybacks: for net operating losses, for *capital losses,* and for the *investment tax credit.* The first two are applied against taxable income and the third against the actual tax. In general, carrybacks are for three years with the earliest year first. Operating losses, the investment tax credit, and the capital loss for corporations, can generally be carried forward for five years. The capital loss for individuals can be carried forward indefinitely.

carrying value (amount). *Book value.*

CASB. Cost Accounting Standards Board. A board of five members authorized by the U.S. Congress to "promulgate cost-accounting standards designed to achieve uniformity and consistency in the cost-accounting principles followed by defense contractors and subcontractors under federal contracts." The *principles* promulgated by the CASB are likely to have considerable weight in practice where the *FASB* has not established a standard.

cash. Currency and coins, negotiable checks, and balances in bank accounts.

cash basis of accounting. In contrast to the *accrual basis of accounting,* a system of accounting in which *revenues* are recognized when *cash* is received and *expenses* are recognized as *expenditures* are made. No attempt is made to *match revenues* and *expenses* in determining *income.*

cash budget. A schedule of expected cash *receipts* and *disbursements.*

cash collection basis. The *installment method* for recognizing *revenue.* Not to be confused with the *cash basis of accounting.*

cash cycle. The period of time that elapses during which *cash* is converted into *inventories,* inventories are converted into *accounts receivable,* and receivables are converted back into cash. *Earnings cycle.*

cash disbursements journal. A specialized *journal* used to record *expenditures* by *cash* and by *check.* If a *check register* is also used, the cash disbursements journal records only expenditures of currency and coins.

cash discount. A reduction in sales or purchase price allowed for prompt payment.

cash dividend. See *dividend.*

cash equivalent value. A term used to describe the amount for which an *asset* could be sold. *Market value.*

cash flow. Cash *receipts* minus *disbursements* from a given *asset,* or group of assets, for a given period.

cash flow statement. A statement similar to the typical *statement of changes in financial position* where the flows of cash, rather than of *working capital,* are explained.

cashier's check. A bank's own *check* drawn on itself and signed by the cashier or other authorized official. It is a direct obligation of the bank. Compare with *certified check.*

cash receipts journal. A special *journal* used to record all *receipts* of *cash.*

cash (surrender) value of life insurance. An amount equal, not to the face value of the policy to be paid in event of death, but to the amount that could be realized if the policy were immediately

canceled and traded with the insurance company for cash.

cash yield. See *yield.*

central corporate expenses. General *overhead expenses* incurred in running the corporate headquarters and related supporting activities of a corporation. These expenses are treated as *period expenses.* Contrast with *manufacturing overhead.*

certificate. The document that is the physical embodiment of a *bond* or a *share of stock.* A term sometimes used for the *auditor's report.*

certificate of deposit. Federal law constrains the *rate of interest* that banks can pay. Under current law banks are allowed to pay a higher rate than the one allowed on a *time deposit* if the depositor promises to leave funds on deposit for several months or more. When the bank receives such funds, it issues a certificate of deposit. The depositor can withdraw the funds before maturity if a penalty is paid.

certified check. The *check* of a depositor drawn on a bank on the face of which the bank has written the words "accepted" or "certified" with the date and signature of a bank official. The check then becomes an obligation of the bank. Compare with *cashier's check.*

certified financial statement. A financial statement attested to by an independent *auditor* who is a *CPA.*

certified public accountant (CPA). An accountant who has satisfied the statutory and administrative requirements of his or her jurisdiction to be registered or licensed as a public accountant. In addition to passing the Uniform CPA Examination administered by the *AICPA,* the CPA must meet certain educational and moral requirements that differ from jurisdiction to jurisdiction. The jurisdictions are the fifty states, the District of Columbia, Guam, Puerto Rico, and the Virgin Islands.

chain discount. A series of *discount* percentages; for example, if a chain discount of 10 and 5 percent is quoted, then the actual, or *invoice,* price is the nominal, or list, price times .90 times .95.

change fund. Coins and currency issued to cashiers, delivery drivers, and so on.

changes, accounting. See *accounting changes.*

changes in financial position. See *statement of changes in financial position.*

charge. As a noun, a *debit* to an account; as a verb, to debit.

charge off. To treat as a *loss* or *expense* an amount originally recorded as an *asset;* usually the term is used when the charge is not in accord with original expectations.

charter. Document issued by a state government authorizing the creation of a corporation.

chartered accountant (CA). The title used in Australia, Canada, and the United Kingdom for an accountant who has satisfied the requirements of the institute of his or her jurisdiction to be qualified to serve as a *public accountant.* In Canada, each provincial institute or order has the right to administer the examination and set the standards of performance and ethics for Chartered Accountants in its province. For a number of years, however, the provincial organizations have pooled their rights to qualify new members through the Inter-provincial Education Committee and the result is that there are nationally-set and graded examinations given in English and French. The pass/fail grade awarded by the Board of Examiners (a subcommittee of the Inter-provincial Education Committee) is rarely deviated from.

chart of accounts. A list of names and numbers of *accounts* systematically organized.

check. You know what a check is. The Federal Reserve Board defines a check as "a *draft* or order upon a bank or banking house purporting to be drawn upon a deposit of funds for the payment at all events of a certain sum of money to a certain person therein named or to him or his order or to bearer and payable instantly on demand." It must contain the phrase "pay to the order of." The amount shown on the check's face must be clearly readable and it must have the signature of the drawer. Checks need not be dated, although they usually are.

check register. A *journal* to record *checks* issued.

CICA. *Canadian Institute of Chartered Accountants.*

circulating capital. *Working capital.*

clean opinion. See *auditor's report.*

clean surplus concept. The notion that the only entries to the *retained earnings* account are to record net earnings and dividends. Contrast with *current operating performance concept.* This concept, with minor exceptions, is now controlling in *GAAP.* (See *APB Opinions* Nos. 9 and 30.)

clearing account. An account containing amounts to be transferred to another account(s) before the end of the *accounting period.* Examples are the *income summary* account (whose balance is transferred to retained earnings) and the purchases account (whose balance is transferred to *inventory* or to *cost of goods sold*).

close. As a verb, to transfer the *balance* of a *temporary* or *contra* or *adjunct* account to the main account to which it relates; for example, to transfer *revenue* and *expense* accounts directly, or through the *income summary* account, to an *owners' equity* account, or to transfer *purchase discounts* to purchases.

closed account. An account with equal debits and credits. See *ruling an account.*

closing entries. The entries that accomplish the transfer of balances in temporary accounts to the related balance sheet accounts.

closing inventory. *Ending inventory.*

CMA. Certificate in Management Accounting. Awarded by the Institute of Management Accounting of the *National Association of Accountants* to those who pass a set of examinations and meet certain experience and continuing education requirements.

coding of accounts. The numbering of *accounts,* as for a *chart of accounts,* which is particularly necessary for computerized accounting.

coinsurance. Insurance policies that protect against hazards such as fire or water damage often specify that the owner of the property may not collect the full amount of insurance for a loss unless the insurance policy covers at least some specified percentage, usually about 80 percent, of the *replacement cost* of the property. Coinsurance clauses induce the owner to carry full, or nearly-full, coverage.

collateral. Assets pledged by a *borrower* that will be given up if the *loan* is not paid.

collectible. Capable of being converted into cash; now, if due; later, otherwise.

commercial paper. *Short-term notes* issued by corporate borrowers.

commission. Remuneration, usually expressed as a percentage, to employees based upon an activity rate, such as sales.

Committee on Accounting Procedure. Predecessor of the *APB.* The *AICPA's* principle-promulgating body from 1939 through 1959. Its fifty-one pronouncements are called *Accounting Research Bulletins.*

common cost. *Cost* resulting from use of a facility (for example, plant or machines) or a service (for example, fire insurance) that benefits several products or departments and must be allocated to those products or departments. Many writers use common costs and *joint costs* synonymously. We feel that joint costs are more likely to arise from the physical nature of a process, whereas common cost proportions may be altered by management decisions. The difference is, however, one of degree, not of kind. See *joint costs, indirect costs,* and *overhead.*

common-dollar accounting. General *price level adjusted* accounting.

common monetary measuring unit. For U.S. corporations, the dollar. See also *stable monetary unit assumption.*

common-size statement. A *percentage statement.*

common stock. *Stock* representing the class of owners who have residual claims on the assets and earnings of a corporation after all debt and preferred stockholders' claims have been met.

common stock equivalent. A *security* whose primary value arises from its ability to be exchanged for *common shares;* includes *stock options, warrants,* and also *convertible bonds* or *convertible preferred stock* whose cash *yield* for any year within five years of issue is less than two-thirds the *prime rate* at the time of issue.

comparative statements. Financial statements showing information for the same company for different times, usually two successive years. Nearly all published financial statements are in this form. See the General Electric annual report. Contrast with *historical summary.*

compensating balance. When a bank lends funds to a customer, it often requires that the customer keep on deposit in his or her checking account an amount equal to some percentage, say 20 percent, of the loan. The amount required to be left on deposit is the compensating balance. Such amounts effectively increase the *interest rate.* The amounts of such balances must be disclosed in *notes* to the *financial statements.*

completed contract method. Recognizing *revenues*

and *expenses* for a job or order only when it is finished, except that when a loss on the contract is expected, revenues and expenses are recognized in the period where the loss is first forecast.

completed sales basis. See *sales basis of revenue recognition.*

composite depreciation. *Group depreciation* of dissimilar items.

composite life method. *Group depreciation,* which see, for items of unlike kind. The term may be used when a single item, such as a crane, which consists of separate units with differing service lives, such as the chassis, the motor, the lifting mechanism, and so on, is depreciated as a whole rather than treating each of the components separately.

compound entry. A *journal entry* with more than one *debit* or more than one *credit,* or both. See *trade-in transaction* for an example.

compounding period. The time period for which *interest* is calculated. At the end of the period, the interest may be paid to the lender or added (that is, converted) to principal for the next interest-earning period, which is usually a year or some portion of a year.

compound interest. *Interest* calculated on *principal* plus previously undistributed interest.

compound interest depreciation. A method designed to hold the *rate of return* on an asset constant. First find the *internal rate of return* on the cash inflows and outflows of the asset. The periodic depreciation charge is the cash flow for the period less the internal rate of return multiplied by the asset's book value at the beginning of the period. When the cash flows from the asset are constant over time, the method is sometimes called the "annuity method" of depreciation.

comptroller. Same meaning and pronunciation as *controller.*

confirmation. A formal memorandum delivered by the customers or suppliers of a company to its independent *auditor* verifying the amounts shown as receivable or payable.The confirmation document is originally sent by the auditor to the customer. If the auditor asks that the document be returned whether the *balance* is correct or incorrect, then it is called a "positive confirmation." If the auditor asks that the document be returned only if there is an error, it is called a "negative confirmation."

conglomerate. *Holding company.* This term is used when the owned companies are in dissimilar lines of business.

conservatism. A *reporting objective* that calls for anticipation of all *losses* and *expenses* but defers recognition of *gains* or *profits.* In the absence of certainty, events are to be reported in a way that tends to minimize current income.

consignee. See *on consignment.*

consignment. See *on consignment.*

consignor. See *on consignment.*

consistency. Treatment of like *transactions* in the same way in different periods so that financial statements will be more comparable than otherwise. The reporting policy implying that procedures, once adopted, should be followed from period to period by a reporting *entity.* See *accounting changes* for the treatment of inconsistencies.

consol. A *bond* that never matures; a *perpetuity* in the form of a bond. Originally issued by Britain after the Napoleonic wars to consolidate debt issues of that period. The term arose as an abbreviation for "consolidated annuities."

consolidated financial statements. Statements issued by legally separate companies that show financial position and income as they would appear if the companies were one legal *entity.* Such statements reflect an economic, rather than a legal, concept of the *entity.*

consumer price index (CPI). A *price index* computed and issued monthly by the Bureau of Labor Statistics of the U.S. Department of Labor. The index attempts to track the price level of a group of goods and services purchased by the average consumer. Contrast with *GNP Implicit Price Deflator.*

constructive receipt. An item is included in taxable income when the taxpayer can control funds whether or not cash has been received. For example, *interest* added to *principal* in a savings account is deemed to be constructively received.

contingent annuity. An *annuity* whose number of payments depends upon the outcome of an event whose timing is uncertain at the time the annuity is set up; for example, an annuity payable for the life of the *annuitant.*

contingent issue (securities). Securities issuable to specific individuals upon the occurrence of some event, such as the firm's attaining a specified level of earnings.

contingent liability. A potential *liability;* if a specified event were to occur, such as losing a lawsuit, a liability would be recognized. Until the outcome is known, the contingency is merely disclosed in notes rather than shown in the balance sheet accounts. A *material* contingency may lead to a qualified, *"subject to,"* auditor's opinion.

continuing appropriation. A governmental *appropriation* automatically renewed without further legislative action until it is altered or revoked or expended.

continuing operations. See *income from continuing operations.*

continuity of operations. The assumption in accounting that the business *entity* will continue to operate long enough for current plans to be carried out. The *going concern assumption.*

continuous compounding. *Compound interest* where the *compounding period* is every instant of time. See *e* for how to compute the equivalent annual or periodic rate.

continuous inventory method. The *perpetual inventory* method.

contra account. An *account,* such as *accumulated depreciation,* that accumulates subtractions from another account, such as machinery. Contrast with *adjunct account.*

contributed capital. The sum of the balances in *capital stock* accounts plus *capital contributed in excess of par (or stated) value* accounts. *Owners' equity* less *retained earnings.* Contrast with *donated capital.*

contributed surplus. An inferior term for *capital contributed in excess of par value.*

contribution margin. *Revenue* from *sales* less variable *expenses.*

contribution per unit. Selling price less *variable costs* per unit.

contributory. Said of a *pension plan* where employees, as well as employers, make payments to a pension *fund.* Note that the provisions for *vesting* are applicable to the employer's payments. Whatever the degree of vesting of the employer's payments, the employee typically gets back his or her payments, with interest, in case of death, or other cessation of employment, before retirement.

control (controlling) account. A summary *account* that shows totals of entries and balances that appear in individual accounts in a *subsidiary ledger.* Accounts Receivable is a control account backed up with accounts for each customer. The balance in a control account should not be changed unless a corresponding change is made in the subsidiary accounts.

controllable cost. A *cost* whose amount can be influenced by the way in which operations are carried out.

controlled company. A company, a majority of whose voting stock is held by an individual or corporation. Effective control can sometimes be exercised when less than 50 percent of the stock is owned.

controller. The title often used for the chief accountant of an organization. Often spelled *comptroller.*

conversion. The act of exchanging a convertible security for another security.

conversion cost. *Direct labor* costs plus factory *overhead* costs incurred in producing a product. That is, the cost to convert raw materials to finished products.

conversion period. *Compounding period.*

convertible bond. A *bond* that may be converted into a specified number of shares of *capital stock.*

convertible preferred stock. *Preferred stock* that may be converted into a specified number of shares of *common stock.*

copyright. Exclusive right granted by the government to an author, composer, playright and the like for twenty-eight years (renewable for another twenty-eight years) to enjoy the benefit of a piece of written work. The *economic life* of a copyright may be considerably less than the legal life as, for example, the copyright of this book.

corporation. A legal entity authorized by a state to operate under the rules of the entity's *charter.*

correction of errors. See *accounting errors.*

cost. The sacrifice, measured by the *price* paid or required to be paid, to acquire *goods* or *services.* See *acquisition cost* and *replacement cost.* The term "cost" is often used when referring to the valuation of a good or service acquired. When "cost" is used in this sense, a cost is an *asset.* When the benefits of the acquisition (the goods or services acquired) expire, the cost becomes an expense. Some writers, however, use cost and expense as synonyms. Contrast with *expense.*

cost accounting. Classifying, summarizing, recording, reporting, and allocating current or predicted *costs.*

Cost Accounting Standards Board. See *CASB.*

cost center. A unit of activity for which *expenditures* and *expenses* are accumulated.

cost effective. Among alternatives, the one whose benefit, or payoff, divided by cost is highest. Sometimes said of an action whose expected benefits exceed expected costs whether or not there are other alternatives with larger benefit/cost ratios.

cost flow assumption. See *flow assumption.*

cost flows. Costs passing through various classifications within an entity. See *flow of costs* for a diagram.

costing. The process of determining the cost of activities, products, or services. The British word for *cost accounting.*

cost method (for investments). Accounting for an investment in the *capital stock* of another company where the investment is shown at *acquisition cost,* and only *dividends* declared are treated as *revenue.* Used if less than twenty percent of the voting stock is held by the investor.

cost method (for treasury stock). The method of showing *treasury stock* as a *contra* to all other items of *stockholders' equity* in an amount equal to that paid to reacquire the stock.

cost of capital. The average rate per year a company must pay for its *equities.* In efficient capital markets, the *discount rate* that equates the expected *present value* of all future cash flows to common stockholders with the market value of common stock at a given time.

cost of goods manufactured. The sum of all costs allocated to products completed during a period; includes materials, labor, and *overhead.*

cost of goods purchased. Net purchase price of goods acquired plus costs of storage and delivery to the place where the items can be productively used.

cost of goods sold. Inventoriable *costs* that are expensed because the units are sold; equals beginning inventory plus cost of goods purchased or manufactured minus ending inventory.

cost or market, whichever is lower. See *lower of cost or market.*

cost principle. The *principle* that requires reporting *assets* at *historical* or *acquisition cost,* less accumulated *amortization.* This principle is based on the assumption that cost is equal to *fair market value* at the date of acquisition and subsequent changes are not likely to be significant.

cost-recovery method. A method of *revenue* recognition that *credits cost* as collections are received until all costs are recovered. Only after costs are completely recovered is *profit* recognized. To be used only when the total amount of collections is highly uncertain. Contrast with the *installment method* where *pro rata* portions of all collections are credited both to cost and to profit.

cost sheet. Statement that shows all the elements comprising the total cost of an item.

cost-to-cost. The *percentage of completion method* where the estimate of completion is the ratio of costs incurred to date divided by total costs expected to be incurred for the entire project.

cost-volume-profit graph (chart). A graph that shows the relation between *fixed costs, contribution per unit, breakeven point* and *sales.* See *breakeven chart.*

coupon. That portion of a *bond* redeemable at a specified date for *interest* payments. Its physical form is much like a ticket; each coupon is dated and is deposited at a bank, just like a check, for collection or is mailed to the issuer's agent for collection.

coupon rate. Of a *bond,* the amount of annual coupons divided by par value. Contrast with *effective rate.*

covenant. A promise with legal validity.

CPA. See *certified public accountant.* The *AICPA* suggests no periods be shown in the abbreviation.

CPI. *Consumer price index.*

cr. Abbreviation for *credit.*

credit. As a noun, an entry on the right-hand side of an *account.* As a verb, to make an entry on the right-hand side of an account. Records increases in *liabilities, owners' equity,* and *revenues;* records decreases in *assets* and *expenses.* See *debit and credit conventions.* Also the ability or right to buy or borrow in return for a promise to pay later.

credit loss. The amount of *accounts receivables* that is, or is expected to become, *uncollectible.*

credit memorandum. A document used by a seller to inform a buyer that the buyer's *account receivable* is being credited (reduced) because of *errors, returns,* or *allowances.* Also, the document provided by a bank to a depositor to indicate that the depositor's balance is being increased because of some event other than a deposit, such as the collection by the bank of the depositor's *note receivable.*

creditor. One who lends.

cross-reference (index). A number placed by each *account* in a *journal entry* indicating the *ledger* account to which the entry is posted and placing in the ledger the page number of the journal where the entry was made. Used to link the *debit* and *credit* parts of an entry in the ledger accounts back to the original entry in the journal. See *audit trail.*

cross section analysis. Analysis of *financial statements* of various firms for a single period of time, as opposed to time series analysis where statements of a given firm are analyzed over several periods of time.

cumulative dividend. Preferred stock *dividends* that if not paid, accrue as a commitment which must be paid before dividends to common stockholders can be declared.

cumulative preferred stock. *Preferred* stock with *cumulative dividend* rights.

current asset. *Cash* and other *assets* that are expected to be turned into cash, sold, or exchanged within the normal operating cycle of the firm, usually one year. Current assets include *cash, marketable securities, receivables, inventory,* and *current prepayments.*

current cost. *Cost* stated in terms of current market prices rather than in terms of *acquisition cost. Current replacement cost.* See *net realizable value, current selling price.*

current fund. In governmental accounting, a synonym for *general fund.*

current funds. *Cash* and other assets readily convertible into cash. In governmental accounting, funds spent for operating purposes during the current period. Includes *general, special revenue, debt service,* and enterprise funds.

current (gross) margin. See *operating margin (based on replacement costs).*

current liability. A debt or other obligation that must be discharged within a short time, usually one year, normally by expending *current assets.*

current operating performance concept. The notion that reported *income* for a period ought to reflect only ordinary, normal, and recurring operations of that period. A consequence is that *extraordinary* and nonrecurring items are entered directly in the Retained Earnings account. Contrast with *clean surplus concept.* This concept is no longer acceptable. (See *APB Opinions* Nos. 9 and 30.)

current ratio. Sum of *current assets* divided by sum of *current liabilities.* See *ratio.*

current replacement cost. Of an *asset,* the amount currently required to acquire an identical asset (in the same condition and with the same service potential) or an asset capable of rendering the same service at a current *fair market price.* If these two amounts differ, the lower is usually used. See *reproduction cost.*

current selling price. The amount for which an *asset* could be sold as of a given time in an *arm's length* transaction, rather than in a forced sale.

current value accounting. The form of accounting where all assets are shown at *current replacement cost (entry value)* or *current selling price* or *net realizable value (exit value)* and all *liabilities* are shown at *present value.* Entry and exit values may be quite different from each other so there is no general agreement on the precise meaning of current value accounting.

customers' ledger. The *ledger* that shows accounts receivable of individual customers. It is the *subsidiary ledger* for the *controlling account,* Accounts Receivable.

D

DDB. *Double-declining-balance depreciation.*

debenture bond. A *bond* not secured with *collateral.*

debit. As a noun, an entry on the left-hand side of an *account.* As a verb, to make an entry on the left-hand side of an account. Records increases in *assets* and *expenses;* records decreases in *liabilities, owners' equity,* and *revenues.* See *debit and credit conventions.*

debit and credit conventions. The equality of the two sides of the *accounting equation* is maintained by recording equal amounts of *debits* and *credits* for each *transaction.* The conventional use of the *T-account* form and the rules for debit and credit in *balance sheet accounts* are summarized as follows.

debit memorandum

Any Asset Account

Opening Balance	
Increase	Decrease
+	–
Dr.	Cr.
Ending Balance	

Any Liability Account

	Opening Balance
Decrease	Increase
–	+
Dr.	Cr.
	Ending Balance

Any Owners' Equity Account

	Opening Balance
Decrease	Increase
–	+
Dr.	Cr.
	Ending Balance

Revenue and expense accounts belong to the owners' equity group. The relationship and the rules for debit and credit in these accounts can be expressed as follows.

Owners' Equity

Decrease	Increase
–	+
Dr.	Cr.

Expenses		Revenues	
Dr.	Cr.	Dr.	Cr.
+	–	–	+
*			*

*Normal balance prior to closing.

debit memorandum. A document used by a seller to inform a buyer that the seller is debiting (increasing) the amount of the buyer's *account receivable* because of an error. Also, the document provided by a bank to a depositor to indicate that the depositor's *balance* is being decreased because of some event other than payment for a *check,* such as monthly service charges or the printing of checks.

debt. An amount owed. The general name for *notes, bonds, mortgages,* and the like which are evidence of amounts owed.

debt-equity ratio. Total *liabilities* divided by total *equities.* See *ratio.* Sometimes the denominator is merely total *stockholders' equity.* Sometimes the numerator is restricted to long-term *debt.*

debt financing. Raising *funds* by issuing *bonds* or *notes.* Contrast with *equity financing. Leverage.*

debtor. One who borrows.

debt ratio. *Debt-equity ratio.*

debt service fund. In governmental accounting, a *fund* established to account for payment of *interest* and *principal* on all general obligation *debt* other than that payable from special *assessments.*

debt service requirement. The amount of cash required for payments of *interest,* current maturities of *principal* on outstanding *debt,* and payments to *sinking funds* (corporations) or to the *debt service fund* (governmental).

declaration date. Time when a *dividend* is declared by the *board of directors.*

declining-balance depreciation. The method of calculating the periodic *depreciation* charge by multiplying the *book value* at the start of the period by a constant percentage. In pure declining balance depreciation the constant percentage is $1 - \sqrt[n]{s/c}$ where n is the *depreciable life,* s is *salvage value,* and c is *acquisition cost.* See *double-declining-balance depreciation.*

deep discount bonds. Said of *bonds* selling much below (exactly how much is not clear) *par value.* A term sometimes used when there is a presumption that the *face amount* will not be paid at *maturity.*

defalcation. Embezzlement.

default. Failure to pay *interest* or *principal* on a *debt* when due.

deferral method. See *flow-through method* (of accounting for the *investment tax credit*) for definition and contrast.

deferred annuity. An *annuity* whose first payment is made sometime after the end of the first period.

deferred asset. *Deferred charge.*

deferred charge. *Expenditure* not recognized as an *expense* of the period when made but carried forward as an *asset* to be *written off* in future periods, such as for advance rent payments or insurance premiums.

deferred cost. *Deferred charge.*

deferred credit. Sometimes used to indicate *advances from customers.* Also sometimes used to describe the *deferred income tax liability.*

deferred debit. *Deferred charge.*

deferred expense. *Deferred charge.*

deferred gross margin. *Unrealized gross margin.*

deferred income. *Advances from customers.*

deferred income tax (liability). An *indeterminate-term liability* that arises when the pre-tax income shown on the tax return is less than what it would have been had the same *accounting principles* been used in tax returns as used for financial reporting. *APB Opinion* No. 11 requires that the firm debit income tax *expense* and credit deferred income tax with the amount of the taxes delayed by using different accounting principles in tax returns from those used in financial reports. See *timing difference* and *permanent difference.* See *installment sales.* If, as a result of timing differences, cumulative taxable income exceeds cumulative reported income before taxes, the deferred income tax account will have a *debit* balance and will be reported as a *deferred charge.*

See the *Accounting Magic* section of this book for an example calculation.

deferred revenue. Sometimes used to indicate *advances from customers*.

deferred tax. See *deferred income tax*.

deficit. A *debit balance* in the Retained Earnings account; presented on the balance sheet as a *contra* to stockholders' equity.

defined benefit plan. A *pension plan* where the employer promises specific benefits to each employee. The employer's cash contributions and pension expense are adjusted in relation to investment performance of the pension *fund*. Sometimes called a "fixed-benefit" pension plan. Contrast with *money-purchase plan*.

defined contribution plan. A *money purchase (pension) plan*.

deflation. A period of generally declining prices.

demand deposit. *Funds* in a *checking account* at a bank.

demand loan. See *term loan* for definition and contrast.

denominator volume. Capacity measured in expected number of units to be produced this period; divided into *budgeted fixed costs* to obtain fixed costs applied per unit of product.

depletion. Exhaustion or *amortization* of a *wasting asset*, or natural resource. Also see *percentage depletion*.

depletion allowance. See *percentage depletion*.

deposit, sinking fund. Payments made to a *sinking fund*.

deposits in transit. Deposits made by a firm but not yet reflected on the *bank statement*.

depreciable cost. That part of the *cost* of an asset, usually *acquisition cost* less *salvage value*, that is to be charged off over the life of the asset through the process of *depreciation*.

depreciable life. For an *asset*, the time period over which *depreciable cost* is to be allocated. For tax returns, depreciable life may be shorter than estimated *service life*.

depreciation. *Amortization* of *plant assets;* the process of allocating the cost of an asset to the periods of benefit—the *depreciable life*. Classified as a *production cost* or a *period expense*, depending upon the asset and whether *absorption* or *direct costing* is used. Depreciation methods described in this glossary include the *annuity method, appraisal method, composite method, compound interest method, declining-balance method, double-declining-balance method, production method, replacement method, retirement method, straight-line method, sinking-fund method* and *sum-of-the-years'-digits method*.

depreciation reserve. An inferior term for *accumulated depreciation*. See *reserve*. Do not confuse with a replacement *fund*.

Descartes' rule of signs. In a *capital-budgeting* context, the rule says that a series of cash flows will have a non-negative number of *internal rates of return*. The number is equal to the number of variations in the sign of the cash flow series or is less than that number by an even integer. Consider the following series of cash flows, the first occurring now and the others at subsequent yearly intervals: –100, –100, +50, +175, –50, +100. The internal rates of return are the numbers for r that satisfy the equation

$$- 100 - 100/(1 + r) + 50/(1 + r)^2 + 175/(1 + r)^3 \\ - 50/(1 + r)^4 + 100/(1 + r)^5 = 0.$$

The series of cash flows has three variations in sign: a change from minus to plus, a change from plus to minus, and a change from minus to plus. The rule says that this series must have either three or one internal rates of return; in fact, it has only one, about 12 percent. But also see *reinvestment rate*.

differential analysis. Analysis of *incremental costs*.

differential cost. *Incremental cost*.

dilution. A potential reduction in *earnings per share* or *book value* per share by the potential *conversion* of securities or by the potential exercise of *warrants* or *options*.

dilutive. Said of a *security* that would reduce *earnings per share* if it were exchanged for *common stock*.

dipping into LIFO layers. See *LIFO inventory layer*.

direct cost. Cost of *direct material, direct labor,* and *variable overhead* incurred in producing a product. See *prime cost*.

direct costing. The method of allocating costs that assigns only *variable manufacturing costs* to product and treats *fixed manufacturing costs* as *period* expenses. Sometimes called "variable costing."

direct labor (material) cost. Cost of labor (material) applied and assigned directly to a product; contrast with *indirect labor (material)*.

disbursement. Payment by *cash* or by a *check*. See *expenditure*.

DISC. Domestic International Sales Corporation. A U.S. *corporation*, usually a *subsidiary*, whose *income* is primary attributable to exports. *Income tax* on 50 percent of a DISC's income is usually deferred for a long period. Generally, this results in a lower overall corporate tax for the *parent* than would otherwise be incurred.

disclosure. The showing of facts in *financial statements, notes* thereto, or the *auditor's report*.

discontinued operations. See *income from discontinued operations*.

discount. In the context of *compound interest, bonds,* and *notes,* the difference between *face* or *future value* and *present value* of a payment. In the context of *sales* and *purchases,* a reduction in price granted for prompt payment. See also *chain discount, quantity discount,* and *trade discount*.

discounted bailout period. In a *capital budgeting* context, the total time that must elapse before discounted value of net accumulated cash flows from a project, including potential *salvage value* at various times of assets, equal or exceed the *present value* of net accumulated cash outflows. Contrast with *discounted payback period*.

discounted payback period. Amount of time over which the discounted present value of cash inflows from a project equal the discounted *present value* of the cash outflows.

discount factor. One plus the *discount rate.*

discounting a note. See *note receivable discounted* and *factoring.*

discount rate. *Interest rate* used to convert future payments to *present values.*

discounts lapsed (lost). The sum of *discounts* offered for prompt payment that were not taken (or allowed) because of expiration of the discount period. See *terms of sale.*

discovery value accounting. In exploration for natural resources, there is the problem of what to do with the expenditures for exploration. Suppose $10 million is spent to drill ten holes ($1 million each) and that nine of them are dry while one is a gusher containing oil with a *net realizable value* of $40 million. Dry-hole, or successful-efforts, accounting would *expense* $9 million and *capitalize* $1 million to be *depleted* as the oil was lifted from the ground. Full costing would expense nothing but capitalize the $10 million of drilling costs to be depleted as the oil is lifted from the single productive well. Discovery value accounting would capitalize $40 million to be depleted as the oil is lifted, with a $30 million *credit* to *income* or *contributed capital.*

Discussion Memorandum. A neutral discussion of all the issues concerning an accounting problem of current concern to the *FASB.* The publication of such a document usually implies that the FASB is considering issuing a *Statement of Financial Accounting Standards* on this particular problem. The discussion memorandum brings together material about the particular problem to facilitate interaction and comment by those interested in the matter.

dishonored note. A *promissory note* whose maker does not repay the loan at *maturity* for a *term loan,* or on demand, for a *demand loan.*

disintermediation. Federal law regulates the maximum *interest rate* that both banks and savings and loan associations can pay for *time deposits.* When free market interest rates exceed the regulated interest ceiling for such time deposits, some depositors withdraw their funds and invest them elsewhere at a higher interest rate. This process is known as "disintermediation."

distribution expense. *Expense* of selling, advertising, and delivery activities.

dividend. A distribution of *earnings* to owners of a corporation; it may be paid in cash (cash dividend), with stock (stock dividend), with property, or with other securities (dividend in kind). Dividends, except stock dividends, become a legal liability of the corporation when they are declared. Hence, the owner of stock ordinarily recognizes *revenue* when a dividend, other than a stock dividend, is declared. See also *liquidating dividend* and *stock dividend.*

dividends in arrears. Dividends on *cumulative preferred stock* that have not been declared in accordance with the preferred stock contract. Such arrearages must usually be cleared before dividends on *common stock* can be declared.

dividends in kind. See *dividend.*

dividend yield. *Dividends* declared for the year divided by market price of the stock as of a given time of the year.

divisional reporting. *Line of business reporting.*

dollar sign rules. In presenting accounting statements or schedules, place a dollar sign beside the first figure in each column and beside any figure below a horizontal line drawn under the preceding figure. See the statements in the Accounting Magic or U.S. Government annual report sections of this book for examples. The General Electric statements use a modification of this general rule.

dollar value LIFO method. A form of *LIFO* inventory accounting with inventory quantities *(layers)* measured in dollar, rather than physical, terms. Adjustments to account for changing prices are made by use of a specific price index appropriate for the kinds of items in the inventory.

Domestic International Sales Corporation. See *DISC.*

donated capital. A *stockholders' equity* account credited when contributions, such as land or buildings, are freely given to the company. Do not confuse with *contributed capital.*

double-declining-balance depreciation (DDB). *Declining-balance depreciation,* which see, where the constant percentage is $2/n$ and n is the *depreciable life* in periods. Maximum declining-balance rate permitted in the *income tax* laws.

double entry. The system of recording transactions that maintains the equality of the accounting equation; each entry results in recording equal amounts of *debits* and *credits.*

double T-account. *T-account* with an extra horizontal line showing a change in the account balance to be explained by the subsequent entries into the account, such as:

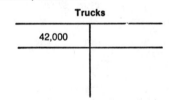

This account shows an increase in the asset account, Trucks, of $42,000 to be explained. Such accounts are useful in preparing the *statement of changes in financial position;* they are not a part of the formal record keeping process.

double taxation. Corporate income is subject to the corporate income tax and the after-tax income, when distributed to owners, is subject to the personal income tax.

doubtful accounts. *Accounts receivable* estimated to be *uncollectible.*

dr. The abbreviation for *debit.*

draft. A written order by the first party, called the drawer, instructing a second party, called the drawee (such as a bank), to pay a third party, called the payee. See also *check, cashier's check, certified check, sight draft,* and *trade acceptance.*

drawee. See *draft.*

drawer. See *draft.*

drawing account. A *temporary account* used in *sole proprietorships* and *partnerships* to record payments to owners or partners during a period.

At the end of the period, the drawing account is closed by crediting it and debiting the owner's or partner's share of income or, perhaps, his or her capital account.

drawings. Payments made to a *sole proprietor* or to a *partner* during a period. See *drawing account.*

dry-hole accounting. See *discovery value accounting* for definition and contrast.

duality. The axiom of *double-entry* record keeping that every *transaction* is broken down into equal *debit* and *credit* amounts.

dual transactions assumption (fiction). In presenting the *statement of changes in financial position,* some transactions not involving *working capital* accounts are reported as though working capital was generated and then used. For example, the issue of *capital stock* in return for the *asset,* land, is reported in the statement of changes in financial position as though stock were issued for *cash* and cash were used to acquire land. Other examples of transactions that require the dual transaction fiction are the issue of a *mortgage* in return for a noncurrent asset and the issue of stock to bondholders in return for their *bonds.*

E

e. The base of natural logarithms; 2.718281828459045.... If *interest* is compounded continuously during a period at stated rate of *r* per period, then the effective *interest rate* is equivalent to interest compounded once per period at rate *i* where $i = e^r - 1$. Tables of e^r are widely available.

earned surplus. A term once used, but no longer considered proper, for *retained earnings.*

earnings. *Income,* or sometimes *profit.*

earnings cycle. The period of time that elapses for a given firm, or the series of transactions, during which *cash* is converted into *goods* and *services,* goods and services are sold to customers, and customers pay for their purchases with cash. *Cash cycle.*

earnings per share (of common stock). *Net income* to common stockholders (net income minus *preferred dividends*) divided by the average number of *common shares* outstanding; but see also *primary earnings per share* and *fully diluted earnings per share.* See *ratio.*

earnings per share (of preferred stock). *Net income* divided by the number of *preferred shares* outstanding. This ratio indicates how well the preferred dividends are covered or protected; it does not indicate a legal share of *earnings.*

earnings, retained. See *retained earnings.*

economic entity. See *entity.*

economic life. The time span over which the benefits of an *asset* are expected to be received. The economic life of a *patent, copyright,* or *franchise* may be less than the legal life. *Service life.*

economic order quantity. In mathematical *inventory* analysis, the optimal amount of stock to order when inventory is reduced to a level called the "re-order point." If *A* represents the *incremental cost* of placing a single order, *D* represents the total demand for a period of time in units, and *H* represents the incremental holding cost during the period per unit of inventory, then the economic order quantity $Q = \sqrt{2AD/H}$. *Q* is sometimes called the "optimal lot size."

effective interest method. A systematic method for amortizing *bond discount* or *premium* that makes the *interest expense* for each period divided by the amount of the net *liability (face amount* minus *discount* or plus *premium)* at the beginning of the period equal to the *yield rate* on the bond at the time of issue. Interest expense for a period is yield rate (at time of issue) multiplied by the net liability at the start of the period. The *amortization* of discount or premium is the *plug* to give equal *debits* and *credits.* (Interest expense is a debit and the amount of coupon payments is a credit.) The bond holder makes a similar calculation.

effective (interest) rate. Of a bond, the *internal rate of return* or *yield to maturity* at the time of issue. Contrast with *coupon rate.* If the bond is issued for a price below *par,* the effective rate is higher than the coupon rate; if it is issued for a price greater than par, then the effective rate is lower than the coupon rate.

efficiency variance. A term used for the *quantity variance* for labor or *variable overhead* in a *standard cost system.*

eliminations. *Work sheet* entries to prepare *consolidated statements* that are made to avoid duplicating the amounts of *assets, liabilities, owners' equity, revenues,* and *expenses* of the consolidated *entity* when the accounts of the *parent* and *subsidiaries* are summed.

employee stock option. See *stock option.*

employer, employee payroll taxes. See *payroll taxes.*

encumbrance. In governmental accounting, an anticipated *expenditure,* or *funds* restricted for anticipated expenditure, such as for outstanding purchase orders. *Appropriations* less expenditures less outstanding encumbrances yields unencumbered balance.

ending inventory. The *cost of inventory* on hand at the end of the *accounting period,* often called "closing inventory." The cost of inventory to be carried to the subsequent period.

endorsee. See *endorser.*

endorsement. See *draft.* The *payee* signs the draft and transfers it to a fourth party, such as the payee's bank.

endorser. The *payee* of a *note* or *draft* signs it, after writing "Pay to the order of X," transfers the note to person X, and presumably receives some benefit, such as cash, in return. The payee who signs over the note is called the endorser and person X is called the endorsee. The endorsee then has the rights of the payee and may in turn become an endorser by endorsing the note to another endorsee.

enterprise. Any business organization, usually defining the accounting *entity.*

enterprise fund. A *fund* established by a governmental unit to account for acquisition, operation, and maintenance of governmental services that are supposed to be self-supporting from user charges, such as for water or airports.

entity. A person, *partnership, corporation,* or other organization. The *accounting entity* for which accounting statements are prepared may not be the same as the entity defined by law. For example, a *sole proprietorship* is an accounting entity but the individual's combined business and personal assets are the legal entity in most jurisdictions. Several affiliated corporations may be separate legal entities while *consolidated financial statements* are prepared for the group of companies operating as a single economic entity.

entity theory. The view of the corporation that emphasizes the form of the *accounting equation* that says *assets = equities.* Contrast with *proprietorship theory.* The entity theory is less concerned with a distinct line between *liabilities* and *stockholders' equity* than is the proprietorship theory. Rather, all equities are provided to the corporation by outsiders who merely have claims of differing legal standings. The entity theory implies using a *multiple-step* income statement.

entry value. The current *cost* of acquiring an asset or service at a *fair-market price. Replacement cost.*

EOQ. *Economic order quantity.*

EPS. *Earnings per share.*

EPVI. *Excess present value index.*

equalization reserve. An inferior title for the allowance account when the *allowance method* is used for such things as maintenance expenses. Periodically, maintenance *expense* is debited and the allowance is credited. As maintenance *expenditures* are actually incurred, the allowance is debited and cash or the other asset expended is credited.

equities. *Liabilities* plus *owners' equity.*

equity. A claim to *assets;* a source of assets.

equity financing. Raising *funds* by issuance of *capital stock.* Contrast with *debt financing.*

equity method. A method of accounting for an *investment* in the stock of another company in which the proportionate share of the earnings of the other company is debited to the investment account and credited to a *revenue* account as earned. When *dividends* are received, *cash* is debited and the investment account is credited. Used in reporting when the investor owns twenty percent or more of the stock of an unconsolidated company. One of the few instances where revenue is recognized without a change in *working capital.*

equity ratio. *Stockholders' equity* divided by total *assets.* See *ratio.*

equivalent production. *Equivalent units.*

equivalent units (of work). The number of units of finished goods that would require the same costs as were actually incurred for production during a period. Used primarily in *process costing* calculations.

ERISA. Employee Retirement Security Income Act of 1974. The federal law that sets *pension plan* requirements.

error accounting. See *accounting errors.*

estimated expenses. See *after cost.*

estimated liabilities. The preferred terminology for estimated costs to be incurred for such uncertain things as repairs under *warranty.* An estimated liability is shown in the *balance sheet.* Contrast with *contingent liability.*

estimated revenue. A term used in governmental accounting to designate revenue expected to accrue during a period whether or not it will be collected during the period. A *budgetary account* usually established at the beginning of the budget period.

estimated salvage value. Synonymous with *salvage value* of an *asset* before its retirement.

estimates, changes in. See *accounting changes.*

excess present value. In a *capital budgeting* context, *present value* of (anticipated net cash inflows minus cash outflows) for a project.

excess present value index. *Excess present value* divided by initial cash outlay.

except for. Qualification in *auditor's report,* usually caused by a change, approved by the auditor, from one acceptable accounting principle or procedure to another.

exchange. The generic term for a transaction (or more technically, a reciprocal transfer) between one entity and another. In another context, the name for a market, such as the New York Stock Exchange.

exchange gain or loss. The phrase used by the *FASB* for *foreign exchange gain or loss.*

exchange rate. The *price* of one country's currency in terms of another country's currency. For example, the British pound might be worth $2.30 at a given time. The exchange rate would be stated as "one pound is worth two dollars and thirty cents" or "one dollar is worth .4348 (=£1/ $2.30) pounds."

excise tax. Tax on the manufacture, sale, or consumption of a commodity.

ex-dividend. Said of a stock at the time when the declared *dividend* becomes the property of the person who owned the stock on the *record date.* The payment date follows the ex-dividend date.

exemption. A term used for various amounts subtracted from gross income to determine taxable income. Not all such subtractions are called "exemptions." See *tax deduction.*

exercise. When the owner of an *option* or *warrant* purchases the security that the option entitles him or her to purchase, he or she has exercised the option or warrant.

exercise price. See *option.*

exit value. The proceeds that would be received if assets were disposed of in an *arm's-length transaction. Current selling price. Net realizable value.*

expected value. The mean or arithmetic *average* of a statistical distribution or series of numbers.

expendable fund. In governmental accounting, a *fund* whose resources, *principal,* and earnings may be distributed.

expenditure. Payment of *cash* to obtain *goods or services.* Virtually synonymous with *disbursement,* except that disbursement is a broader term and includes payments to discharge liabilities.

expense. As a noun, the *cost* of *assets* used up in producing *revenue.* A "gone" asset; an expired cost. Do not confuse with *expenditure* or *disbursement,* which may occur before, when, or after the related expense is recognized. Use the word cost to refer to an item that still has service potential and is an asset. Use the word expense after the asset's service potential has been used. As a verb, to designate a past or current expenditure as a current expense.

expense account. An *account* to accumulate *expenses;* such accounts are closed at the end of the accounting period. A *temporary owners' equity* account. Also used to describe a listing of expenses by an employee submitted to the employer for reimbursement.

experience rating. A term used in insurance, particularly unemployment insurance, to denote changes from ordinary rates to reflect extraordinarily large or small amounts of claims over time by the insured.

expired cost. An *expense* or a *loss.*

exposure draft. A preliminary statement of the *FASB* (or *APB* between 1962 and 1973) which shows the contents of a pronouncement the Board is considering making effective.

external reporting. Reporting to stockholders and the public, as opposed to internal reporting for management's benefit. See *financial accounting* and contrast with *managerial accounting.*

extraordinary item. A *material expense* or *revenue* item characterized both by its unusual nature and infrequency of occurrence that is shown along with its income tax effects separately from ordinary income and *income from discontinued operations* on the *income statement.* A *loss* from an earthquake would probably be classified as an extraordinary item. Gain (or loss) on retirement of *bonds* is treated as an extraordinary item under the terms of *FASB Statement* No. 4.

F

face amount (value). The nominal amount due at *maturity* from a *bond* or *note.* The corresponding amount of a stock certificate is best called the *par* or *stated value,* whichever is applicable.

factoring. The process of buying *notes* or *accounts receivable* at a *discount* from the holder to whom the debt is owed; from the holder's point of view, the selling of such notes or accounts. When a single note is involved, the process is called "discounting a note."

factory. Used synonymously with *manufacturing* as an adjective.

factory burden. Manufacturing *overhead.*

factory cost. *Manufacturing cost.*

factory expense. Manufacturing *overhead.*

factory overhead. Usually an item of *manufacturing cost* other than *direct labor* or *direct materials.*

fair market price (value). Price (value) determined at *arm's length* between a willing buyer and a willing seller, each acting rationally in their own self interest. May be estimated in the absence of a monetary transaction.

fair presentation (fairness). When the *auditor's report* says that the *financial statements* "present fairly...," the auditor means that the accounting alternatives used by the entity are all in accordance with *GAAP.* In recent years, however, courts are finding that conformity with *generally acceptable accounting principles* may be insufficient grounds for an opinion that the statements are fair.

FASB. Financial Accounting Standards Board. An independent board responsible, since 1973, for establishing *generally accepted accounting principles.* Its official pronouncements are called "Statements of Financial Accounting Standards" and "Interpretations of Financial Accounting Standards." See *Discussion Memorandum.*

FASB Interpretation. An official statement of the *FASB* interpreting the meaning of *Accounting Research Bulletins, APB Opinions,* and *Statements of Financial Accounting Standards.*

favorable variance. An excess of *standard cost* over actual cost.

federal income tax. *Income tax* levied by the U.S. government on individuals and corporations.

Federal Unemployment Tax Act. See *FUTA.*

FEI. *Financial Executives Institute.*

FICA. Federal Insurance Contributions Act. The law that sets *"Social Security" taxes* and benefits.

fiduciary. Someone responsible for the custody or administration of property belonging to another, such as an executor (of an estate), agent, receiver (in *bankruptcy*), or trustee (of a trust).

FIFO. First-in, first-out; an *inventory flow assumption* by which *ending inventory* cost is determined from most recent purchases and *cost of goods sold* is determined from oldest purchases including beginning inventory. See *LISH.* Contrast with *LIFO.*

finance. As a verb, to supply with *funds* through the *issue* of stocks, bonds, notes, or mortgages, or through the retention of earnings.

financial accounting. The accounting for *assets, equities, revenues,* and *expenses* of a business. Primarily concerned with the historical reporting of the *financial position* and operations of an *entity* to external users. Contrast with *managerial accounting.*

Financial Accounting Standards Board. *FASB.*

Financial Executives Institute. An organization of financial executives, such as chief accountants, *controllers,* and treasurers, of large businesses.

financial expense. An *expense* incurred in raising *funds.*

financial position (condition). Statement of the *assets* and *equities* of a firm displayed on the *balance sheet* statement.

financial ratio. See *ratio.*

financial statements. The *balance sheet, income statement, statement of retained earnings, statement of changes in financial position,* and *notes* thereto.

financial structure. *Capital structure.*

financing lease. A *lease* treated by the lessee as both the borrowing of funds and the acquisition of an *asset* to be *amortized.* Both the *liability* and the asset are recognized on the balance sheet. Expenses consist of *interest* on the *debt* and *amortization* of the asset. The lessor treats the lease as the sale of the asset in return for a series of future cash receipts. Contrast with *operating* *lease.* Note that the same lease may, in some cases, be treated as a financing lease by the lessor and an operating lease by the lessee.

finished goods. Manufactured product ready for sale; a *current asset (inventory) account.*

firm. Informally, any business entity. (Strictly speaking, a firm is a *partnership.)*

first-in, first-out. See *FIFO.*

fiscal year. A period of twelve consecutive months chosen by a business as the *accounting period* for annual reports. May or may not be a *natural business year* or a calendar year.

FISH. An acronym, conceived by George H. Sorter, for *first-in, still-here.* FISH is the same cost flow assumption as *LIFO.* Many readers of accounting statements find it easier to think about inventory questions in terms of items still on hand. Think of LIFO in connection with *cost of goods sold* but of FISH in connection with *ending inventory.* See *LISH.*

fixed assets. *Plant assets.*

fixed-benefit plan. A *defined benefit (pension) plan.*

fixed budget. A plan that provides for specified amounts of *expenditures* and *receipts* that do not vary with activity levels. Sometimes called a "static budget." Contrast with *flexible budget.*

fixed cost (expense). An *expenditure* or *expense* that does not vary with volume of activity, at least in the short run.

fixed liability. *Long-term* liability.

flexible budget. *Budget* that projects expenditures as a function of activity levels. Contrast with *fixed budget.*

float. *Checks* that have been *credited* to the depositor's bank account, but not yet *debited* to the *drawer's* bank account.

flow. The change in the amount of an item over time. Contrast with *stock.*

flow assumption. When a *withdrawal* is made from *inventory,* the cost of the withdrawal must be determined by a flow assumption if *specific identification* of units is not used. The usual flow assumptions are *FIFO, LIFO,* and *weighted-average.*

flow of costs. *Costs* passing through various classifications within an *entity.* See the diagram below for a summary of *product* and *period cost* flows.

flow-through method. Accounting for the *investment tax credit* to show all income statement benefits of the credit in the year of acquisition, rather than spreading them over the life of the asset acquired, called the "deferral method." The *APB* preferred the deferral method in Opinion No. 2 (1962) but accepted the flow-through method in Opinion No. 4 (1964). See the Accounting Magic section for examples of both methods. Sometimes also used in connection with *depreciation* accounting where *straight-line method* is used for financial reporting and an *accelerated* method for tax reporting. Followers of the flow-through method would not recognize a *deferred tax liability.* APB Opinion No. 11 prohibited the use of the flow-through approach in this connection.

FOB. Free on board some location (for example, FOB shipping point; FOB destination); the *invoice* price includes delivery at seller's expense to that location. Title to goods usually passes from

FLOW OF COSTS (AND SALES REVENUE)*

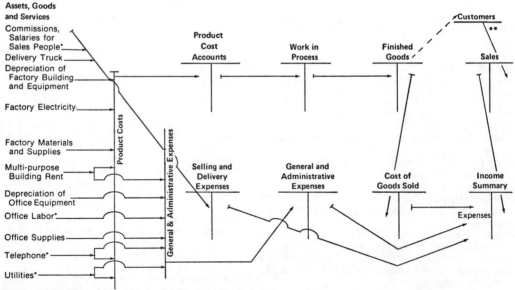

*The credit in the entry to record these items is usually to a payable; for all others, the credit is usually to an asset, or to an asset contra account.

**When sales to customers are recorded, the Sales account is credited. The debit is usually to Cash or Accounts Receivable.

seller to buyer at the FOB location.

footing. Adding a column of figures.

footnotes. More detailed information than that provided in the *income statement, balance sheet, statement of retained earnings,* and *statement of changes in financial position;* these are considered an integral part of the statements and are covered by the *auditor's report.* Sometimes called "notes."

forecast. An estimate or projection of costs or revenues or both.

foreign exchange gain or loss. Gain or loss from holding *net* foreign *monetary items* during a period when the *exchange rate* changes. See General Electric annual report at note 6.

Form 10-K. See *10-K.*

franchise. A privilege granted or sold, such as to use a name or to sell products or services.

free on board. *FOB.*

freight-in. The *cost* of freight or shipping in acquiring *inventory,* preferably treated as a part of the cost of *inventory.* Often shown temporarily in an *adjunct account* which is closed at the end of the period with other purchase accounts to inventory account.

freight-out. The *cost* of freight or shipping in selling *inventory,* treated as a selling *expense* in the period of sale.

full costing. *Absorption costing.* See *discovery value accounting* for another definition in the context of accounting for natural resources.

full disclosure. The reporting policy requiring that all significant or *material* information is to be presented in the financial statements. See *fair presentation.*

fully diluted earnings per share. Smallest *earnings per share* figure on *common stock* that can be obtained by computing an earnings per share for all possible combinations of assumed *exercise* or *conversion* of *potentially dilutive securities.* Must be reported on the *income statement* if it is less than 97 percent of earnings available to common stockholders divided by the average number of common shares outstanding during the period.

fully vested. Said of a *pension plan* when an employee (or his or her estate) has rights to all the benefits purchased with the employer's contributions to the plan even if the employee is not employed by this employer at the time of retirement.

function. In governmental accounting, said of a group of related activities for accomplishing a service or regulatory program for which the governmental unit is responsible. In mathematics, a rule for associating a number, called the dependent variable, with another number or numbers, called independent variables.

functional classification. *Income statement* reporting form in which *expenses* are reported by functions, that is, cost of goods sold, administrative expenses, selling expenses; contrast with *natural classification.*

fund. An *asset* or group of assets set aside for a specific purpose.

fund balance. In governmental accounting context, the excess of assets of a *fund* over its liabilities and reserves; the not-for-profit equivalent of

stockholders' equity.

funded. Said of a *pension plan* or other obligation when *funds* have been set aside for meeting the obligation when it becomes due. The federal law for pension plans requires that all *normal costs* be funded as recognized. In addition, *past and prior service costs* of pension plans must be funded over 30 or over 40 years, depending upon the circumstances.

funding. Replacing *short-term* liabilities with *long-term* debt.

funds. Generally *working capital;* current assets less current liabilities. Sometimes used to refer to *cash* or to cash and *marketable securities.*

funds provided by operations. An important subtotal in the *statement of changes in financial position.* This amount is the total of revenues producing *funds* less *expenses* requiring funds. Often, the amount is shown as *net income* plus expenses not requiring funds (such as depreciation charges) minus revenues not producing funds (such as revenues recognized under the *equity method* of accounting for a long-term investment).

funds statement. An informal name often used for the *statement of changes in financial position.*

funny money. Said of securities such as *convertible preferred stock, convertible bonds, options,* and *warrants* which have aspects of *common stock* equity but which did not reduce reported *earnings per share* prior to the issuance of *APB Opinions* No. 9 in 1967 and No. 15 in 1969.

FUTA. Federal Unemployment Tax Act which provides for taxes to be collected at the federal level, to help subsidize the individual states' administration of their unemployment compensation programs.

G

GAAP. *Generally accepted accounting principles.* A plural noun.

gain. Excess of *revenues* over *expenses* from a specific transaction. Frequently used in the context of describing a transaction not part of a firm's typical, day-to-day operations.

general debt. Debt of a governmental unit legally payable from general revenues and backed by the full faith and credit of the governmental unit.

General Electric Annual Report. Another section of this book.

general expenses. *Operating expenses* other than those specifically assigned to cost of goods sold, selling, and administration.

general fixed asset (group of accounts). Accounts showing those long-term assets of a governmental unit not accounted for in *enterprise, trust,* or intragovernmental service funds.

general fund. Assets and liabilities of a nonprofit entity not specifically earmarked for other purposes; the primary operating fund of a governmental unit.

general journal. The formal record where transactions, or summaries of similar transactions, are recorded in *journal entry* form as they occur. Use of the adjective "general" usually implies that there are also various *special journals,* such as *check register* or *sales journal,* in use.

general ledger. The name for the formal *ledger* containing all of the financial statement accounts. It has equal debits and credits as evidenced by the *trial balance.* Some of the accounts in the general ledger may be *controlling accounts,* supported by details contained in *subsidiary ledgers.*

generally accepted accounting principles (GAAP). As previously defined by the *APB* and now by the *FASB,* the conventions, rules, and procedures necessary to define accepted accounting practice at a particular time; includes both broad guidelines and relatively detailed practices and procedures.

generally accepted auditing standards. The standards, as opposed to particular procedures, promulgated by the *AICPA* (in *Statement on Auditing Standards* No. 1) which concern "the auditor's professional qualities" and "the judgment exercised by him in the performance of his examination and in his report." Currently, there are ten such standards, three general ones (concerned with proficiency, independence, and degree of care to be exercised), three standards of field work, and four standards of reporting. The first standard of reporting requires that the *auditor's report* state whether or not the *financial statements* are prepared in accordance with *generally accepted accounting principles.* Thus the typical auditor's report says that the examination was conducted in accordance with generally accepted auditing standards and that the statements are prepared in accordance with generally accepted accounting principles.

general partner. Member of *partnership* personally liable for all debts of the partnership; contrast with *limited partner.*

general price index. A measure of the aggregate prices of a wide range of goods and services in the economy at one time relative to the prices during a base period. See *consumer price index* and *GNP Implicit Price Deflator.* Contrast with *specific price index.*

general price level adjusted statements. See *price level adjusted statements.*

general price level changes. Changes in the aggregate prices of a wide range of goods and services in the economy. These price changes are measured using a *general price index.* Contrast with *specific price changes.*

general purchasing power of the dollar. The command of the dollar over a wide range of goods and services in the economy. The general purchasing power of the dollar is inversely related to changes in a general price index. See *general price index.*

GNP Implicit Price Deflator (Index). A *price index* issued quarterly by the Office of Business Economics of the U.S. Department of Commerce. This index attempts to trace the price level of all *goods and services* comprising the *gross national product.* Contrast with *consumer price index.*

going-concern assumption. For accounting purposes a business is assumed to remain in operation long enough for all its current plans to be carried out. This assumption is part of the justification for the *acquisition cost* basis, rather than a *liquidation* or *exit value* basis, of accounting.

going public. Said of a business when its *shares* become widely traded, rather than being closely held by relatively few *stockholders.* Issuing shares to the general investing public.

goods. Items of merchandise, supplies, raw materials, or finished goods. Sometimes the meaning of "goods" is extended to include all *tangible* items, as in the phrase "goods and services."

goods available for sale. The sum of *beginning inventory* plus all acquisitions, or purchases, during an *accounting period.*

goods in process. *Work in process.*

goodwill. The excess of cost of an acquired firm or operating unit over the current or *fair market value* of *net assets* of the acquired unit. Informally used to indicate the value of good customer relations, high employee morale, a well-respected business name, and so on, which are expected to result in greater than normal earning power.

goodwill method. A method of accounting for the *admission* of a new partner to a *partnership* when the new partner is to be credited with an amount of capital greater than the value of the *tangible* assets contributed. See *bonus method* for a description and contrast.

graded vesting. Said of a *pension plan* where not all employee benefits are currently *vested.* By law, the benefits must become vested according to one of several formulas as time passes.

gross. Not adjusted or reduced by deductions or subtractions. Contrast with *net.*

gross margin. *Net sales* minus *cost of goods sold.*

gross margin percentage. $100 \times (1 - cost\ of\ goods\ sold/net\ sales) = 100 \times (gross\ margin/net\ sales).$

gross national product (GNP). The market value within a nation for a year of all goods and services produced as measured by final sales of goods and services to individuals, corporations, and governments plus the excess of exports over imports.

gross price method (of recording purchase or sales discounts). The *purchase* (or *sale*) is recorded at its *invoice price,* not deducting the amounts of *discounts* available. Discounts taken are recorded in a *contra* account to purchases (or sales). Information on discounts lapsed is not made available, and for this reason, most firms prefer the *net-price method* of recording purchase discounts.

gross profit. *Gross margin.*

gross profit method. A method of estimating *ending inventory* amounts. *Cost of goods sold* is measured as some fraction of sales; and then the *inventory equation* is then used to value *ending inventory.*

gross profit ratio. *Gross margin* divided by *net sales.*

gross sales. All *sales* at *invoice* prices, not reduced by *discounts, allowances, returns,* or other adjustments.

group depreciation. A method of calculating *depreciation* charges where similar assets are combined, rather than depreciated separately. No gain or loss is recognized on retirement of items from the group until the last item in the group is sold or retired. See *composite life method.*

H

hidden reserve. The term refers to an amount by which *owners' equity* has been understated, perhaps deliberately. The understatement arises from an undervaluation of *assets* or overvaluation of *liabilities.* By undervaluing assets on this period's *balance sheet, net income* in some future period can be made to look artificially high by disposing of the asset: actual *revenues* less artificially-low cost of assets sold yields artificially-high net income. There is no *account* that has this title.

historical cost. *Acquisition cost; original cost; a sunk cost.*

historical summary. A part of the *annual report* to stockholders that shows important items, such as *net income, revenues, expenses, asset* and *equity* totals, *earnings per share,* and the like, for five or ten periods including the current one. Usually not as much detail is shown in the historical summary as in *comparative statements,* which typically report as much detail for the immediately preceding year as for the current year. Annual reports may contain both comparative statements and a historical summary. See pages 86-87.

holding company. A company that confines its activities to owning *stock* in, and supervising management of, other companies. A holding company usually owns a controlling interest in, that is more than 50 percent of the voting stock of, the companies whose stock it holds. Contrast with *mutual fund.* See *conglomerate.*

holding gain or loss. Difference between end-of-period price and beginning-of-period price of an asset held during the period. Ordinarily, realized holding gains and losses are not separately reported in financial statements. See *inventory profit* for further refinement, including *gains* on *assets* sold during the period.

horizontal analysis. *Time series analysis.*

human resource accounting. A term used to describe a variety of proposals that seek to report and emphasize the importance of human resources— knowledgeable, trained, and loyal employees—in a company's earning process and total assets.

hypothecation. The *pledging* of property, without transfer of title or possession, to secure a loan.

I

I. *Identity matrix.*

ideal standard costs. *Standard costs* set equal to those that would be incurred under the best possible conditions.

identity matrix. A square *matrix* with ones on the main diagonal and zeros elsewhere; a matrix I such that for any other matrix A, $IA = AI = A$. The matrix equivalent to the number one.

IIA. *Institute of Internal Auditors.*

imprest fund. *Petty cash fund.*

improvement. An *expenditure* to extend the useful life of an *asset* or to improve its performance (rate of output, cost) over that of the original asset. Such expenditures are *capitalized* as part of the asset's cost. Contrast with *maintenance* and *repair.*

imputed cost. A cost that does not appear in accounting records, such as the *interest* that could be earned on cash spent to acquire inventories rather than, say, government bonds. Or, consider a firm that owns the buildings it occupies. This firm has an imputed cost for rent in an amount equal to what it would have to pay to use similar buildings owned by another.

imputed interest. See *interest, imputed.*

income. Excess of *revenues* over *expenses* for a period. Sometimes used with an appropriate modifier to refer to the various intermediate amounts shown in a *multiple-step income statement.* Sometimes used to refer to revenues, as in "rental income."

income accounts. *Revenue* and *expense accounts.*

income distribution account. *Temporary account* sometimes debited when *dividends* are declared; closed to *retained earnings.*

income from continuing operations. As defined by *APB Option* No. 30, all *revenues* less all *expenses* except for the following: results of operations, including income tax effects, that have been or will be discontinued; *gains* or *losses,* including income tax effects, on disposal of segments of the business; gains or losses, including income tax effects, from *extraordinary items;* and the cumulative effect of *accounting changes.*

income from discontinued operations. *Income,* net of tax effects, from parts of the business that have been discontinued during the period or are to be discontinued in the near future. Such items are reported on a separate line of the *income statement* after *income from continuing operations* but before *extraordinary items.*

income (revenue) bond. See *special revenue debt.*

income statement. The statement of *revenues, expenses, gains,* and *losses* for the period ending with *net income* for the period. The *earnings per share* amount is usually shown on the income statement; the *reconciliation* of beginning and ending balances of *retained earnings* may also be shown in a combined statement of income and retained earnings. See *income from continuing operations, income from discontinued operations, extraordinary items, multiple-step, single-step.*

income summary. An *account* used in problem solving that serves as a surrogate for the income statement. All *revenues* are closed to the Income Summary as *credits* and all *expenses,* as *debits.* The *balance* in the account, after all other *closing entries* are made, is then closed to the retained earnings or other *owners' equity* account and represents *net income* for the period.

income tax. An annual tax levied by the federal and other governments on the income of an entity. An *expense;* if not paid, a *liability.*

income tax allocation. See *deferred tax liability* and *tax allocation: intrastatement.*

incremental cost. *Costs* that will be incurred (saved) if an activity is undertaken (stopped).

indenture. See *bond indenture.*

independence. The mental attitude required of the *CPA* in performing the *attest* function. It implies impartiality and that the members of the auditing CPA firm own no stock in the corporation being audited.

independent accountant. The *CPA* who performs the *attest* function for a firm.

indeterminate-term liability. A *liability* lacking the criterion of being due at a definite time. This term is our own coinage to encompass the *deferred income tax liability*.

indexation. An attempt by lawmakers or parties to a contract, to cope with the effects of *inflation*. Amounts fixed in law or contracts are "indexed" when these amounts change as a given measure of price changes. For example, a so-called escalator clause in a labor contract might provide that hourly wages will be increased as the *consumer price index* increases. Many economists have suggested the indexation of numbers fixed in the *income tax* laws. If, for example, the personal *exemption* is $750 at the start of the period, prices rise by 10 percent during the period, and the personal exemption is indexed, then the personal exemption would automatically rise to $825 (= $750 + .10 × $750) at the end of the period.

indirect costs. Costs of production not easily associated with the production of specific goods and services; *overhead costs*. May be *allocated* on some arbitrary basis to specific products or departments.

indirect labor (material) cost. An *indirect cost* for labor (material).

individual proprietorship. *Sole proprietorship*.

inflation. A time of generally rising prices.

information system. A system, sometimes formal and sometimes informal, for collecting, processing, and communicating data that are useful for the managerial functions of decision making, planning, and control, and for financial reporting under the *attest* requirement.

insolvent. Unable to pay debts when due. Said of a company even though *assets* exceed *liabilities*.

installment. Partial payment of a debt or collection of a receivable.

installment contracts receivable. The name used for *accounts receivable* when the *installment method* of recognizing revenue is used. Its *contra, unrealized gross margin*, is shown on the balance sheet as a subtraction from the amount receivable.

installment (sales) method. Recognizing *revenue* and *expense* (or *gross margin*) from a sales transaction in proportion to the fraction of the selling price collected during a period. See *unrealized* (and *realized*) *gross margin*.

installment sales. Sales on account where the buyer promises to pay in several separate payments, called *installments*. Sometimes are, but need not be, accounted for on the *installment method*. If installment sales are accounted for with the sales *basis of revenue recognition* for financial reporting but with the installment method for income tax returns, then a *deferred income tax liability* arises.

Institute of Internal Auditors. The national association for accountants who are engaged in internal auditing employed by business firms.

insurance. A contract for reimbursement of specific losses; purchased with insurance premiums. Self-insurance is not insurance but merely the willingness to assume risk of incurring losses while saving the premium.

intangible asset. A nonphysical, *noncurrent* asset such as a *copyright, patent, trademark, goodwill,* and *capitalized* advertising cost.

intercompany elimination. See *eliminations*.

intercompany profit. If one *affiliated company* sells to another, and the goods remain in the second company's *inventory* at the end of the period, then the first company's *profit* has not been realized by a sale to an outsider. That profit is called "intercompany profit" and is eliminated from net *income* in *consolidated income statements* or when the *equity method* is used.

interest. The charge or cost for using money; frequently expressed as a rate per period, usually one year, called the interest rate.

interest factor. One plus the *interest* rate.

interest, imputed. If a borrower merely promises to pay a single amount, sometime later than the present, then the *present value* of the promise is less than the *face amount* to be paid at *maturity*. The difference between the face amount and the present value of a promise is called imputed interest. See also *imputed cost*.

interest rate. See *interest*.

inter-fund accounts. In governmental accounting, the accounts that show transactions between funds, especially inter-fund receivables and payables.

interim statements. Statements issued for periods less than the regular, annual *accounting period*. Most corporations are required to issue interim statements on a quarterly basis. The basic issue in preparing interim reports is whether their purpose is to report on the interim period (1) as a self-contained accounting period, or (2) as an integral part of the year of which they are a part so that forecasts of annual performance can be made. *APB Opinion* No. 28 and the *SEC* require that interim reports be constructed largely to satisfy the second purpose.

internal audit. An *audit* conducted by employees to ascertain whether or not *internal control* procedures are working, as opposed to an external audit conducted by a *CPA*.

internal control. The procedures used by a business in attempting to insure that operations are carried out or recorded as planned. Particularly in the context of cash transactions, often referred to as an "internal check."

internal rate of return. The discount rate that equates the net *present value* of a stream of cash flows, including the initial investment, to zero.

Internal Revenue Service (IRS). Agency of the U.S. Treasury Department responsible for administering the Internal Revenue Code and collecting income, and certain other, taxes.

internal reporting. Reporting for management's use in planning and control; contrast with *external reporting* for financial statement users.

International Accounting Standards Committee.

An organization that promotes the establishment of international accounting standards.

interpolation. The estimation of an unknown number intermediate between two (or more) known numbers.

Interpretations of Statements of Financial Accounting Standards. See *FASB Interpretations*.

in the black (red). Operating at a profit (loss).

inventoriable costs. *Costs* that "attach" to products. *Product costs (assets)* as opposed to *period expenses*.

inventory. As a noun, the *balance* in an asset *account* such as raw materials, supplies, work in process, and finished goods. As a verb, to calculate the *cost* of goods on hand at a given time or to physically count items on hand.

inventory equation. *Beginning inventory + net additions – withdrawals = ending inventory*. Ordinarily, additions are net purchases and withdrawals are *cost of goods sold*. Notice that ending inventory, to be shown on the balance sheet, and cost of goods sold, to be shown on the income statement, are not independent of each other. The larger is one, the smaller must be the other. In valuing inventories, beginning inventory and net purchases are usually known. In some inventory methods (for example, some applications of the *retail inventory method*), cost of goods sold is measured and the equation is used to find the cost of ending inventory. In most methods, cost of ending inventory is measured and the equation is used to find the cost of goods sold (withdrawals).

inventory layer. See *LIFO inventory layer*.

inventory holding gains. See *inventory profit*.

inventory profit. This term has several different meanings. Consider the following data:

	Number of Units	Total Acquisition Cost of Units
Beginning Inventory	100	$ 1,000
Purchases During Period (at various prices)	1,000	$12,000
Sales During Period at $16 per unit	900	10,500*
Ending Inventory	200	2,500*

*These two costs require a cost flow assumption for inventory. FIFO is assumed.

Assume, further, that the average selling price during the period has been $16 per unit and that the replacement cost of a unit at the end of the period is $13. Then the following calculations can be performed.

Goods Available for Sale During Period Valued at Replacement Cost (1,100 × $13)	$14,300
Acquisition Cost of Goods Available for Sale During Period	13,000
Holding Gains During Period	$ 1,300

The total of holding gains during the period are split into realized and unrealized portions, using the *cost flow assumption*, as follows:

Revenues from Sales (900 × $16)	$14,400
Less Replacement Cost of Goods Sold (900 × $13)	11,700
Operating Margin	$ 2,700
Replacement Cost of Goods Sold (900 × $13)	$11,700
Less Acquisition Cost of Goods Sold (FIFO)	10,500
Realized Holding Gain	$ 1,200

Replacement Cost of Ending Inventory (200 × $13)	$ 2,600
Less Acquisition Cost of Ending Inventory (FIFO)	2,500
Unrealized Holding Gain	$ 100

The *gross margin* on sales as reported in the *income statement* is revenues from sales less *acquisition cost of goods sold*. In the example, gross margin is $3,900 (= $14,400 – $10,500). This gross margin is always equal to the *operating margin* plus the realized holding gain ($2,700 + $1,200 = $3,900).

The *SEC*, in its *Accounting Series Releases*, uses the term "inventory profit" to refer to the realized holding gain, $1,200 in the example. The SEC requires that this inventory profit be disclosed in *notes* to the *financial statements* if the amount is *material*. The amount will usually be material in periods of rising prices when a *FIFO* cost flow assumption is used, as in the example.

The computations can be somewhat more complex than shown in the example here. The replacement cost of goods sold can be computed as of the times of sale, rather than at the end of the period. This requires *perpetual inventory* records and, for that reason, we suspect that most firms which report "inventory profit" do so approximately as we show here.

Others use the term "inventory profit" to refer to the unrealized holding gain—the excess of current replacement cost of ending inventory over its acquisition cost. Still others use the term "inventory profit" to refer to the total holding gains, whether realized or not. Total holding gains can always be computed as the replacement cost of goods available for sale (which is beginning inventory plus purchases valued at replacement cost) less the acquisition cost of goods available for sale.

In periods of rising prices and increasing inventories, the realized holding gains under a FIFO cost flow assumption will be larger than under LIFO. The unrealized holding gains under LIFO will be larger than under FIFO.

inventory turnover. Number of times the average *inventory* has been sold during a period; *cost of goods sold* for a period divided by average inventory for the period. See *ratio*.

invested capital. *Contributed capital*.

investment. An *expenditure* to acquire property or other assets in order to produce *revenue;* the *asset* so acquired; hence a *current* expenditure made in anticipation of future income. Said of *securities* of other companies held for the long term and shown in a separate section of the *balance sheet;* in this context, contrast with *marketable securities*.

investment tax credit. A reduction in income tax liability granted by the federal government to

29

firms that buy new equipment. This item is deducted from the tax bill, not from pre-tax income. The tax credit has been a given percentage of the purchase price of certain assets purchased. The actual rules and rates have changed over the years. See *flow-through method* and *carry forward*.

invoice. A document showing the details of a sale or purchase transaction.

issue. When a corporation exchanges its stock (or bonds) for cash or other assets, the corporation is said to issue, not sell, that stock (or bonds). Also used in the context of withdrawing supplies or materials from inventory for use in operations and drawing of a *check*.

issued shares. Those shares of *authorized capital stock* of a *corporation* that have been distributed to the stockholders. See *issue*. Shares of *treasury stock* are legally issued but are not considered to be *outstanding* for the purpose of voting, *dividend declarations,* and *earnings per share* calculations.

J

job cost sheet. A schedule showing actual or budgeted inputs for a special order.

job development credit. The name used for the *investment tax credit* in the 1971 tax law on this subject.

job-order costing. Accumulation of *costs* for a particular identifiable batch of products, known as a job, as it moves through production.

joint cost. Cost of simultaneously producing or otherwise acquiring two or more products, called joint products, that must, by the nature of the process, be produced or acquired together, such as the cost of beef and hides of cattle. Other examples include central *corporate expenses, overhead* of a department when several products are manufactured, and *basket purchases*.

joint product. One of two or more outputs from a process that must be produced or acquired simultaneously. See *by-product* and *joint cost*.

journal. The place where transactions are recorded as they occur. The book of original entry.

journal entry. A recording in a *journal,* of equal *debits* and *credits,* with an explanation of the *transaction,* if necessary.

journalize. To make an entry in a *journal*.

Journal of Accountancy. A monthly publication of the *AICPA*.

Journal of Accounting Research. Scholarly journal containing articles on theoretical and empirical aspects of accounting. Published three times a year by the Graduate School of Business of the University of Chicago.

journal voucher. A *voucher* documenting a transaction, leading to an entry in the *journal*.

K

kiting. This term means slightly different things in banking and auditing contexts. In both, however, it refers to the wrongful practice of taking advantage of the *float,* the time that elapses between the deposit of a *check* in one bank and its collection at another. In the banking context, an individual deposits in Bank A a check written on Bank B. He (or she) then writes checks against the deposit created in Bank A. Several days later, he deposits in Bank B a check written on Bank A, to cover the original check written on Bank B. Still later, he deposits in Bank A a check written on Bank B. The process of covering the deposit in Bank A with a check written on Bank B and vice versa is continued until an actual deposit of cash can be arranged. In the auditing context, kiting refers to a form of *window dressing* where the amount of the account Cash in Bank is made to appear larger than it actually is by depositing in Bank A a check written on Bank B without recording the check written on Bank B in the *check register* until after the close of the *accounting period*.

L

labor variances. The *price* (or *rate*) and *quantity* (or *usage*) *variance* for *direct labor* inputs in a *standard cost system*.

land. An *asset shown at acquisition cost* plus the *cost* of any nondepreciable *improvements*. In accounting, implies use as a plant or office site, rather than as a *natural resource,* such as timberland.

lapping (accounts receivable). The theft, by an employee, of cash sent in by a customer to discharge the latter's *payable*. The theft from the first customer is concealed by using cash received from a second customer. The theft from the second customer is concealed by using the cash received from a third customer, and so on. The process is continued until the thief returns the funds or can make the theft permanent by creating a fictitious *expense* or receivable write off, or until the fraud is discovered.

lapse. To expire; said of, for example, an insurance policy or discounts made available for prompt payment that are not taken.

last-in, first-out. See *LIFO*.

layer. See *LIFO inventory layer*.

lead time. The time that elapses between order-placing and receipt of the ordered *goods or services*.

lease. A contract calling for the lessee (user) to pay the lessor (owner) for the use of an asset. A cancelable lease is one the lessee can cancel at any time. A noncancelable lease requires payments from the lessee for the life of the lease and usually has many of the economic characteristics of *debt financing*. A noncancelable lease meets the usual criteria to be classified as a *liability* but sometimes under *GAAP,* need not be shown as a liability. The *SEC* requires disclosure in notes to the financial statements of the commitments for noncancelable leases. See *financing lease* and *operating lease*.

leasehold. The *asset* representing the right of the *lessee* to use leased property. See *lease* and *leasehold improvement*.

leasehold improvement. An *improvement* to leased property. Should be *amortized* over *service life* or the life of the lease, whichever is shorter.

least and latest rule. Pay the least amount of taxes as late as possible within the law to minimize the *present value* of tax payments for a given set of operations.

ledger. A book of accounts. See *general ledger* and *subsidiary ledger*. Contrast with *journal*.

legal capital. *Par* or *stated value* of issued *capital stock*. The amount of *contributed capital* that, according to state law, must remain permanently in the firm as protection for creditors.

legal entity. See *entity*.

lender. See *loan*.

lessee. See *lease*.

lessor. See *lease*.

leverage. Refers to the use of *long-term* debt, in addition to *equity,* securities for raising *funds*.

leveraged lease. A special form of lease involving three parties—a *lender,* a *lessor,* and a *lessee.* The lender, such as a bank or insurance company, lends a portion, say 80 percent, of the cash required for the acquisition of an *asset.* The lessor puts up the remainder, say 20 percent, of the cash required. The lessor acquires the asset with the cash, using the asset as security for the loan and leases it to the lessee on a *noncancelable* basis. The lessee makes periodic lease payments to the lessor, who in turn makes payments on the loan to the lender. Typically, the lessor has no obligation for the debt to the lender other than transferring a portion of the receipts from the lessee. If the lessee should default on required lease payments, then the lender can repossess the leased asset. The lessor is usually entitled to deductions for tax purposes for depreciation on the asset, for interest expense on the loan from the lender, and for any investment tax credit. The lease is leveraged in the sense that the lessor, who enjoys most of the risks and rewards of ownership, usually borrows most of the funds needed to acquire the asset. See *leverage*.

liability. Usually, a legal obligation to pay a definite or reasonably certain amount at a definite or reasonably certain time in return for a current benefit. Some of the criteria are not met by items classified as liabilities where there are special circumstances. Examples are *pension* liabilities, estimates of future *warranty* expenditures, and *deferred tax liabilities.* See *indeterminate-term liability.* Other items meet the criteria to be a liability but are not shown as such. For example, noncancelable leases, which are sometimes disclosed only in footnotes; see *lease*.

lien. The right of person A to satisfy a claim against person B by holding B's property as security or by seizing B's property.

life annuity. A *contingent annuity* in which payments cease at death of a specified person(s), usually the *annuitant(s)*.

LIFO. An *inventory* flow assumption where the *cost of goods sold* is the cost of the most recently acquired units and the *ending inventory cost* is determined from costs of the oldest units. Contrast with *FIFO.* In periods of rising prices and increasing inventories, LIFO leads to higher reported expenses and therefore lower reported income and lower balance sheet inventories than does FIFO. See the example in the Accounting Magic section of this book. See also *FISH* and *inventory profit*.

LIFO, dollar value method. See *dollar value LIFO method*.

LIFO inventory layer. The *ending inventory* for a period is likely to be larger than the *beginning inventory.* Under a *LIFO cost flow assumption,* this increase in physical quantities is given a value determined by the prices of the earliest purchases during the year. The LIFO inventory then consists of layers, sometimes called "slices," which typically consist of relatively small amounts of physical quantities from each of the past several years. Each layer carries the prices from near the beginning of the period when it was acquired. The earliest layers will typically (in periods of rising prices) have prices very much less than current prices. If inventory quantities should decline in a subsequent period, the latest layers enter cost of goods sold first.

limited liability. Stockholders of corporations are not personally liable for debts of the company.

limited partner. Member of a *partnership* not personally liable for debts of the partnership; every partnership must have at least one *general partner* who is fully liable.

line of business reporting. Reporting of income, and sometimes assets, by *segments of a business,* usually classified by nature of products sold but sometimes by geographical area where goods are produced or sold. Sometimes called "segment reporting." *Central corporate expenses* are usually allocated to the segments, although these reports may be more useful when such expenses are separately disclosed. See the excerpt from the General Electric annual report (on page 61 of this book for an example).

line of credit. An agreement with a bank or set of banks for short-term borrowings on demand.

liquid. Said of a business with a substantial amount (the amount is unspecified) of *working capital,* especially *quick assets*.

liquid assets. *Cash, marketable securities,* and, sometimes, *current receivables*.

liquidating dividend. *Dividend* declared in the winding up of a business to distribute the assets of the company to the stockholders. Usually treated as a return of *investment,* not as *revenue*.

liquidation. Payment of a debt. Sale of assets in closing down a business or a segment thereof.

liquidation value per share. The amount each *share* of stock will receive if the corporation is dissolved. For *preferred stock* with a *liquidation preference,* a stated amount per share.

LISH. An acronym, conceived by George H. Sorter, for *last-in, still-here.* LISH is the same cost flow assumption as *FIFO.* Many readers of accounting statements find it easier to think about inventory questions in terms of items still on hand. Think of FIFO in connection with *cost of goods sold* but of LISH in connection with *ending inventory.* See *FISH*.

list price. The published or nominally quoted price for goods.

list-price method. See *trade-in transaction*.

loan. An arrangement where the owner of property, called the lender, allows someone else, called the borrower, the use of the property for a period of time that is usually specified in the agreement setting up the loan. The borrower promises to return the property to the lender and, often, to make a payment for use of the property. Generally used when the property is *cash* and the payment for its use is *interest*.

long-lived (term) asset. An asset whose benefits are expected to be received over several years. A *noncurrent* asset, usually includes *investments, plant assets,* and *intangibles*.

long-term (construction) contract accounting. The *percentage of completion method* of *revenue* recognition.

loss. Excess of *cost* over net proceeds for a single transaction; negative *income* for a period. A cost expiration that produced no *revenue*.

lower of cost or market. A basis for *inventory* valuation where the inventory value is set at the lower of *acquisition cost* or *current replacement cost* (market), subject to the following constraints: First, the market value of an item used in the computation cannot exceed its *net realizable value*—an amount equal to selling price less reasonable costs to complete production and to sell the item. Second, the market value of an item used in the computation cannot be less than the net realizable value minus the normal *profit* ordinarily realized on disposition of completed items of this type. The lower of cost or market valuation is chosen as the lower of acquisition cost or replacement cost (market) subject to the upper and lower bounds on replacement cost established in the first two steps. The method for valuing by lower of cost or market is easier to remember and use when the method is translated into symbols as follows: Let: *AC* represent acquisition cost, *RC* represent replacement cost, *NRV* represent net realizable value, and *PROF* represent the normal profit. Then the lower of cost or market valuation is:

minimum [*AC*, *NRV*, maximum(*RC*, *NRV* - *PROF*)].

In words, find the maximum of replacement cost and net realizable value minus normal profit. Call that quantity *MAX*. Then choose the smallest of acquisition cost, net realizable value, and *MAX*. (The minimum of *NRV* and *MAX* is the "market" figure used in the computation.) The following example illustrates the application of the rule for lower of cost or market when the normal profit margin is nine cents ($.09) per unit.

	Item			
	1	**2**	**3**	**4**
(a) Acquisition Cost	$ .90	$ .97	$ .96	$ .90
(b) Net Realizable Value	.95	.95	.95	.95
(c) Net Realizable Value Less Normal Profit Margin	.86	.86	.86	.86
(d) Replacement Cost	.92	.96	.92	.85
(e) Maximum [(d), (c)] = MAX	.92	.96	.92	.86
(f) Lower of Cost of Market = Minimum [(a), (b), (e)]	.90	.95	.92	.86

Notice in this illustration that each of the four possible valuations is used once to determine lower of cost or market. Item 1 uses acquisition cost; Item 2 uses net realizable value; Item 3 uses replacement cost; and Item 4 uses net realizable value less normal profit.

Lower of cost or market cannot be used for tax returns in combination with a *LIFO* flow assumption.

lump-sum acquisition. *Basket purchase.*

M

maintenance. *Expenditures* undertaken to preserve an *asset's* service potential for its originally-intended life; these expenditures are treated as *period expenses* or *product costs*. Contrast with *improvement*. See *repair*.

make-or-buy decision. A managerial decision about whether the firm should produce a product internally or purchase it from others. Proper make-or-buy decisions in the short run result only when *opportunity costs* are the only costs considered in decision making.

maker (of note) (of check). One who signs a *note* to borrow. One who signs a *check*; in this context, synonomous with drawer; see *draft*.

management. Executive authority that operates a business.

Management Accounting. Monthly publication of the *NAA*.

management (managerial) accounting. Reporting designed to enhance the ability of management to do its job of decision making, planning, and control; contrast with *financial accounting*.

manufacturing cost. Costs of producing goods, usually in a factory.

manufacturing expense. Another, less useful, title for *manufacturing overhead*.

manufacturing overhead. General manufacturing *costs* incurred in providing a capacity to carry on productive activities but which are not directly associated with identifiable units of product. Treated as a *product cost* under *absorption costing* but as an *expense* of the period under *direct costing*.

margin. *Revenue* less specified expenses. See *contribution margin, gross margin* and *current margin*.

marginal cost. *Incremental cost* per unit.

marginal costing. *Direct costing*.

marginal revenue. The increment in *revenue* from sale of one extra unit of product.

margin of safety. Excess of actual, or budgeted, sales over *breakeven* sales. Usually expressed in dollars; may be expressed in units of product.

markdown. The reduction below an originally established retail price.

marketable securities. *Stocks* and *bonds* of other companies held that can be readily sold on stock exchanges or over-the-counter markets and that the company plans to sell as cash is needed. Classified as *current* assets and as part of *working capital*.

market price. See *fair market price*.

market rate. The rate of *interest* a company must pay to borrow *funds* currently. See *effective rate.*

markon. An amount originally added to *cost* to obtain *list price.* Usually expressed as a percentage of cost. Further increases in list price are called *markups;* decreases are called *markdowns.*

markup. An amount originally added to cost. Usually expressed as a percentage of selling price. Also refers to an increase above an originally-established retail price. See *markon.*

markup percentage. *Markup* divided by selling price.

matching convention. The concept of recognizing cost expirations (*expenses*) in the same accounting period when the related *revenues* are recognized.

material. As an adjective, it means relatively important. See *materiality.* Currently, no operational definition exists. As a noun, *raw material.*

materiality. The concept that accounting should disclose separately only those events that are relatively important (no operable definition yet exists) for the business or for understanding its statements.

material variances. *Price* and *quantity variances* for *direct materials* in *standard cost systems.* Sometimes used to mean variances that are significant; see *materiality.*

matrix. A rectangular array of numbers or mathematical symbols.

matrix inverse. For a given square *matrix,* A, the square matrix inverse is the matrix, A^{-1}, such that $AA^{-1} = A^{-1} A = I$, the *identity matrix.* Not all square matrices have inverses. Those that do not are called singular; those that do are nonsingular.

maturity. The date at which an obligation, such as the *principal* of a *bond* or a *note,* becomes due.

maturity value. The amount expected to be collected when a loan reaches *maturity.* Depending upon the context, the amount may be *principal* or principal and *interest.*

merchandise. *Finished goods* bought by a retailer for resale. Contrast with finished goods of a manufacturing business.

merchandise turnover. *Inventory turnover* for merchandise; see *ratio.*

merchandising business. As opposed to a manufacturing or service business, one that buys *finished goods* for resale.

merger. The joining of two or more businesses into a single *economic entity.*

minority interest. A *balance sheet account* on *consolidated statements* showing the *equity* in a *subsidiary* company allocable to those who are not part of the controlling (majority) interest. May be classified either as stockholders' equity or as a liability of *indeterminate term* on the consolidated balance sheet. On the *income statement,* the minority's interest in current income must be subtracted to arrive at consolidated *net income* for the period.

minority investment. A holding of less than 50 percent of the *voting stock* in another corporation. Accounted for with the *cost method* when less than 20 percent is held, and with the *equity method* otherwise. See *mutual fund.*

minutes book. A record of all actions authorized at corporate *board of directors'* or stockholders' meeting.

mixed cost. A *semifixed* or a *semivariable* cost.

modified cash basis. The *cash basis of accounting* with long-term assets accounted for with the *accrual basis of accounting.*

monetary assets, liabilities. See *monetary items.*

monetary gain or loss. The *gain* or *loss* in general purchasing power as a result of holding *monetary assets* or liabilities during a period when the *general purchasing power of the dollar* changes. During periods of *inflation,* holders of net monetary assets lose, and holders of net monetary liabilities gain, general purchasing power. During periods of *deflation,* holders of net monetary assets gain, and holders of net monetary liabilities lose, general purchasing power.

monetary items. Amounts fixed in terms of dollars by statute or contract. *Cash, accounts receivable, accounts payable,* and *debt.* The distinction between monetary and nonmonetary items is important for general *price level adjusted statements* and for *foreign exchange gain or loss* computations. In the foreign exchange context, account amounts denominated in dollars are not monetary items while amounts denominated in any other currency are monetary.

money. A word seldom used with precision in accounting, at least in part because economists have not yet agreed on its definition. Economists use the term to refer to both a medium of exchange and a unit of value. See *cash* and *monetary items.*

money-purchase plan. A *pension plan* where the employer contributes a specified amount of cash each year to each employee's pension fund. Benefits ultimately received by the employee are not specifically defined but depend on the rate of return on the cash invested. Sometimes called a "defined-contribution" pension plan. Contrast with *defined-benefit plan.* As of the mid-1970's, most corporate pension plans were defined benefit plans because both the law and *generally accepted accounting principles* for pensions made defined benefit plans more attractive than money purchase plans. The federal pension law of 1974 makes money purchase plans relatively more attractive than they had been. We expect the number of money-purchase plans to increase. See *ERISA.*

mortality table. Data on life expectancies or probabilities of death for persons of specified ages and sex.

mortgage. A claim given by the borrower (mortgagor) to the lender (mortgagee) against the borrower's property in return for a loan.

moving average. An *average* computed on observations over time. As a new observation becomes available, the oldest one is dropped so that the average is always computed for the same number of observations and only the most recent ones. Sometimes, however, this term is used synonymously with *weighted-average.*

moving average method. *Weighted-average method.*

multiple-step. Said of an *income* statement where various classes of *expenses* and *losses* are subtracted from *revenues* to show intermediate items such as *operating income,* income of the enterprise (operating income plus *interest* income), income to investors (income of the enterprise less *income taxes*), net income to shareholders (income to investors less interest charges), and income retained (income to stockholders less dividends). See *entity theory.*

municipal bond. A *bond* issued by a village, town, city, county, state, or other public body. *Interest* on such bonds is generally exempt from federal *income taxes* and from some state income taxes. Sometimes referred to as "tax exempts."

mutual fund. An investment company that issues its own stock to the public and uses the proceeds to invest in securities of other companies. A mutual fund usually owns less than five or ten percent of the stock of any one company and accounts for its investments using current *market values.* Contrast with *holding company.*

N

National Association of Accountants (NAA). A national society generally open to all engaged in activities closely associated with *managerial accounting.* Oversees the administration of the *CMA* Examinations through the Institute of Management Accounting.

natural business year. A twelve month period chosen as the reporting period so that the end of the period coincides with a low point in activity or inventories. See *ratio* for a discussion of analyses of financial statements of companies using a natural business year.

natural classification. *Income statement* reporting form in which *expenses* are classified by nature of items, that is materials, wages, salaries, insurance, and taxes, as well as depreciation. Contrast with *functional classification.*

natural resources. Timberland, oil and gas wells, ore deposits, and other products of nature that have economic value. The cost of natural resources is subject to *depletion.* Often called "wasting assets." See also *discovery value accounting.*

negotiable. Legally capable of being transferred by endorsement. Usually said of *checks* and *notes* and sometimes of *stocks* and *bearer bonds.*

negative confirmation. See *confirmation.*

net. Reduced by all relevant deductions.

net assets. *Owners' equity;* total *assets* minus total *liabilities.*

net current assets. *Working capital = current assets – current liabilities.*

net income. The excess of all *revenues* and *gains* for a period over all *expenses* and *losses* of the period.

net loss. The excess of all *expenses* and *losses* for a period over all *revenues* and *gains* of the period. Negative *net income.*

net markup. In the context of *retail inventory methods,* markups less markup cancellations; a figure which usually ignores *markdowns* and markdown cancellations.

net of tax method. A nonsanctioned method for dealing with the problem of income tax allocation; described in *APB* Opinion No. 11. Deferred tax items are subtracted from specific asset amounts rather than being shown as a deferred credit or liability.

net of tax reporting. Reporting, such as for *income from discontinued operations, extraordinary items,* and *prior-period adjustments,* where the amounts presented in *financial statements* have been adjusted for all income tax effects. For example, if an extraordinary loss amounted to $10,000 and the average tax rate were 40 percent, then the extraordinary item would be reported "net of taxes" as a $6,000 loss. Hence, all income taxes may not be reported on one line of the income statement. The taxes will be allocated to *income from continuing operations,* income from discontinued operations, extraordinary items, and prior-period adjustments.

net present value. Discounted or *present value* of all cash inflows and outflows of a project or from an *investment* at a given *discount rate.*

net price method (of recording purchase or sales discounts). The *purchase* (or *sale*) is recorded at its *invoice* price less all *discounts* made available under the assumption that nearly all discounts will be taken. Discounts lapsed through failure to pay promptly are recorded in an *adjunct account* to purchases (or sales) or in the purchasing context, to an *expense* account. In the context of purchases, management usually prefers to know about the amount of discounts lost because of inefficient operations, not the amounts taken, so that most managers prefer the net price method to the *gross price method.*

net realizable value. Selling price of an item less reasonable further costs to make the item ready for sale and to sell it.

net sales. Sales (at gross invoice amount) less *returns, allowances,* freight paid for customers, and *discounts* taken.

net working capital. *Working capital;* the "net" is redundant in accounting. Financial analysts sometimes mean *current* assets when they speak of working capital, so for them the "net" is not redundant.

net worth. A misleading term, to be avoided, that means the same as *owners' equity.* See the Penn Central annual report.

New York Stock Exchange (NYSE). A public market where various corporate *securities* are traded.

nominal accounts. *Temporary accounts* as opposed to *balance sheet accounts.* All nominal accounts are *closed* at the end of each *accounting period.*

noncancelable. See *lease.*

noncontributory. Said of a *pension plan* where only the employer makes payments to a pension *fund.* Contrast with *contributory.*

noncurrent. Due more than one year hence.

nonexpendable fund. A governmental fund, whose *principal,* and sometimes earnings, may not be spent.

noninterest-bearing note. A *note* which bears no explicit interest. The *present value* of such a note at any time before *maturity* is less than the *face* *value* so long as *interest rates* are positive. *APB Opinion* No. 21 requires that the present value, not face value, of long-term noninterest-bearing notes be reported as the *asset* or *liability* amount in financial statements.

nonmonetary items. All items that are not monetary; see *monetary items.*

nonoperating. In the *income statement* context, said of revenues and expenses arising from transactions incidental to the company's main line(s) of business. In the *statement of changes in financial position* context, said of all sources or uses of *working capital* other than working capital provided by operations.

nonprofit corporation. An incorporated *entity,* such as a hospital, with no owners who share in the earnings. It usually emphasizes providing services rather than maximizing income.

nonrecurring. Said of an event that is not expected to happen often for a given firm. Under *APB* Opinion No. 30, the effects of such events should be disclosed separately, but as part of *ordinary* items unless the event is also unusual. See *extraordinary* item.

no par. Said of *stock* without a *par value.*

normal cost. *Pension plan expenses* incurred during an *accounting period* for employment services performed during that period. Contrast with *past* and *prior service cost* and see *funded.*

normal spoilage. Costs incurred because of ordinary amounts of spoilage; such costs should be prorated to units produced as *product costs.* Contrast with *abnormal spoilage.*

normal volume. The amount produced in units during a period if *capacity* is used as planned.

note. An unconditional written promise by the maker (borrower) to pay a certain amount on demand or at a certain future time. See *footnotes* for another context.

note receivable discounted. A *note* assigned by the holder to another. If the note is assigned with recourse, it is the *contingent liability* of the assignor until the debt is paid. See *factoring.*

number of days sales in inventory (or receivable). Days of average inventory on hand (or average collection period for receivables). See *ratio.*

NYSE. *New York Stock Exchange.*

O

OASD(H)I. *Old Age, Survivors, Disability, and (Hospital) Insurance.*

objective. See *reporting objective* and *objectivity.*

objectivity. The reporting policy implying that formal recognition will not be given to an event in financial statements until the magnitude of the events can be measured with reasonable accuracy and is subject to independent verification.

obsolescence. A decline in *market value* of an *asset* caused by improved alternatives becoming available that will be more *cost-effective;* the decline in market value is unrelated to physical changes in the asset itself.

off balance sheet financing. A description often used for a *long-term, noncancelable lease* accounted for as an *operating lease.*

Old Age, Survivors, Disability and (Hospital) Insurance. The technical name for Social Security under the Federal Insurance Contribution Act (FICA).

on (open) account. Said of a *purchase* or *sale* when payment is expected sometime after delivery and no *note* evidencing the *debt* is given or received. When a sale (purchase) is made on open account, *accounts receivable (payable)* is *debited (credited).*

on consignment. Said of goods delivered by the owner (the consignor) to another (the consignee) to be sold by the other person; the owner is entitled to the return of the property or payment of an amount agreed upon in advance.

open account. Any *account* with a nonzero debit or credit *balance.* See *on (open) account.*

operating. An adjective used to refer to *revenue* and *expense* items relating to the company's main line(s) of business.

operating accounts. *Revenue, expense,* and *production cost accounts.* Contrast with *balance sheet accounts.*

operating cycle. *Earnings cycle.*

operating expenses. *Expenses* incurred in the course of *ordinary* activities of an *entity.* Frequently, a narrower classification including only *selling, general,* and *administrative expenses,* thereby excluding *cost of goods sold, interest,* and *income tax* expenses.

operating lease. A *lease* accounted for by the *lessee* without showing an *asset* for the lease rights *(leasehold)* or a *liability* for the lease payment obligations. Rental payments of the lessee are merely shown as *expenses* of the period. The lessor keeps the asset on his or her *books* and shows the rental payments as *revenues.* Contrast with *financing lease.* Note that the same lease may, in some cases, be treated as a financing lease by the lessor and an operating lease by the lessee.

operating margin (based on replacement costs). *Revenues* from *sales* minus current *replacement cost* of goods sold. A measure of operating efficiency that is independent of the *cost flow assumption* for *inventory.* Sometimes called "current (gross) margin." See *inventory profit* for example computations.

opinion. The *auditor's report* containing an attestation or lack thereof. Also, *APB Opinion.*

opportunity cost. The *present value* of the *income* (or *costs*) that could be earned (or saved) from using an *asset* in its best alternative use to the one being considered.

option. The legal right to buy something during a specified period at a specified price, called the *exercise* price. Employee stock options should not be confused with put and call options traded in various public markets.

ordinary annuity. An *annuity in arrears.*

ordinary income. For income tax purposes, reportable *income* not qualifying as *capital gains.*

organization costs. The *costs* incurred in planning and establishing an *entity;* example of an *intangible* asset. Often, since the amounts are not *material,* the costs are treated as *expenses* in the period incurred even though the *expenditures* clearly provide future benefits and should be treated as *assets*.

original cost. *Acquisition cost.* In public-utility accounting, the acquisition cost to the *entity* first devoting the asset to public use.

original entry. Entry in a *journal*.

outlay. The amount of an *expenditure*.

out-of-pocket. Said of an *expenditure* usually paid for with cash. An *incremental cost*.

output. Physical quantity or monetary measurement of *goods* and *services* produced.

outside director. A member of a corporate board of directors who is not a company officer and does not participate in the corporation's day-to-day management.

outstanding. Unpaid or uncollected. When said of *stock,* the shares issued less *treasury stock*. When said of checks, it means a check issued that did not clear the *drawer's* bank prior to the *bank statement* date.

over-and-short. Title for an *expense account* used to account for small differences between book balances of actual cash and actual cash and vouchers or receipts in *petty cash* or *change funds*.

overapplied (overabsorbed) overhead. An excess of costs applied, or *charged,* to product for a period over actual *overhead* costs during the period. A *credit balance* in an overhead account after overhead is assigned to product.

overdraft. A check written on a checking account containing less funds than the amount of the check.

overhead costs. Any *cost* not specifically or directly associated with the production of identifiable goods and services. Sometimes called "burden" or "indirect costs" and, in Britain, "oncosts." Frequently limited to manufacturing overhead. See *central corporate expenses* and *manufacturing overhead*.

overhead rate. Standard, or other predetermined, rate at which *overhead costs* are applied to products or to services.

owners' equity. *Proprietorship; assets* minus *liabilities; paid-in capital* plus *retained earnings* of a corporation; partners' capital accounts in a *partnership;* owner's capital account in a *sole proprietorship*.

P

paid-in capital. Sum of balances in *capital stock* and *capital contributed in excess of par (or stated) value* accounts. Same as *contributed capital* (minus *donated capital*).

paper profit. A *gain* not yet realized through a *transaction*. An *unrealized holding gain*.

parent company. Company owning more than 50 percent of the voting shares of another company, called the *subsidiary*.

partially funded. Said of a *pension plan* where not all earned benefits have been funded. See *funded* for funding requirements.

partially vested. Said of a *pension plan* where not all employee benefits are *vested*. See *graded vesting*.

participating dividend. *Dividend* paid to preferred stockholders in addition to the minimum pre-

ferred dividends when the *preferred stock* contract allows such sharing in earnings. Usually applies after dividends on *common stock* have reached a certain level.

participating preferred stock. *Preferred stock* with rights to *participating dividends*.

partner's drawing. A payment to a partner to be charged against his or her share of income or capital. The name of a *temporary account* to record such payments.

partnership. Contractual arrangement between individuals to share resources and operations in a jointly run business. See *general* and *limited partner* and *Uniform Partnership Act*.

par value. *Face amount* of a *security*.

par value method. The method of accounting for *treasury stock* that *debits* a common stock account with the *par value* of the shares reacquired and allocates the remaining debits between the *additional paid-in capital* and *retained earnings* accounts. Contrast with *cost method*.

past service cost. *Present value* at a given time of a *pension plan's* unrecognized, and usually unfunded, benefits assigned to employees for their service before the inception of the plan. A part of *prior service cost*. See *prior service cost* for disclosure rules. See *funded*. Contrast with *normal cost*.

patent. Exclusive right granted by the government to an inventor for seventeen years to enjoy the fruits of an invention. An asset if acquired by purchase. If developed internally, the development costs are *expensed* when incurred under current *GAAP*.

payable. Unpaid but not necessarily due or past due.

pay as you go. Said of an *income tax* scheme where periodic payments of income taxes are made during the period when the income to be taxed is being earned; in contrast to a scheme where no payments are due until the end of, or after, the period whose income is being taxed. (Called PAYE—pay as you earn—in Britain.) Sometimes this phrase is used to describe an *unfunded pension plan,* where payments to pension plan beneficiaries are made from general corporate funds, not from cash previously contributed to a pension fund. Not acceptable as a method of accounting for pension plans.

payback period. Amount of time that must elapse before the cash inflows from a project equal the cash outflows.

payback reciprocal. One divided by the *payback period*. This number approximates the *internal rate of return* on a project when the project life is more than twice the payback period and the cash inflows are identical in every period after the initial investment.

PAYE. See *pay as you go*.

payee. The entity to whom a cash payment is made or who will receive the stated amount of money on a check. See *draft*.

payout ratio. *Common stock dividends* declared for a year divided by net *income* to common stock for the year. A term used by financial analysts. Contrast with *dividend yield*.

payroll taxes. Taxes levied because salaries or wages are paid; for example, *FICA* and unemployment compensation insurance taxes. Typically, the employer pays a portion and withholds part of the employee's wages for the other portion.

pension fund. *Fund,* the assets of which are to be paid to retired ex-employees, usually as a *life annuity.* Usually held by an independent trustee and then is not an *asset* of the firm.

pension plan. Details or provisions of employer's contract with employees for paying retirement *annuities* or other benefits. See *funded, vested, normal cost, past service cost, prior service cost, money-purchase plan,* and *defined-benefit plan.*

per books. An expression used to refer to the *book value* of an item.

percent. Any number, expressed as a decimal, multiplied by 100.

percentage depletion (allowance). Deductible *expense* allowed in some cases by the federal *income tax* regulations; computed as a percentage of gross income from a *natural resource* independent of the unamortized cost of the asset. Since the amount of the total deductions for tax purposes is usually greater than the cost of the asset being *depleted,* many people think the deduction is an unfair tax advantage or "loophole."

percentage of completion method. Recognizing *revenues* and *expenses* on a job, order, or contract (a) in proportion to the *costs* incurred for the period divided by total costs expected to be incurred for the job or order, or (b) in proportion to engineers' estimates of the incremental degree of completion of the job, order, or contract during the period. Contrast with *completed contract method.*

percentage statement. A statement containing, in addition to dollar amounts, ratios of dollar amounts to some base. In a percentage *income statement,* the base is usually either *net sales* or total *revenues* and in a percentage *balance sheet,* the base is usually total *assets.*

period. *Accounting period.*

period cost. An inferior term for *period expense.*

period expense (charge). *Expenditure,* usually based upon the passage of time, charged to operations of the accounting period rather than *capitalized* as an asset. Contrast with *product cost.*

periodic inventory. A method of recording *inventory* that uses data on beginning inventory, additions to inventories, and ending inventory in order to find the cost of withdrawals from inventory.

periodic procedures. The process of making *adjusting entries, closing entries,* and preparing the *financial statements,* usually by use of *trial balances* and *work sheets.*

permanent account. An account which appears on the *balance sheet;* contrast with *temporary account.*

permanent difference. Difference between reported income and taxable income that will never be reversed and, hence, requires no entry in the *deferred income tax (liability)* account. An example is the difference between taxable and reportable income from interest earned on state and municipal bonds. Contrast with *timing difference* and see *deferred tax liability.*

perpetual annuity. *Perpetuity.*

perpetual inventory. Records on quantities and amounts of *inventory* that are changed or made current with each physical addition to or withdrawal from the stock of goods; an inventory so recorded. The records will show the physical quantities and, frequently, the dollar valuations that should be on hand at any time.

perpetuity. An *annuity* whose payments continue forever. The *present value* of a perpetuity in *arrears* is p/r where p is the periodic payment and r is the *interest rate* per period.

personal account. *Drawing account.*

petty cash fund. Currency maintained for expenditures that are conveniently made with cash on hand.

physical verification. *Verification,* by an *auditor,* performed by actually inspecting items in *inventory, plant assets,* and the like. May be based on statistical sampling procedures. Contrasted with mere checking of written records.

plant. *Plant assets.*

plant assets. Buildings, machinery, land, and natural resources. The phrase "property, plant, and equipment" is, therefore, a redundancy. In this context, "plant" means buildings.

pledging. The borrower assigns *assets* as security or *collateral* for repayment of a loan.

pledging of receivables. The process of using expected collections on amounts receivable as *collateral* for a loan. The borrower remains responsible for collecting the receivable but promises to use the proceeds for repaying the debt.

plow back. To retain earnings for continued investment in the business.

plug. In making a *journal entry,* often all *debits* are known, as are all but one of the *credits* (or vice versa). Since *double-entry* bookkeeping requires equal debits and credits, the unknown quantity can be determined by subtracting the sum of the known credits from the sum of all the debits (or vice versa). This process is known as plugging. The unknown found is called the plug. For example, if a *discount* on *bonds payable* is being *amortized* with the *straight-line method,* then *interest expense* is a plug: interest expense = interest payable + discount amortization. See *trade-in transaction* for an example.

pooling of interests method. Accounting for a *business combination* by merely adding together the *book value* of the *assets* and *equities* of the combined firms. Contrast with *purchase method.* Generally leads to a higher reported *net income* for the combined firms than would be reported had the business combination been accounted for as a purchase. See *APB Opinion* No. 16 for the conditions that must be met before the pooling of interests treatment is acceptable.

positive confirmation. See *confirmation.*

post. To record entries in an *account* in a *ledger;* usually the entries are copied from a *journal.*

post-closing trial balance. *Trial balance* taken after all *temporary accounts* have been closed.

post-statement events. Events with *material* impact that occur between the end of the *accounting period* and the formal publication of the *financial statements*. Such events must be disclosed in notes for the auditor to give a *clean opinion,* even though the events are subsequent to the period being reported on.

potentially dilutive. A *security* which may be converted into, or exchanged for, common stock and thereby reduce reported *earnings per share. Options, warrants, convertible bonds,* and *convertible preferred stock.*

pre-closing trial balance. *Trial balance* taken at the end of the period before *closing entries*. In this sense, an *adjusted trial balance*. Sometimes taken before *adjusting entries* and then is synonymous with *unadjusted trial balance*. The hyphen is often omitted in spelling.

predetermined (factory) overhead rate. Rate used in applying *overhead* to products or departments developed at the start of a period by dividing estimated overhead cost by the estimated number of units of overhead allocation base (or *denominator volume*) activity.

pre-emptive right. The privilege of a stockholder to maintain a proportionate share of ownership by purchasing a proportionate share of any new stock issues.

preference as to assets. The rights of *preferred stockholders* to receive certain payments in case of dissolution before common stockholders receive payments.

preferred stock. *Capital stock* with a claim to income or assets after bondholders but before *common stock. Dividends* on preferred stock are income distributions, not expenses. See *cumulative preferred stock.*

premium. The excess of issue (or market) price over *par value*. For a different context, see *insurance.*

premium on capital stock. Alternative but inferior title for *capital contributed in excess of par (or stated) value.*

prepaid expense. An *expenditure* that leads to a *deferred charge* or *prepayment;* strictly speaking, a contradiction in terms for an *expense* is a gone asset and this title refers to past *expenditures,* such as for rent or insurance premiums, that still have future benefits and are *assets.*

prepaid income. An inferior alternative title for *advances from customers*. An item should not be called *revenue* or *income* until goods are delivered or services are rendered.

prepayments. *Deferred charges. Assets* representing *expenditures* for future benefits. Rent and insurance premiums paid in advance are usually classified as *current* prepayments.

present value. Value today of an amount or amounts to be paid or received later, discounted at some *interest rate.*

price. The quantity of one *good* or *service,* usually *cash,* asked in return for a unit of another good or service. See *fair market price.*

price-earnings ratio. At a given time, the market value of a company's *common stock,* per share, divided by the *earnings per* common *share* for the past year. See *ratio.*

price index. A series of numbers, one for each period, that purports to represent some *average* of prices for a series of periods, relative to a base period.

price level. The number from a *price index* series for a given period or date.

price level adjusted statements. *Financial statements* expressed in terms of dollars of uniform purchasing power. *Nonmonetary* items are restated to reflect changes in general *price levels* since the time specific *assets* were acquired and *liabilities* were incurred. A *gain* or *loss* is recognized on *monetary items* as they are held over time periods when the general *price level* changes. Conventional financial statements show *historical costs* and ignore differences in purchasing power in different periods.

price variance. In accounting for *standard costs,* (actual cost per unit – standard cost per unit) times quantity purchased.

primary earnings per share. Net *income* to *common stockholders* plus *interest (net of tax* effects) or *dividends* paid on *common stock equivalents* divided by (weighted-average of common shares outstanding plus the net increase in the number of common shares that would become *outstanding* if all common stock equivalents were exchanged for common shares with cash proceeds, if any, used to retire common shares).

prime cost. Sum of *direct materials* plus *direct labor* costs assigned to product.

prime rate. The rate for loans charged by commercial banks to their most preferred risks. For the *earnings-per-share* purpose of deciding whether a security is or is not a *common stock equivalent,* the corporation should use the rate in effect at the bank at which it does business or an average of such rates if the corporation does business with more than one bank. The *Federal Reserve Bulletin* is considered the authoritative source of information about historical prime rates.

principal. An amount on which *interest* is charged or earned.

principle. See *generally accepted accounting principles.*

prior-period adjustment. A *debit* or *credit* made directly to *retained earnings* (that does not affect *income* for the period) to adjust retained earnings for such things as lawsuit settlements and changes in *income tax expense* of prior periods. Theory would suggest that corrections of errors in accounting estimates (such as the *depreciable life* or *salvage value* of an asset) should be treated as adjustments to retained earnings. But *GAAP* require that corrections of such estimates flow through current, and perhaps future, *income statements*. See *accounting changes* and *accounting errors.*

prior service cost. *Present value* at a given time of a *pension plan's* unrecognized benefits assigned to employees for their service before that given time. Includes *past service cost*. Such obligations are not recognized as liabilities in the accounting records, but must be disclosed in the notes to the financial statements. Contrast with *normal cost.*

See *funded*. See the General Electric annual report at notes 39-41 for examples.

proceeds. The *funds* received from disposition of assets or from the issue of securities.

process costing. A method of *cost accounting* based on average costs (total cost divided by the *equivalent units* of work done in a period). Typically used for assembly lines or for products that are produced in a series of steps that are more continuous than discrete.

product. *Goods* or *services* produced.

product cost. Any *manufacturing cost* that can be inventoried. See *flow of costs* for example and contrast with *period expenses*.

production cost. *Manufacturing cost.*

production cost account. A *temporary account* for collecting *manufacturing costs* during a period.

production method (depreciation). The depreciable asset is given a *depreciable life* measured, not in elapsed time, but in units of output or perhaps in units of time of actual use. Then the *depreciation* charge for a period is a portion of depreciable cost equal to a fraction determined by dividing the actual output produced during the period by the expected total output to be produced over the life of the asset. Sometimes called the "units of production (or output) method."

production method (revenue recognition). *Percentage of completion method* for recognizing *revenue*.

profit. Excess of *revenues* over *expenses* for a *transaction;* sometimes used synonymously with *net income* for the period.

profitability accounting. *Responsibility accounting.*

profit and loss sharing ratio. The fraction of *net income* or loss allocable to a partner in a *partnership*. Need not be the same fraction as the partner's share of capital.

profit and loss statement. *Income statement.*

profit center. A segment of a business responsible for its own *revenues* and *expenses*.

profit margin. Sales minus all expenses as a single amount. Frequently used to mean the ratio of sales minus all *operating* expenses divided by sales.

profit maximization. The doctrine that a given set of operations should be accounted for so as to make reported *net income* as large as possible. Contrast with *conservatism*. This concept in accounting is slightly different from the profit maximizing concept in economics where the doctrine states that businesses should be run to maximize the present value of the firm's wealth, generally by equating *marginal costs* and *marginal revenues*.

profit-volume graph. See *breakeven chart*.

profit-volume ratio. Net *income* divided by net sales in dollars.

pro forma statements. Hypothetical statements. Financial statements as they would appear if some event, such as a *merger* or increased production and sales, had occurred or were to occur. Pro forma is often spelled as one word.

progressive tax. Tax for which the rate increases as the taxed base, such as income, increases. Contrast with *regressive tax*.

projected financial statement. *Pro forma* financial statement.

promissory note. An unconditional written promise to pay a specified sum of money on demand or at a specified date.

proof of journal. The process of checking arithmetic accuracy of *journal entries* by testing for the equality of all *debits* with all *credits* since the last previous proof.

property dividend. A *dividend in kind*.

proprietary accounts. See *budgetary accounts* for contrast in context of governmental accounting.

proprietorship. *Assets* minus *liabilities* of an *entity;* equals *contributed capital* plus *retained earnings*.

proprietorship theory. The view of the corporation that emphasizes the form of the *accounting equation* that says *assets – liabilities = stockholders' equity*. Contrast with *entity theory*. The major implication of a choice between these theories deals with the treatment of *subsidiaries*. For example, the view that *minority interest* is an *indeterminate-term liability* is based on the proprietorship theory. The proprietorship theory implies using a *single-step income statement*.

prorate. To *allocate* in proportion to some base; for example, to allocate *service department* costs in proportion to hours of service used by the benefited departments.

prospectus. Formal written document describing *securities* to be issued. See *proxy*.

protest fee. Fee charged by banks or other financial agencies when items (such as checks) presented for collection cannot be collected.

provision. Often the exact amount of an *expense* is uncertain, but must be recognized currently anyway. The entry for the estimated expense, such as for *income taxes* or expected costs under *warranty,* is:

Expense (Estimated) X
Liability (Estimated) X

In American usage, the term "provision" is often used in the expense account title of the above entry. Thus, Provision for Income Taxes is used to mean the estimate of income tax expense. (In British usage, the term "provision" is used in the title for the estimated liability of the above entry, so that Provision for Income Taxes is a balance sheet account.)

proxy. Written authorization given by one person to another so that the second person can act for the first, such as to vote shares of stock. Of particular significance to accountants because the *SEC* presumes that financial information is distributed by management along with its proxy solicitations.

public accountant. Generally, this term is synonymous with *certified public accountant*. In some jurisdictions individuals have been licensed as public accountants without being CPA's; such public accountants may not perform the *attest* function.

public accounting. That portion of accounting primarily involving the *attest* function, culminating in the *auditor's report*.

PuPU. An acronym for *p*urchasing *p*ower *u*nit. Some, including the Chief Accountant of the *SEC,* who think *general price level adjusted* accounting is not particularly useful, poke fun at it by calling it "PuPu accounting."

purchase allowance. A reduction in sales *invoice price* usually granted because the *goods* received by the purchaser were not exactly as ordered. The goods are not returned to the seller, but are purchased at a price lower than originally agreed upon.

purchase discount. A reduction in sales *invoice price* granted for prompt payment. See *sales discount* and *terms of sale.*

purchase method. Accounting for a *business combination* by adding the acquired company's assets at the price paid for them to the acquiring company's assets. Contrast with *pooling of interests method.* Since the acquired assets are put on the books at current, rather than original costs, the *amortization expenses* are usually larger (and reported income, smaller) than for the same business combination accounted for as a pooling of interests.

purchase order. Document authorizing a seller to deliver goods with payment to be made later.

Q

qualified report (opinion). *Auditor's* report containing a statement that the auditor was unable to complete a satisfactory examination of all things considered relevant or that the auditor has doubts about the financial impact of some item reported in the financial statements. See *except for* and *subject to.*

qualified (stock) option (plan). Said of a compensation scheme in which *options* to purchase *stock* are granted to employees and in which the implicit compensation is neither tax deductible as an *expense* by the employer nor taxable *income* to the employee.

quantity discount. A reduction in purchase price as quantity purchased increases; amount of the discount is constrained by law (Robinson-Patman Act). Not to be confused with *purchase discount.*

quantity variance. In *standard cost* systems, the standard price per unit times (actual quantity used minus standard quantity that should be used).

quasi-reorganization. A *reorganization* where no new company is formed or no court has intervened, as would happen in *bankruptcy.* The primary purpose is to absorb a *deficit* and get a "fresh start."

quick assets. *Assets* readily convertible into *cash;* includes cash, *marketable securities* and *receivables.*

quick ratio. *Acid test* ratio. See *ratio.*

R

R & D. See *research and development.*

rate of return (on total capital). See *ratio* and *all capital earnings rate.*

rate variance. *Price variance.*

ratio. The number resulting when one number is divided by another. Ratios are generally used to assess aspects of profitability, solvency, and liquidity. The commonly used financial ratios are of essentially two kinds:

(1) those that summarize some aspect of operations for a period, usually a year, and

(2) those that summarize some aspect of *financial position* at a given moment—the moment for which a balance sheet has been prepared.

The table on the next page lists the most common financial ratios and shows separately both the numerator and denominator used to calculate the ratio.

For all ratios that require an average balance during the period, the average is most often derived as one-half the sum of the beginning and ending balances. Sophisticated analysts recognize, however, that when companies use a fiscal year different from the calendar year, this averaging of beginning and ending balances may be misleading. Consider, for example, the *all capital earnings rate* of Sears, Roebuck & Company whose fiscal year ends on January 31. Sears chooses a January 31 closing date at least in part because inventories are at a low level and are therefore easy to count—the Christmas merchandise has been sold and the Easter merchandise has not yet all been received. Furthermore, by January 31, most Christmas purchases have been paid for or returned, so receivable amounts are not unusually large. Thus at January 31, the amount of total assets is lower than at many other times during the year. Consequently, the denominator of the all capital earnings rate, total assets, for Sears is more likely to represent the smallest amount of total assets on hand during the year than the average amount. The all capital earnings rate for Sears and other companies who choose a fiscal year-end to coincide with low points in the inventory cycle is likely to be larger than if a more accurate estimate of the average amounts of total assets were used.

raw material. Goods purchased for use in manufacturing a product.

reacquired stock. *Treasury stock.*

real accounts. *Balance sheet accounts;* as opposed to *nominal accounts.* See *permanent accounts.*

real estate. *Land* and its *improvements,* such as landscaping and roads but not buildings.

realizable value. *Market value* or, sometimes, *net realizable value.*

realization convention. The accounting practice of delaying the recognition of *gains* and *losses* from changes in the market price of *assets* until the assets are sold. However, unrealized losses on *inventory* and *marketable securities* are recognized prior to sale when the *lower-of-cost-or-market* valuation basis is used.

realize. To convert into *funds.* See *recognize.*

realized holding gain. See *inventory profit* for definition and an example.

rearrangement costs. *Costs* of re-installing an asset, perhaps in a different location. Should be *capitalized* as part of the asset's cost, just as is original installation cost.

recapitalization. *Reorganization.*

FINANCIAL RATIOS DEFINED

Ratio	Numerator	Denominator
Ratios Summarizing Operations of a Period		
All Capital Earnings Rate	Net Income + Minority Share of After-tax Income + Interest Charges Net of Tax Effects[1]	Average of Total Assets during the Period.
Rate of Return on Stockholders' Equity	Net Income	Average Stockholders' Equity during the Period
Rate of Return on Common-Stock Equity	Net Income — Preferred Stock Dividends	Average Common Stockholders' Equity during the Period
Earnings per Share on Common Stock[2]	Net Income — Preferred Stock Dividends	Average Number of Common Shares Outstanding during the Period
Operating Ratio Based Upon Revenues	Total Expenses	Total Revenues
Operating Ratio Based Upon Net Sales	Total Expenses	Net Sales
Inventory Turnover	Cost of Goods Sold	Average Inventory during the Period
Days of Average Inventory on Hand	365	Inventory Turnover
Receivables Turnover	Net Sales on Account	Average Accounts Receivable during the Period
Average Collection Period of Receivables	365	Receivables Turnover
Asset Turnover	Net Sales	Average Assets during the Period
Turnover of Plant and Equipment	Net Sales	Average of Land, Buildings, and Equipment Accounts during the Period
Times Interest Earned	Income before Interest and Income Tax Charges[3]	Interest Charges
Ratios Summarizing Financial Position at a Moment in Time		
Current Ratio	Total Current Assets	Total Current Liabilities
Acid-Test or Quick Ratio	Quick Assets (Ordinarily: Cash, Marketable Securities, and Receivables[4])	Total Current Liabilities
Equity Ratio[5]	Total Stockholders' Equity	Total Equities (=Total Assets)
Debt-Equity Ratio[6]	Total Liabilities	Total Equities
Book Value per Share of Common Stock	Total Stockholders' Equity — Preferred Stockholders' Equity	Number of Common Shares Outstanding
Price-Earnings Ratio	Market Price per Share of Common Stock	Earnings per Share of Common Stock for the Last Year

[1]Interest charges net of tax effects = $(1 - t) \times$ interest charges where t is the average tax rate.
[2]See *primary earnings per share* and *fully diluted earnings per share* for complications when there are residual securities outstanding.
[3]May be merely income before interest charges.
[4]Receivables should be excluded for some businesses and inventories should be included for others. In practice, however, neither of these realistic adjustments is made.
[5]Sometimes called the *worth-debt ratio.*
[6]We include minority interest in total liabilities.

receipt. Acquisition of *cash.*

receivable. Any *collectible* whether or not it is currently due.

receivables turnover. See *ratio* and the General Electric annual report at note 59.

reciprocal holdings. Company A owns stock of Company B and Company B owns stock of Company A.

recognize. To enter a transaction in the books. Some writers use "recognize" to indicate that an event has been *journalized* and use "realize" only for those events that affect the *income statement.*

reconciliation. A calculation that shows how one balance or figure is derived systematically from another, such as a *reconciliation of retained earnings* or a *bank reconciliation schedule.* See *articulate.*

record date. *Dividends* are paid on payment date to those who own the stock on the record date.

recourse. See *note receivable discounted.*

redemption. Retirement by the issuer, usually by a purchase or *call,* of *stocks* or *bonds.*

redemption premium. *Call premium.*

redemption value. The price to be paid by a corporation to retire *bonds* or *preferred stock* if called before *maturity.*

refunding bond issue. Said of a *bond* issue whose proceeds are used to retire bonds already *outstanding.*

register. Collection of consecutive entries, or other information, in chronological order, such as a check register or an insurance register, which lists all insurance policies owned. If entries are recorded, it may serve as a *journal.*

registered bond. *Principal* of such a *bond* and *interest,* if registered as to interest, is paid to the owner listed on the books of the issuer. As opposed to a bearer bond where the possessor of the bond is entitled to interest and principal.

registrar. An *agent,* usually a bank or trust company, appointed by a corporation to keep track of the names of stockholders and distributions of earnings.

registration statement. Statement required by the Securities Act of 1933 of most companies wishing to *issue securities* to the public or by the Securities Exchange Act of 1934 of a company wishing to have its securities traded in public markets. The statement discloses financial data and other items of interest to potential investors.

regressive tax. Tax for which the rate decreases as the taxed base, such as income, increases. Contrast with *progressive tax.*

Regulation S-X. The *SEC*'s regulation specifying the form and content of financial reports to the SEC.

reinvestment rate. In a *capital budgeting* context, the rate at which cash inflows from a project occurring before the project's completion are invested. Once such a rate is assumed, there will never be multiple *internal rates of return.* See *Descartes' rule of signs.*

relative sales value method. A method for *allocating joint costs* in proportion to *net realizable values* of the joint products. For example, joint products A and B together cost $100 and A sells for $60 while B sells for $90. Then A would be allocated ($60/$150)×$100=.40×$100=$40 of cost while B would be allocated ($90/$150)×$100=$60 of cost.

relevant cost. *Incremental cost.*

relevant range. Activity levels over which costs are linear or for which *flexible budget* estimates and *breakeven charts* will remain valid.

remittance advice. Information on a *check* stub, or on a document attached to a check by the *drawer,* which tells the *payee* why a payment is being made.

rent. A charge for the use of land, buildings, or other assets.

re-order point. See *economic order quantity.*

reorganization. A major change in the *capital structure* of a corporation that leads to changes in the rights, interests, and implied ownership of the various security owners. Usually results from a *merger* or agreement by senior security holders to take action to forestall *bankruptcy.*

repair. An *expenditure* to restore an *asset's* service potential after damage or after prolonged use. In the second sense, after prolonged use, the difference between repairs and maintenance is one of degree and not of kind. Treated as an *expense* of the period when incurred. Because repairs and maintenance are treated similarly in this regard, the distinction is not important. Contrast with *improvement.*

replacement cost. For an asset, the current fair market price to purchase another, similar asset (with the same future benefit or service potential). *Current cost.* See *reproduction cost.*

replacement method of depreciation. The original-cost *depreciation* charge is augmented by an amount based upon a portion of the difference between the *current replacement cost* of the asset and its *original cost.*

report. *Financial statement; auditor's report.*

reporting objectives (policies). The general doctrines underlying accounting. These include *full disclosure, objectivity, consistency, conservatism,* the assumption of *continuity of operations,* and *materiality.*

reproduction cost. The *cost* necessary to construct an *asset* similar in all important respects to another asset for which a *current value* is wanted but not readily available from market prices. See *replacement cost.*

requisition. A formal written order or request, such as for withdrawal of supplies from the storeroom.

resale value. *Exit value. Net realizable value.*

research and development. Research is activity aimed at discovering new knowledge in hopes that such activity will be useful in creating a new product, process, or service or improving a present product, process, or service. Development is the translation of research findings or other knowledge into a new or improved product, process, or service. The *FASB* requires that costs of such activities be *expensed* as incurred on the grounds that the future benefits are too uncertain to warrant *capitalization* as an *asset.* This treatment seems questionable to us because we wonder why firms would continue to undertake R & D if there were no expectation of future benefit; if future benefits exist, then the *costs* should be assets.

reserve. When properly used in accounting, the term refers to an account that appropriates *retained earnings* and restricts dividend declarations. Appropriating retained earnings is itself a poor and slowly vanishing practice, so the word should seldom be used in accounting. In addition, used in the past to indicate an asset *contra* (for example, "reserve for depreciation") or an *estimated liability* (for example, "reserve for warranty costs"). In any case, reserve accounts have credit balances and are not pools of *funds* as the unwary reader might infer. If a company has set aside a pool of *cash (or marketable securities)*, then that cash will be called a *fund*.

No other word in accounting is so misunderstood and misused by laymen and "experts" who should know better. A leading unabridged dictionary defines *reserve* as "Cash, or assets readily convertible into cash, held aside, as by a corporation, bank, state or national government, etc. to meet expected or unexpected demands." This definition is absolutely wrong in accounting. Reserves are not funds. For example, a contingency fund of $10,000 is created by depositing cash in a fund and this entry is made:

Dr. Contingency Fund 10,000
    Cr. Cash 10,000

The following entry may accompany this entry, if retained earnings are to be appropriated:

Dr. Retained Earnings 10,000
    Cr. Reserve for Contingencies 10,000

The transaction leading to the first entry is an event of economic significance. The second entry has little economic impact for most firms. The problem with the word *reserves* arises because the second entry can be made without the first—a company can create a reserve, that is appropriate retained earnings, without creating a fund. The problem is at least in part caused by the fact that in common usage, "reserve" means a pool of assets, as in the phrase "oil reserves." The *Internal Revenue Service* does not help in dispelling confusion about the term *reserves*. The federal *income tax* return for corporations uses the title "Reserve for Bad Debts" to mean the "Allowance for Uncollectible Accounts" and speaks of the "Reserve Method" in referring to the *allowance method* for estimating *revenue* or *income* reductions from estimated *uncollectibles*.

residual security. A *potentially dilutive security*. *Options, warrants, convertible bonds,* and *convertible preferred stock*.

residual value. At any time, the estimated, or actual, *net realizable value* of an *asset,* usually a depreciable *plant asset*. In the context of depreciation accounting, this term is equivalent to *salvage value* and is preferable to *scrap value*, because the asset need not be scrapped. Sometimes used to mean net *book value*. In the context of a *noncancelable* lease, the estimated value of the leased asset at the end of the lease period. See *lease*.

responsibility accounting. Accounting for a business by considering various units as separate entities, or *profit centers,* giving management of each unit responsibility for the unit's *revenues* and *expenses*. Sometimes called "activity accounting." See *transfer price*.

restricted assets. Governmental resources restricted by legal or contractual requirements for specific purposes.

restricted retained earnings. That part of *retained earnings* not legally available for *dividends*. See *retained earnings, appropriated*. Bond indentures and other loan contracts can curtail the legal ability of the corporation to declare dividends without formally requiring a retained earnings appropriation.

retail inventory method. Ascertaining *inventory* amounts for financial statements by using ratios of cost to selling price. That is, *cost of sales* = (1 — *markup percentage*) ×*sales;* and *ending inventory* = (1 — *markup percentage*) × *ending inventory* at retail prices.

retained earnings. Net *income* over the life of a corporation less all income distributions (including capitalization through stock dividends); *owners' equity* less *contributed capital*.

retained earnings, appropriated. An *account* set up by crediting it and debiting *retained earnings*. Used to indicate that a portion of retained earnings is not available for dividends. The practice of appropriating retained earnings is misleading unless all capital is earmarked with its use, which is not practical. Use of formal retained earnings appropriations is declining.

retained earnings statement. *Generally accepted accounting principles* require that whenever *comparative balance sheets* and an *income statement* are presented, there must also be presented a *reconciliation* of the beginning and ending balances in the *retained earnings account*. This reconciliation can appear in a separate statement, in a combined statement of income and retained earnings or in the balance sheet.

retirement method of depreciation. A method under which no *depreciation* charges are made until the asset is about to be retired. Such a method is based upon the assumption that the asset's services per unit of time do not diminish until the asset itself expires. The assumption is not realistic in most cases and the method is seldom used. This "method" is not actually depreciation, which is a systematic allocation of costs to the periods of benefit.

retirement plan. *Pension plan*.

return. A schedule of information required by governmental bodies, such as the tax return required by the *Internal Revenue Service*. Also the physical return of merchandise. See also *return on investment*.

return of capital investment (capital). A payment to owners *debited* to an *owners' equity account* other than *retained earnings*.

return on investment (capital). *Income* (before distributions to suppliers of capital) for a period.

As a rate, this amount divided by average total assets. *Interest,* net of tax effects, should be added back to *net income* for the numerator. See *ratio.*

revenue. The monetary measure of a service rendered. Do not confuse with *receipt* of funds which may occur before, when, or after revenue is recognized.

revenue-cost graph. See *breakeven chart.*

revenue expenditure. A phrase sometimes used to mean *expense* in contrast to a capital *expenditure* to acquire an *asset* or to discharge a *liability.* Avoid using this phrase.

revenue received in advance. An inferior term for *advances from customers.*

reversal (reversing) entry. An *entry* in which all *debits* and *credits* are the credits and debits, respectively, of another entry, and in the same amounts. It is usually made on the first day of an *accounting period* to reverse a previous *adjusting entry,* usually an *accrual.* The purpose of such entries is to make the bookkeeper's tasks easier. Suppose that salaries are paid every other Friday, with paychecks compensating employees for the two weeks just ended. Total salaries accrue at the rate of $5,000 per five-day work week. The bookkeeper is accustomed to making the following entry every other Friday:

(1) Salary Expense 10,000
    Cash 10,000
    To record salary expense and salary payments.

If paychecks are delivered to employees on Friday, December 26, 1975, then the *adjusting entry* made on December 31 (or, perhaps, later) to record accrued salaries for December 29, 30, and 31 would be:

(2) Salary Expense 3,000
    Salaries Payable 3,000
    To charge 1975 operations with all salaries earned in 1975.

The Salary Expense account would be closed as part of the December 31 *closing entries.* On the next pay day, January 9, the salary entry would have to be:

(3) Salary Expense 7,000
    Salaries Payable 3,000
    Cash 10,000
    To record salary payments split between expense for 1976 (7 days) and liability carried over from 1975 (3 days).

To make entry (3), the bookkeeper must look back into the records to see how much of the debit is to Salaries Payable accrued from the previous year so that total debits are properly split between 1976 expense and the liability carried over from 1975. Notice that this entry forces the bookkeeper both (a) to refer to balances in old accounts and (b) to make an entry different from the one customarily made, entry (1).

The reversing entry, made just after the books have been closed for 1975, makes the salary entry for January 9, 1976, the same as that made on all other Friday pay days. The reversing entry merely *reverses* the adjusting entry (2):

(4) Salaries Payable 3,000
    Salary Expense 3,000
    To reverse the adjusting entry.

This entry results in a zero balance in the Salaries Payable account and a *credit* balance in the Salary Expense account. If entry (4) is made just after the books are closed for 1975, then the entry on January 9 will be the customary entry (1). Entries (4) and (1) together have exactly the same effect as entry (3).

The procedure for using reversal entries is as follows: The required adjustment to record an accrual (*payable* or *receivable*) is made at the end of an *accounting period;* the closing entry is made as usual; as of the first day of the following period, an entry is made reversing the adjusting entry; when a payment is made (or received), the entry is recorded as though no adjusting entry had been recorded. Whether or not reversal entries are used affects the record-keeping procedures, but not the financial statements.

Also used to describe the entry reversing an incorrect entry before recording the correct entry.

reverse stock split. A stock split in which the number of shares *outstanding* is decreased. See *stock split.*

revolving fund. A *fund* whose amounts are continually expended and then replenished; for example, a *petty cash fund.*

revolving loan. A *loan* which is expected to be renewed at *maturity.*

right. The privilege to subscribe to new *stock* issues or to purchase stock. Usually, rights are contained in securities called *warrants* and the warrants can be sold to others. See also *preemptive right.*

risk. A measure of the variability of the *return on investment.* For a given expected amount of return, most people prefer less risk to more risk. Therefore, in rational markets, investments with more risk usually promise, or are expected to yield, a higher rate of return than investments with lower risk. Most people use "risk" and "uncertainty" as synonyms. In technical language, however, these terms have different meanings. "Risk" is used when the probabilities attached to the various outcomes are known, such as the probabilities of heads or tails in the flip of a fair coin. "Uncertainty" refers to an event where the probabilities of the outcomes, such as winning or losing a lawsuit, can only be estimated.

risk-adjusted discount rate. In a *capital budgeting* context, a decision maker compares projects by comparing their *net present values* for a given *interest* rate, usually the *cost of capital.* If a given project's outcome is considered to be much more or much less risky than the normal undertakings of the company, then the interest rate will be increased (if the project is more risky) or decreased (if less risky) and the rate used is said to be risk-adjusted.

risk premium. Extra compensation paid to an employee or extra interest paid to a lender, over amounts usually considered normal, in return for their undertaking to engage in activities more risky than normal.

royalty. Compensation for the use of property, usually copyrighted material or natural resources, expressed as a percentage of receipts from using the property or as an account per unit produced.

rule of 69. An amount of money invested at r percent per period will double in 69/r + .35 periods. This approximation is accurate to one-tenth of a period for interest rates between ¼ and 100 percent per period. For example, at 10 percent per period, the rule says a given sum will double in 69/10 + .35 = 7.25 periods. At 10 percent per period, a given sum doubles in 7.27+ periods.

rule of 72. An amount of money invested at r percent per period will double in 72/r periods. A reasonable approximation but not nearly as accurate as the *rule of 69*. For example, at 10 percent per period, the rule says a given sum will double in 72/10 = 7.2 periods.

rule of 78. The rule followed by many finance companies for allocating earnings on *loans* among the months of a year on the sum-of-the-months'-digits basis. The sum of the digits from 1 through 12 is 78, so 12/78 of the year's earnings are allocated to the first month, 11/78 to the second month, and so on. See *sum-of-the-years'-digits depreciation.*

ruling an account. The process of summarizing a series of entries in an *account* by computing a new *balance* and drawing double lines to indicate the information above the double lines has been summarized in the new balance. The process is illustrated below. The steps are as follows. (1) Compute the sum of all *debit* entries including opening debit balance, if any—$1,364.16. (2) Compute the sum of all credit entries including opening credit balance, if any—$13.57. (3) If the amount in (1) is larger than the amount in (2), then write the excess as a credit with a check mark—$1,364.16 – $13.57 = $1,350.59. (4) Add both debit and credit columns, which should both now sum

to the same amount, and show that identical total at the foot of both columns. (5) Draw double lines under those numbers and write the excess of debits over credits as the new debit balance with a check mark. (6) If the amount in (2) is larger than the amount in (1), then write the excess as a debit with a check mark. (7) Do steps (4) and (5) except that the excess becomes the new credit balance. (8) If the amount in (1) is equal to the amount in (2), then the balance is zero and only the totals with the double lines beneath them need be shown.

This process is illustrated below.

S

salary. Compensation earned by managers, administrators, professionals, not based on an hourly rate. Contrast with *wage.*

sale. A *revenue* transaction where *goods* or *services* are delivered to a customer in return for cash or a contractual obligation to pay.

sale and leaseback. Phrase used to describe a *financing* transaction where improved property is sold but is taken back for use on a long-term *lease.* Such transactions often have advantageous income tax effects.

sales allowance. A reduction in sales *invoice* price usually given because the goods received by the buyer are not exactly what was ordered. The amounts of such adjustments are often accumulated by the seller in a temporary *revenue contra account* having this, or a similar, title.

sales basis of revenue recognition. *Revenue* is recognized, not as goods are produced nor as orders are received, but only when the sale (delivery) has been consummated and cash or a legal receivable obtained. Most revenue is recognized on this basis. Compare with the *percentage of completion method* and the *installment method.* Identical with the *completed contract*

An Open Account, Ruled and Balanced

(Steps indicated in parentheses correspond to steps described in "ruling an account".)

	Date		Explanation	Ref.	Debit		Date		Explanation	Ref.	Credit		
	1975						1975						
	Jan.	13		VR	121	37	Sept.	15		J		42	
	Mar.	20		VR	56	42	Nov.	12		J	13	15	
	June	5		J	1,138	09	Dec.	31	Balance	✓	1,350	59	(3)
	Aug.	18		J	1	21							
	Nov.	20		VR	38	43							
	Dec.	7		VR	8	64							
(4)					1,364	16					1,364	16	(4)
	1976						1976						
(5)	Jan.	1	Balance	✓	1,350	59							

method but this latter term is ordinarily used only for *long-term* construction projects.

sales discount. Reduction in sales *invoice* price usually offered for prompt payment. See *terms of sale* and *2/10, n/30.*

sales return. The physical return of merchandise; the amounts of such returns are often accumulated by the seller in a temporary *revenue contra account.*

sales, uncollectible accounts adjustment. The preferred title for the *contra-revenue account* to recognize estimated reductions in income caused by accounts receivable that will not be collected. Called *bad debt expense* and treated as an expense, rather than an adjustment to revenue, when the write-off method is used. See *allowance for uncollectibles* and *allowance method.*

sales value method. *Relative sales value method.*

salvage value. Actual or estimated selling price, net of removal or disposal costs, of a used *plant asset* to be sold or otherwise retired. See *residual value.*

schedule. Supporting set of calculations which show how figures in a statement or tax return are derived.

scientific method. *Effective interest method* of *amortizing bond discount* or *premium.*

scrap value. *Salvage value* assuming item is to be junked. A *net realizable value.*

SEC. Securities and Exchange Commission, an agency authorized by the U.S. Congress to regulate, among other things, the financial reporting practices of most public corporations. The SEC has indicated that it will usually allow the *FASB* to set accounting principles but it reserves the right to require more disclosure than required by the FASB. The SEC's accounting requirements are stated in its *Accounting Series Releases* (ASR) and *Regulation S-X.* See also *registration statement* and *10-K.*

secret reserve. *Hidden reserve.*

Securities and Exchange Commission. *SEC.*

security. Document that indicates ownership or indebtedness.

segment (of a business). As defined by *APB Opinion* No. 30, "a component of an *entity* whose activities represent a separate major line of business or class of customer...[It may be] a *subsidiary,* a division, or a department,...provided that its *assets,* results of *operations,* and activities can be clearly distinguished, physically and operationally for financial reporting purposes, from the other assets, results of operations, and activities of the entity."

segment reporting. *Line of business reporting.*

self-balancing. A set of records with equal *debits* and *credits* such as the *ledger* (but not individual accounts), the *balance sheet,* and a *fund* in nonprofit accounting.

self-insurance. See *insurance.*

selling and administrative expenses. *Expenses* not specifically identifiable with, nor assigned to, production.

semifixed costs. *Costs* that increase with activity as a step function.

semivariable costs. *Costs* that increase strictly linearly with activity but that are positive at zero activity level. Royalty fees of two percent of sales are variable; royalty fees of $1,000 per year plus two percent of sales are semivariable.

serial bonds. An *issue* of *bonds* that mature in part at one date, another part on another date, and so on; the various maturity dates usually are equally spaced. Contrast with *term bonds.*

service basis of depreciation. *Production method.*

service department. A department, such as the personnel or computer department, that provides services to other departments, rather than direct work on salable product.

service life. Period of expected usefulness of an asset; may not coincide with *depreciable life* for income tax purposes.

service potential. The future benefits embodied in an item that cause the item to be classified as an *asset.* Without service potential, there are no future benefits and the item should not be classified as an asset.

services. Useful work done by a person, a machine, or an organization. See *goods and services.*

setup. The time or costs required to prepare production equipment for doing a job.

share. A unit of *stock* representing ownership in a corporation.

short-term. Current; ordinarily, due within one year.

shrinkage. An excess of *inventory* shown on the *books* over actual physical quantities on hand. Can result from theft or shoplifting as well as from evaporation or general wear and tear.

sight draft. A demand for payment drawn by a person to whom money is owed. The *draft* is presented to the borrower's (the debtor's) bank in expectation that the borrower will authorize its bank to disburse the funds. Such drafts are often used when a seller sells goods to a new customer in a different city. The seller is not sure whether the buyer will pay the bill. The seller sends the *bill* of lading, or other evidence of ownership of the goods, along with a sight draft to the buyer's bank. The buyer is therefore notified that if the goods are to be released to the buyer, the bank must be instructed to honor the sight draft. Once the sight draft is honored, the bill of lading or other document evidencing ownership is handed over to the buyer and the goods become the property of the buyer.

simple interest. *Interest* calculated on *principal* where interest earned during periods before maturity of the loan is neither added to the principal nor paid to the lender. *Interest = principal × interest rate × time.* Seldom used in economic calculations except for periods less than one year. Contrast with *compound interest.*

single-entry accounting. Accounting that is neither *self-balancing* nor *articulated;* that is, it does not rely on equal *debits* and *credits. No journal entries* are made. *Plugging* is required to derive *owners' equity* for the *balance sheet.*

single proprietorship. *Sole proprietorship.*

single step. Said of an *income statement* where all *ordinary revenue* and *gain* items are shown first and totaled. Then all ordinary *expenses* and *losses* are totaled. Their difference, plus the effect of *income from discontinued operations* and *extraordinary items,* is shown as *net income.* Contrast with *multiple-step* and see *proprietorship theory.*

sinking fund. *Assets* and their earnings earmarked for the retirement of bonds or other long-term obligations. Earnings of sinking fund investments are taxable income of the company.

sinking fund method of depreciation. The periodic charge is an amount so that when the charges are considered to be an *annuity,* the value of the annuity at the end of depreciable life is equal to the *acquisition cost* of the asset. In theory, the charge for a period ought also to include interest on the accumulated depreciation at the start of the period as well. A *fund* of cash is not necessarily, or even usually, accumulated.

skeleton account. *T-account.*

slide. The name of the error made by a bookkeeper in recording the digits of a number correctly with the decimal point misplaced; for example, recording $123.40 as $1,234.00 or as $12.34.

soak-up method. The *equity method.*

Social Security taxes. Taxes levied by the federal government on both employers and employees to provide *funds* to pay retired persons (or their survivors) who are entitled to receive such payments, either because they paid Social Security taxes themselves or because the Congress has declared them eligible. See *Old Age, Survivors, Disability,* and *(Hospital) Insurance.*

sole proprietorship. All *owner's equity* belongs to one person.

solvent. Able to meet debts when due.

sound value. A phrase used mainly in appraisals of *fixed assets* to mean *fair market value* or *replacement cost* in present condition.

source of funds. Any *transaction* that increases *working capital.*

sources and uses statement. *Statement of changes in financial position.*

SOYD. *Sum-of-the-years'-digits depreciation.*

special assessment. A compulsory levy made by a governmental unit on property to pay the costs of a specific improvement, or service, presumed not to benefit the general public but only the owners of the property so assessed. Accounted for in a special assessment fund.

special journal. A *journal,* such as a sales journal or cash disbursements journal, to record *transactions* of a similar nature that occur frequently.

special revenue debt. Debt of a governmental unit backed only by revenues from specific sources such as tolls from a bridge.

specific identification method. Method for valuing *ending inventory* and *cost of goods sold* by identifying actual units sold and in inventory and summing the actual costs of those individual units.

specific price changes. Changes in the market prices of specific *goods and services.* Contrast with *general price level changes.*

specific price index. A measure of the price of a specific good or service, or a small group of similar goods or services, at one time relative to the price during a base period. Contrast with *general price index.* See *dollar-value LIFO method.*

spending variance. In *standard cost systems,* the *rate* or *price variance* for *overhead costs.*

split. *Stock split.* Sometimes called "splitup."

splitoff point. The point where all costs are no longer *joint costs* but can be identified with individual products or perhaps with a smaller number of *joint products.*

spread sheet. A *work sheet* organized like a *matrix* that provides a two-way classification of accounting data. The rows and columns are both labeled with *account* titles. An entry in a row represents a *debit* while an entry in a column represents a *credit.* Thus, the number "100" in the "cash" row and the "accounts receivable" column records an entry debiting cash and crediting accounts receivable for $100. A given row total indicates all debit entries to the account represented by that row and a given column total indicates the sum of all credit entries to the account represented by that column.

squeeze. A term sometimes used for *plug.*

stabilized accounting. General *price-level adjusted accounting.*

stable monetary unit assumption. In spite of *inflation* that appears to be a way of life, the assumption that underlies *historical cost* accounting—namely that current dollars and dollars of previous years can be meaningfully added together. No specific recognition is given to changing values of the dollar in the usual *financial statements.* See *price level adjusted statements.*

standard cost. Anticipated *cost* of producing a unit of output; a predetermined cost to be assigned to products produced.

standard cost system. *Product costing* using *standard costs* rather than actual costs. May be based on either *absorption* or *direct costing* principles.

standard price (rate). Unit price established for materials or labor used in *standard cost systems.*

stated capital. Amount of capital contributed by stockholders. Sometimes used to mean *legal capital.*

stated value. A term used for *capital stock,* only if no *par value* is indicated. Where there is a stated value per share, it may be set by the directors (in which case, capital *contributed in excess of stated value* may come into being).

statement of affairs. A *balance sheet* showing immediate *liquidation* amounts, rather than *historical costs,* usually prepared when *insolvency* or *bankruptcy* is imminent.

statement of changes in financial position. As defined by *APB Opinion* No. 19, a statement which explains the changes in *working capital* (or cash) balances during a period and shows the changes in the working capital (or cash) accounts themselves. Sometimes called the "funds statement."

Statement of Financial Accounting Standards. See *FASB.*

statement of financial position. *Balance sheet.*

statement of retained earnings (income). A statement that reconciles the beginning-of-period and end-of-period balances in the *retained earnings* account. It shows the effects of *earnings, dividend* *declarations,* and *prior-period adjustments.*

Statements on Auditing Standards. No. 1 of this series (1973) codifies all statements on auditing standards previously promulgated by the *AICPA.* Later numbers deal with specific auditing standards and procedures.

static budget. *Fixed budget.*

step cost. *Semifixed cost.*

step-down method. The method for *allocating service department* costs that starts by allocating one service department's costs to *production departments* and to all other service departments. Then a second service department's costs, including costs allocated from the first, are allocated to production departments and to all other service departments except the first one. In this fashion, the costs of all service departments, including previous allocations, are allocated to production departments and to those service departments whose costs have not yet been allocated.

stock. *Inventory. Capital stock.* A measure of the amount of something on hand at a specific time; in this sense, contrast with *flow.*

stock dividend. A so-called *dividend* where additional *shares* of *capital stock* are distributed, without cash payments, to existing shareholders. It results in a *debit* to *retained earnings* in the amount of the market value of the shares issued and a *credit* to *capital stock* accounts. It is ordinarily used to indicate that earnings retained have been permanently reinvested in the business. Contrast with a *stock split,* which requires no entry in the capital stock accounts other than a notation that the *par* or *stated value* per share has been changed.

stockholders' equity. *Proprietorship* or *owners' equity* of a corporation.

stock option. The right to purchase a specified number of shares of *stock* for a specified price at specified times, usually granted to employees. Contrast with *warrant.*

stock right. See *right.*

stock split. Increase in the number of common shares outstanding resulting from the issuance of additional shares to existing stockholders without additional capital contributions by them. Does not increase the total *par* (or *stated*) *value* of *common stock* outstanding because par (or stated) value per share is reduced in inverse proportion. A three-for-one stock split reduces par (or stated) value per share to one-third of its former amount. Stock splits are usually limited to distributions that increase the number of shares outstanding by 20 percent or more. Compare with *stock dividend.*

stock subscriptions. See *subscription* and *subscribed stock.*

stock warrant. See *warrant.*

stores. *Raw materials,* parts, and supplies.

straight debt value. An estimate of what the *market value* of a *convertible bond* would be if the bond did not contain a conversion privilege.

straight-line depreciation. If the *depreciable life* is n periods, then the periodic *depreciation* charge is $1/n$ of the *depreciable cost.* Results in equal periodic charges and is sometimes called "straight-time depreciation."

subject to. Qualifications in an *auditor's report* usually caused by a *material* uncertainty in the valuation of an item, such as future promised payments from a foreign government or outcome of pending litigation.

subscribed stock. A *stockholders' equity* account showing the capital that will be contributed as soon as the subscription price is collected. A subscription is a legal contract so that an entry is made debiting a receivable and crediting subscribed stock as soon as the stock is subscribed.

subscription. Agreement to buy a *security,* or to purchase periodicals such as magazines.

subsequent events. *Post-statement events.*

subsidiary. Said of a company more than 50 percent of whose voting stock is owned by another.

subsidiary (ledger) accounts. The *accounts* in a *subsidiary ledger.*

subsidiary ledger. The *ledger* that contains the detailed accounts whose total is shown in a *controlling account* of the *general ledger.*

successful-efforts accounting. In petroleum accounting, the *capitalization* of the drilling costs of only those wells which contain oil. See *discovery value accounting* for an example.

summary of significant accounting principles. *APB* Opinion No. 22 requires that every *annual report* summarize the significant *accounting principles* used in compiling the annual report. This summary may be a separate exhibit or the first *note* to the financial statements.

sum-of-the-years'-digits depreciation. An *accelerated depreciation* method for an asset with *depreciable life* of n years where the charge in period i ($i = 1, \ldots, n$) is the fraction $(n + 1 - i)/[n(n + 1)/2]$ of the *depreciable cost.* If an asset has a depreciable cost of \$15,000 and a five-year depreciable life, for example, the depreciation charges would be \$5,000 ($= 5/15 \times \$15,000$) in the first year, \$4,000 in the second, \$3,000 in the third, \$2,000 in the fourth, and \$1,000 in the fifth.

sunk cost. *Costs* incurred in the past that are not affected by, and hence irrelevant for, current decisions. Contrast with *incremental costs* and *imputed costs.* For example, the *acquisition cost* of machinery is irrelevant to a decision of whether or not to scrap the machinery. The current *exit value* of the machine is the imputed cost of continuing to own it and the cost of, say, electricity to run the machine is an incremental cost of its operation.

supplementary statements (schedules). Statements (schedules) in addition to the four basic *financial statements* (including the retained earnings reconciliation as a basic statement).

surplus. A word once used but now considered poor terminology; prefaced by "earned" to mean *retained earnings* and prefaced by "capital" to mean *capital contributed in excess of par* (or *stated*) *value.*

surplus reserves. Of all the words in accounting, *reserve* is the most objectionable and *surplus* is the second most objectionable. This phrase, then, has nothing to recommend it. It means, simply, *appropriated retained earnings.*

suspense account. A *temporary account* used to record part of a transaction prior to final analysis of that transaction. For example, if a business regularly classifies all sales into a dozen or more different categories but wants to deposit the proceeds of cash sales every day, it may credit a sales suspense account pending detailed classification of all sales into sales, type 1; sales, type 2; and so on.

S-X. See *Regulation S-X*.

SYD. *Sum-of-the-years'-digits depreciation.*

T

T-account. Account form shaped like the letter T with the title above the horizontal line. *Debits* are shown to the left of the vertical line; *credits,* to the right.

take-home pay. The amount of a paycheck; earned wages or *salary* reduced by deductions for *income taxes, Social Security taxes,* contributions to fringe benefit plans, union dues, and so on. Take-home pay might be as little as 60 percent of earned compensation.

taking a bath. To incur a large loss. See *big bath*.

tangible. Having physical form.

target cost. *Standard cost.*

tax. A nonpenal, but compulsory, charge levied by a government on income, consumption, wealth, or other bases for the benefit of all those governed. The term does not include fines or specific charges for benefits accruing only to those paying the charges, such as licenses, permits, special assessments, admissions fees, and tolls.

tax allocation: inter-period. See *deferred income tax liability*.

tax allocation: intra-statement. The showing of income tax effects on *extraordinary items, income from discontinued operations,* and *prior period adjustments* along with these items, separately from income taxes on other income. See *net of tax reporting*.

tax avoidance. See *tax shelter*.

tax credit. A subtraction from taxes otherwise payable, contrast with *tax deduction*.

tax deduction. A subtraction from *revenues* and *gains* to arrive at taxable income. Tax deductions are technically different from tax *exemptions,* but the effect of both is to reduce gross income in computing taxable income. Both are different from *tax credits,* which are subtracted from the computed tax itself in determining taxes payable.

tax evasion. The fraudulent understatement of taxable income or overstatement of deductions and expenses or both. Contrast with *tax shelter*.

tax exempts. See *municipal bonds*.

tax shelter. The legal avoidance of, or reduction in, *income taxes* resulting from a careful reading of the complex income tax regulations and the subsequent rearrangement of financial affairs to take advantage of the regulations. Often the term is used pejoratively, but the courts have long held that an individual or corporation has no obligation to pay taxes any larger than the legal minimum. If the public concludes that a given tax shelter is "unfair," then the laws and regulations can be changed. Sometimes used to refer to the investment that permits tax avoidance.

tax shield. The amount of an *expense* that reduces taxable income but does not require *working capital,* such as *depreciation*. Sometimes this term is expanded to include expenses that reduce taxable income and use working capital. A depreciation deduction (or *R & D expense* in the expanded sense) of $10,000 provides a tax shield of $4,800 when the marginal tax rate is 48 percent.

temporary account. *Account* that does not appear on the *balance sheet*. *Revenue* and *expense* accounts, their *adjuncts* and *contras, production cost accounts, income distribution accounts,* and purchases-related accounts (which are closed to the various inventories). Sometimes called a "nominal account."

temporary difference. See *timing difference*.

temporary investments. Investments in *marketable securities* that the owner intends to sell within a short time, usually one year, and hence classified as *current assets*.

10-K. The name of the annual report required by the *SEC* of nearly all publicly-held corporations. This report contains more information than the *annual report* to stockholders. Corporations must send a copy of the 10-K to those stockholders who request it.

term bonds. A *bond issue* whose component bonds all mature at the same time. Contrast with *serial bonds*.

term loan. A loan with a *maturity* date, as opposed to a demand loan which is due whenever the lender requests payment. In practice bankers and auditors use this phrase only for loans for a year or more.

terms of sale. The conditions governing payment for a sale. For example, the terms *2/10, n(et)/30* mean that if payment is made within ten days of the invoice date, a *discount* of two percent from *invoice* price can be taken; the invoice amount must be paid, in any event, within thirty days or it becomes overdue.

tickler file. A collection of vouchers or other memorandums arranged chronologically to remind the person in charge of certain duties to make payments (or to do other tasks) as scheduled.

time-adjusted rate of return. *Internal rate of return*.

time cost. *Period cost.*

time deposit. Cash in a bank earning interest; contrast with *demand deposit*.

time series analysis. See *cross section analysis* for definition and contrast.

times-interest earned. Ratio of pre-tax *income* plus *interest* charges to interest charges. See *ratio*.

timing difference. A difference between taxable income and pre-tax income reported to stockholders that will be reversed in a subsequent period and requires an entry in the *deferred income tax* account. For example, the use of *accelerated depreciation* for tax returns and *straight-line depreciation* for financial reporting. See *Accounting Magic* for an example.

trade acceptance. A *draft* drawn by a seller which is

presented for signature (acceptance) to the buyer at the time goods are purchased and which then becomes the equivalent of a *note receivable* of the seller and the *note payable* of the buyer.

trade discount. A *discount* from *list price* offered to all customers of a given type. Contrast with a *discount* offered for prompt payment and *quantity discount.*

trade-in. Acquiring a new *asset* in exchange for a used one and perhaps additional cash. See *boot* and *trade-in transaction.*

trade-in transaction. The accounting for a trade-in depends upon whether or not the asset received is "similar" to the asset traded in and whether the accounting is for *financial statements* or for *income tax* returns. Assume an old asset cost $5,000, has $3,000 of *accumulated depreciation* (after recording depreciation to the date of the trade-in), and hence has a *book value* of $2,000. The old asset appears to have a market value of $1,500, according to price quotations in used-asset markets. The old asset is traded-in on a new asset with a list price of $10,000. The old asset and $5,500 cash (*boot*) are given for the new asset. The generic entry for the trade-in transaction is:

New Asset	A	
Accumulated Depreciation (Old Asset).....	3,000	
Adjustment on Exchange of Asset	B or	B
Old Asset		5,000
Cash.................................		5,500

(1) the *list-price* method of accounting for trade-ins rests on the assumption that the list price of the new asset closely approximates its market value. The new asset is recorded at its list price (A = $10,000 in the example); B is a *plug* (= $2,500 credit in the example). If B requires a *debit* plug, the Adjustment on Exchange of Asset is a *loss;* if a *credit* plug is required (as in the example), the adjustment is a *gain.*

(2) Another theoretically sound method of accounting for trade-ins rests on the assumption that the price quotation from used-asset markets gives a more reliable measure of the market value of the old asset than is the list price a reliable measure of the market value of the new asset. This method uses the *fair market value* of the old asset, $1,500 in the example, to determine B (= $2,000 book value – $1,500 assumed proceeds on disposition = $500 debit or loss). The exchange results in a loss if the book value of the old asset exceeds its market value and in a gain if the market value exceeds the book value. The new asset is recorded on the books by plugging for A (= $7,000 in the example).

(3) For income tax reporting, no gain or loss may be recognized on the trade-in. Thus the new asset is recorded on the books by assuming B is zero and plugging for A (= $7,500 in the example). In practice, firms that wish to recognize the loss currently will sell the old asset directly, rather than trading it in, and acquire the new asset entirely for cash.

(4) *Generally accepted accounting principles (APB Opinion* No. 29) require a variant of these methods. The basic method is (1) or (2), depending upon whether the list price of the new asset (1) or the quotation of the old asset's market value (2) is the more reliable indication of market value. If, when applying the basic method, a debit entry, or loss, is required for the Adjustment on Exchange of Asset, then the trade-in is recorded as described in (1) or (2) and the full amount of the loss is recognized currently. If, however, a credit entry, or gain, is required for the Adjustment on Exchange of Asset, then the amount of gain recognized currently depends upon whether or not the old asset and the new asset are "similar." If the assets are not similar, then the entire gain is recognized currently. If the assets are similar and cash is not received by the party trading in, then no gain is recognized and the treatment is like that in (3); i.e., B = O, plug for A. If the assets are similar and cash is received by the party trading in—a rare case—then a portion of the gain is recognized currently. The portion of the gain recognized currently is the fraction *cash received/market value of old asset.* (When the list-price method, (1), is used, the market value of the old asset is assumed to be the list price of the new asset plus the amount of cash received by the party trading in.)

The results of applying GAAP to the example can be summarized as follows:

More Reliable Information	Old Asset Compared with New Asset	
	Similar	Not Similar
New Asset List Price	A =$7,500	A = $10,000
	B = 0	B = 2,500 gain
Old Asset Market Price...	A =$7,000	A =$ 7,000
	B = 500 loss	B = 500 loss

trademark. A distinctive name, sign, or symbol. Exclusive rights to use a trademark are granted by the federal government for twenty-eight years and can be renewed for another twenty-eight years.

trade payables (receivables). *Payable (receivables)* arising in the ordinary course of business transactions. Most accounts payable (receivable) are of this kind.

trading on the equity. Said of a firm engaging in *debt financing;* frequently said of a firm doing so to a degree considered abnormal for a firm of its kind. *Leverage.*

transaction. An exchange between the accounting *entity* and another party, or parties, that leads to an accounting entry. Sometimes used to describe any event that requires a *journal entry.*

transfer agent. Usually a bank or trust company *designated* by a corporation to make legal transfers of *stock (bonds)* and, perhaps, to pay *dividends (coupons).*

transfer price. A substitute for a *market,* or *arm's-length, price* used in *profit center,* or *responsibility, accounting* when one segment of the business "sells" to another segment. Incentives of profit center managers will not coincide with the best interests of the entire business unless transfer prices are properly set.

translation gain (or loss). *Foreign exchange gain (or loss).*

transportation-in. *Freight-in.*

treasury bond. A bond issued by a corporation and then reacquired; such bonds are treated as retired when reacquired and an *extraordinary gain* or *loss* on reacquisition is recognized. See General Electric annual report at note 76. Also, a *bond* issued by the U.S. Treasury Department.

treasury stock. *Capital stock* issued and then reacquired by the corporation. Such reacquisitions result in a reduction of *stockholders' equity,* and are usually shown on the balance sheet as *contra* to stockholders' equity. Neither *gain* nor *loss* is recognized on transactions involving treasury stock. Any difference between the amounts paid and received for treasury stock transactions are debited (if positive) or credited (if negative) to *additional paid-in capital.* See *cost method* and *par value method.* See General Electric annual report at notes 23, 79, and 80.

trial balance. A listing of *account balances;* all accounts with *debit* balances are totaled separately from accounts with *credit* balances. The two totals should be equal. Trial balances are taken as a partial check of the arithmetic accuracy of the entries previously made. See *adjusted, pre-closing, post-closing, unadjusted trial balance.*

turnover. The number of times that *assets,* such as *inventory* or *accounts receivable,* are replaced on average during the period. Accounts receivable turnover, for example, is total sales on account for a period divided by average accounts receivable balance for the period. See *ratio.*

two-T-account method. A method for computing either (1) *foreign exchange gains and losses* or (2) *monetary gains* and *losses* for *general price level adjusted statements.* The left-hand *T-account* shows actual net balances of *monetary items* and the right-hand T-account shows implied *(common) dollar* amounts.

2/10, n(et)/30. See *terms of sale.*

U

unadjusted trial balance. *Trial balance* before *adjusting* and *closing entries* are made at the end of the period.

unappropriated retained earnings. *Retained earnings* not appropriated and therefore against which *dividends* can be charged in the absence of retained earnings restrictions. See *restricted retained earnings.*

uncertainty. See *risk* for definition and contrast.

uncollectible account. An *account receivable* that will not be paid by the *debtor.* If the preferable *allowance method* is used, the entry on judging a specific account to be uncollectible is to *debit* the allowance for uncollectibles account and to *credit* the specific account receivable. See *sales, uncollectible accounts adjustment.*

unconsolidated subsidiary. A *subsidiary* not consolidated and, hence, accounted for on the *equity method.*

uncontrollable cost. The opposite of *controllable cost.*

underapplied (underabsorbed) overhead. An excess of actual *overhead* costs for a period over costs applied, or charged, to products produced during the period. A *debit balance* in an overhead account after overhead is assigned to product.

underlying document. The record, memorandum, *voucher,* or other signal that is the authority for making an *entry* into a *journal.*

underwriter. One who agrees to purchase an entire *security issue* for a specified price, usually for resale to others.

unearned income (revenue). *Advances from customers;* strictly speaking, a contradiction in terms.

unemployment tax. See *FUTA.*

unencumbered appropriation. In governmental accounting, portion of an *appropriation* not yet spent or *encumbered.*

unexpired cost. An *asset.*

unfavorable variance. In *standard cost* accounting, an excess of actual cost over standard cost assigned to product.

unfunded. Not *funded.* An obligation or *liability,* usually for *pension costs,* exists but no *funds* have been set aside to discharge the obligation or liability.

Uniform Partnership Act. A model law, enacted by many states, to govern the relations between partners where the *partnership* agreement fails to specify the agreed-upon treatment.

unissued capital stock. *Stock* authorized but not yet issued.

units of production method. The *production method of depreciation.*

unlimited liability. The liability of *general partners* or a sole proprietor for all debts of the *partnership* or *sole proprietorship.*

unqualified opinion. See *auditor's report.*

unrealized appreciation. An *unrealized holding gain;* frequently used in the context of *marketable securities.*

unrealized gross margin (profit). A *contra* account to *installment accounts receivable* used with the *installment method* of revenue recognition. Shows the amount of profit that will eventually be realized when the receivable is collected.

unrealized holding gain. See *inventory profit* for definition and an example.

unrecovered cost. *Book value* of an *asset.*

usage variance. *Quantity variance.*

useful life. *Service life.*

use of funds. Any *transaction* that reduces *working capital.*

V

valuation account. A *contra account.* When *inventories* or *marketable securities* are shown at *cost* and the *lower-of-cost-or-market* valuation basis is to be used, often any declines in market value below cost will be credited to a valuation account. In this way, the acquisition cost and the amounts of price declines below cost can both be shown.

value. Monetary worth; the term is usually so subjective that it ought not to be used unless most people would agree on the amount; not to be confused with *cost*. See *fair market value*.

value added. *Cost* of a product or *work in process*, minus the cost of the materials purchased for the product or work in process.

value variance. *Price variance*.

variable annuity. An *annuity* whose periodic payments depend upon some uncertain outcome, such as stock market prices.

variable budget. *Flexible budget*.

variable costing. *Direct costing*.

variable costs. *Costs* that change as activity levels change. Strictly speaking, variable costs are zero when the activity level is zero. See *semivariable costs*.

variance. Difference between actual and *standard costs* or between *budgeted* and actual *expenditures* or, sometimes, *expenses*. In accounting, the word has a completely different meaning from its meaning in statistics, where it is a measure of dispersion of a distribution.

variance analysis. The investigation of the causes of *variances* in a *standard cost system*. This term has a different meaning in statistics.

variation analysis. Analysis of the causes of changes in items of interest in financial statements such as net *income* or *gross margin*.

vendor. A seller. Sometimes spelled "vender."

verifiable. A qualitative *objective* of financial reporting specifying that items in *financial statements* can be checked by tracing back to supporting *invoices*, canceled *checks*, and other physical pieces of evidence.

verification. The auditor's act of reviewing or checking items in *financial statements* by tracing back to supporting *invoices*, canceled *checks*, and other business documents, or sending out *confirmations* to be returned. Compare with *physical verification*.

vertical analysis. Analysis of *percentage statements* of a single firm as of a given date, as opposed to *horizontal* or *time series analysis* where items are compared over time or across firms.

vested. Said of *pension plan* benefits that are not contingent on the employee continuing to work for the employer.

volume variance. *Capacity variance*.

voucher. A document that serves to recognize a *liability* and authorize the disbursement of cash. Sometimes used to refer to the written evidence documenting an *accounting entry*, as in the term *journal voucher*.

voucher system. A method for controlling cash that requires each check to be authorized with an approved *voucher*. No cash disbursements are made.

W

wage. Compensation of employees based on time worked or output of product for manual labor. But see *take-home pay*.

warrant. A certificate entitling the owner to buy a specified amount of stock at a specified time(s) for a specified price. Differs from a *stock option* only in that options are granted to employees and warrants are sold to the public. See *right*.

warranty. A promise by a seller to correct deficiencies in products sold. When warranties are given, good accounting practice recognizes an estimate of warranty *expense* and an *estimated liability* at the time of sale.

wash sale. The sale and purchase of the same or similar *asset* within a short time period. For *income tax* purposes, *losses* on a sale of stock may not be recognized if equivalent stock is purchased within thirty days before or thirty days after the date of sale.

wasting asset. A *natural resource* having a limited *useful life* and, hence, subject to *amortization* called *depletion*. Examples are timberland, oil and gas wells, and ore deposits.

watered stock. *Stock* issued for *assets* with *fair market value* less than *par* of *stated value*. The assets are put onto the books at the overstated values. The term originated from a former practice of cattlemen who fed cattle large quantities of salt to make them thirsty. The cattle then drank a lot of water before being taken to market. This was done to make the cattle appear heavier and more valuable than they would have been otherwise.

weighted average. An *average* computed by counting each occurrence of an item, not merely the number of different items. For example, if one unit is purchased for $1 and two units are purchased for $2 each, then the simple average of the transaction prices is $1.50 but the weighted average cost of the three items is $5/3 = $1.67. Contrast with *moving average*.

weighted-average inventory method. Valuing either *withdrawals* or *ending inventory* at the *weighted average* purchase price of all units on hand at the time of withdrawal or of computing ending inventory. The *inventory equation* is used to calculate the other quantity. If the *perpetual inventory* method is in use, often called the "moving-average method."

window dressing. The attempt to make financial statements show *operating* results, or *financial position*, more favorable than would be otherwise shown.

withdrawals. *Assets* distributed to an owner. *Partner's drawings*. See *inventory equation* for another context.

withholding. Deductions from *salaries* or *wages*, usually for *income taxes*, to be remitted by the employer, in the employee's name, to the taxing authority.

working capital. *Current assets* minus *current liabilities*. The *statement of changes in financial position* usually explains the changes in working capital for a period.

working capital provided by operations. See *funds provided by operations*.

working papers. The schedules and analyses prepared by the *auditor* in carrying out investigations prior to issuing an *opinion* on *financial statements*.

work in process. Partially completed product; an *asset* which is classified as *inventory*.

work sheet. A tabular schedule for convenient summary of *adjusting* and *closing entries*. The work sheet usually begins with an *unadjusted trial balance*. Adjusting entries are shown in the next two columns, one for *debits* and one for *credits*. The horizontal sum of each line is then carried to the right into either the *income statement* or *balance sheet* columns, as appropriate. The *plug* to equate the income statement column totals is the income, if a debit plug is required, or loss, if a credit plus is required, for the period. That income will be closed to retained earnings on the balance sheet. The income statement credit columns are the revenues for the period and the debit columns are the expenses (and revenue *contras*) to be shown on the income statement.

An example of a work sheet is shown here for Caralex Stores, Inc. for the quarter ending September 30, 1975. The company last closed its books on June 30, 1975. The Expense Control Account is used to record various expenses not shown in separate accounts (see *control account*). The numbers in parentheses on the work sheet correspond to the adjusting entries explained below.

(1) A deposit of $1,250 was made up, journalized and posted on September 30, but actually was not deposited in the bank until October 1.

Undeposited Cash 1,250
    Cash in Bank   1,250
To reverse entry prematurely recorded.

CARALEX STORES, INC.
Work Sheet — Quarter Ending September 30, 1975

	Unadjusted Trial Balance		Adjustments				Income Statement		Balance Sheet	
	Dr.	Cr.	Dr.		Cr.		Dr.	Cr.	Dr.	Cr.
Accounts Payable		32,400								32,400
Accounts Receivable........	94,000		(2)	650					94,650	
Accumulated Depreciation..		17,000			(7)	500				17,500
Advances by Customers.....					(2)	650				650
Allowance for Uncollectible Accounts.................		1,400			(6)	3,200				4,600
Bonus Expense.............			(12)	752			752			
Bonus Payable					(12)	752				752
Capital Stock...............		160,000								160,000
Cash in Bank..............	8,270				(1)	1,250			7,020	
Cost of Goods Sold........			(3)	246,000			246,000			
Expense Control Account...	62,960		(4)	260	(5)	1,200	62,800			
			(7)	500	(8)	1,400				
			(9)	1,680						
Furniture and Fixtures	25,000								25,000	
Income Tax Expense			(13)	2,160			2,160			
Income Tax Payable					(13)	2,160				2,160
Interest Expense...........	620		(11)	100			720			
Interest Revenue					(10)	240		240		
Interest Payable		400			(11)	100				500
Interest Receivable	80		(10)	240					320	
Merchandise Inventory......	376,000				(3)	246,000			130,000	
Notes Payable..............		24,000								24,000
Notes Receivable	9,600								9,600	
Payroll Taxes Payable		360			(9)	1,680				2,040
Prepaid Insurance	1,560				(4)	260			1,300	
Prepaid Rent	1,200		(5)	1,200					2,400	
Retained Earnings		13,860								13,860
Sales		326,000						326,000		
Sales Returns and Allowances...............	6,000						6,000			
Sales Tax Payable		9,600								9,600
Sales, Uncollectible Accounts Adjustment.....			(6)	3,200			3,200			
Supplies Inventory..........	1,200		(8)	1,400					2,600	
Undeposited Cash	500		(1)	1,250					1,750	
Withheld Income Tax		1,970								1,970
Column Totals	586,990	586,990		259,392		259,392	321,632	326,240	274,640	270,032
Net Income for Quarter							4,608			4,608
							326,240	326,240	274,640	274,640

(2) The net debit balances of accounts receivable from customers is \$94,000. A review of individual customers' accounts reveals that several individual accounts have credit balances totaling \$650. Thus, the gross amount of account receivable is \$94,650.

Accounts Receivable.................... 650
  Advances by Customers   650
To set up advances by customers who have made payments on accounts or returned goods for credit.

(3) The merchandise inventory on hand at September 30 is \$130,000.

Cost of Goods Sold...................246,000
  Merchandise Inventory..............   246,000
To record reduction in inventory as cost of goods sold. \$376,000 – \$130,000 = \$246,000.

(4) The insurance policies all expire on January 1, 1977. No payments on insurance policies were made this quarter.

Expense Control Account 260
  Prepaid Insurance   260
The insurance policies provide 18 months' coverage as of June 30, 1975.
To record insurance expired for three months; 3/18 × \$1,560 = \$260.

(5) The rent is \$1,200 per month and has been paid through November 30, 1975. When the rent was paid, it was debited to Rent Expense, a component of the Expense Control Account.

Prepaid Rent 1,200
  Expense Control Account   1,200
To set up two months' prepaid rent as of September 30. Prepaid rent was \$1,200; As a result of this entry, it is \$2,400.

(6) The estimated uncollectibles to arise from sales of the quarter are 1 percent of net sales.

Sales, Uncollectible Accounts
  Adjustment............................3,200
    Allowance for Uncollectible
      Accounts.........................   3,200
.01 × (\$326,000 – \$6,000) = \$3,200.

(7) Depreciation on furniture and fixtures is 8 percent of cost per year.

Expense Control Account 500
  Accumulated Depreciation   500
3/12 × .08 × \$25,000 = \$500.

(8) The cost of all supplies purchased is debited to Supplies Expense, a component of the Expense Control Account. The Supplies Inventory at September 30 is \$2,600.

Supplies Inventory...................... 1,400
  Expense Control Account   1,400
To set up supplies inventory at \$2,600.

(9) The employer's share of payroll taxes has been paid through September 1. The employer's share for September is calculated to be \$1,680.

Expense Control Account 1,680
  Payroll Taxes Payable   1,680
To record Payroll Tax Expense for September as a component of the Expense Control Account.

(10) The Notes Receivable account contains a 10-percent note for \$9,600 dated June 1, 1975, and due December 1, 1975.

Interest Receivable 240
  Interest Revenue   240
3/12 × .10 × \$9,600 = \$240.

(11) The Notes Payable account contains a single 10-percent note for \$24,000 dated July 15, 1975, and due January 16, 1976. Interest has been accrued on the 15th of each month.

Interest Expense......................... 100
  Interest Payable   100
Interest expense per month is \$200 (= 1/12 × .10 × \$24,000). The balance of the Interest Payable on the note should be \$500 (= 2½ × \$200). To adjust interest expense for the quarter and interest payable as of September 30.

(12) The manager is to be paid a bonus of 10 percent of the pretax income of the enterprise exclusive of the bonus.

Bonus Expense.......................... 752
  Bonus Payable   752
From Income Statement columns: .10 × (\$240 + \$326,000 – \$246,000 – \$66,000 – \$2,160 – \$720 – \$6,000) = \$752.

(13) The income tax for the quarter is estimated to be \$2,160.

Income Tax Expense 2,160
  Income Taxes Payable   2,160
To record income tax expense for quarter.

Work sheet is also used to refer to *schedules* for determining other items appearing on the *financial statements* that require adjustment or compilation.

worth. *Value.* See *net worth.*

worth-debt ratio. Reciprocal of the *debt-equity ratio.* See *ratio.*

write down. *Write off,* except that not all the asset's cost is charged to expense or *loss.* Generally used for nonrecurring items.

write off. *Charge* an *asset* to *expense* or *loss;* that is, *debit* expense (or loss) and *credit* asset.

writeoff method. A method for treating *uncollectible accounts* that charges *bad debt expense* and credits accounts receivable of specific customers as uncollectible amounts are identified. May not be used when uncollectible amounts are significant and can be estimated. See *sales, uncollectible* *accounts adjustment* and the *allowance method* for contrast.

write up. To increase the recorded *cost* of an *asset* with no corresponding *disbursement* of *funds;* that is, *debit* asset and *credit revenue* or, perhaps, *owners' equity.* Seldom done since currently accepted accounting principles are based on actual transactions.

Y

yield. *Internal rate of return* on a stream of cash flows. Cash yield is cash flow divided by book value. See also *dividend yield.*

yield to maturity. At a given time, the *internal rate of return* of a series of cash flows, usually said of a *bond.* Sometimes called the "effective rate."

Z

zero salvage value. If the *salvage value* of a *depreciable asset* is estimated to be less than 10 percent of its *cost,* then the tax regulations permit an assumption of zero salvage value in computing *depreciation* for federal *income tax* purposes. This convention is often used in financial reporting as well.

Accounting Magic

Generally accepted accounting principles permit alternative treatments for certain accounting events. Which treatment a company chooses will affect the financial statements that the company issues. In this section, we show how alternative accounting treatments of identical events can lead to reported income figures that are perhaps surprisingly different from each other.[1]

The Scenario

On January 1, two companies start in business. The two companies are exactly alike in all respects except for their accounting treatment of several events. Conservative Company chooses the accounting alternatives that will minimize its reported income while High Flyer Company chooses the alternatives that will maximize its reported income. Both companies choose, where possible, accounting methods that will minimize income taxes. The following events occur during the year.

1. Both companies issue common stock to raise the funds necessary to commence a merchandising business.
2. Both companies purchase $7,000,000 worth of equipment that is assumed to have zero salvage value and a depreciable life of 10 years.
3. Both companies make the following purchases of merchandise inventory:

Date	Units Purchased		Unit Price		Cost of Purchase
January 1	85,000	@	$60	=	$ 5,100,000
May 1	95,000	@	$63	=	5,985,000
September 1	100,000	@	$68	=	6,800,000
Total...............................	280,000				$17,885,000

4. During the year, both companies sell 210,000 units at an average price of $100 each so that each realizes sales revenues of $21,000,000.
5. During the year, both companies have selling, general and administrative expenses, excluding officers' salaries, of $3,350,000.
6. At the end of the year, both the companies "pay" bonuses worth $120,000 to officers for jobs well done in addition to the $350,000 paid to them during the year in salaries. Conservative Company pays cash bonuses of $120,000 while High Flyer Company awards options for purchasing shares of common stock to its officers. Comparable options have market value of $120,000.

Accounting Alternatives

At the end of the year both companies prepare financial statements. Both must decide how to report the various events that occurred during the year. The following decisions made by each company are all generally acceptable.

---

[1]The title for this example, "Accounting Magic," and indeed the inspiration for its preparation come from an article by Leonard Spacek, "Business Success Requires an Understanding of Unsolved Problems of Accounting and Financial Reporting," Arthur Andersen Pamphlet (September 25, 1959), pp. 19-28. Since the time Spacek prepared his illustration, there have been changes in generally accepted accounting principles, but several of the alternatives we illustrate were illustrated by him, too.

Inventory Cost Flow Assumption. Since not all goods purchased during the year were sold, each company must make an assumption about the cost of goods sold to be shown on the income statement and, simultaneously, about the cost of ending inventory to be shown on the balance sheet. Conservative Company makes a last-in, first-out (LIFO) cost flow assumption while High Flyer Company makes a first-in, first-out (FIFO) assumption. Since the beginning inventory is zero, the cost of goods available for sale by each company is equal to the purchases of $17,885,000 during the year. Both companies have 70,000 units in ending inventory. Conservative Company, using LIFO, reports a cost of goods sold of $13,685,000 (= $17,885,000 – 70,000 × $60) while High Flyer Company reports a cost of goods sold of $13,125,000 (= $17,885,000 – 70,000 × $68.) Income tax regulations require a company to use LIFO in its financial statements if it uses LIFO for its tax return. High Flyer Company desires not to use LIFO in its financial statements and therefore foregoes the savings in taxes from using LIFO on its tax returns.

Depreciation. Conservative Company decides to depreciate its equipment using the double-declining-balance method on both its tax return and its financial statements. High Flyer Company decides to use the straight-line method in reporting income to stockholders but the double-declining-balance method in its tax return. Conservative Company therefore reports depreciation expense of $1,400,000 (= 2 × 1/10 × $7,000,000) while High Flyer Company reports depreciation expense of $700,000 (= 1/10 × $7,000,000) to stockholders and $1,400,000 on its tax return.

ACCOUNTING MAGIC COMPARATIVE INCOME STATEMENTS
For the Year Ending December 31

	Conservative Company		High Flyer Company	
	Financial Statement	Tax Return	Financial Statement	Tax Return
	(Amounts in Thousands Except Per Share Amounts)			
Sales Revenues	$21,000	$21,000	$21,000	$21,000
Expenses				
Cost of Goods Sold	$13,685	$13,685	$13,125	$13,125
Depreciation on Equipment	1,400	1,400	700	1,400 [b]
Officers' Compensation:				
Salaries	350	350	350	350
Cash Bonuses	120	120	—	—
Stock Options	—	—	0	0
Other Selling, General and Administrative Expenses	3,350	3,350	3,350	3,350
Expenses before Income Taxes	$18,905	$18,905	$17,525	$18,225
Income before Taxes	$ 2,095	$ 2,095	$ 3,475	$ 2,775
Income Tax Expense[a]	922		955	
Net Income	$ 1,173		$ 2,520	
Earnings Per Share in Dollars (500,000 Shares Outstanding)	$ 2.35		$ 5.04	

[a] Computation of Income Tax Expense:

Income Before Taxes	$ 2,095	$ 2,095	$ 3,475	$ 2,775
Income Tax on Current Income (20 percent of first $25,000 plus 22 percent of next $25,000 plus 48 percent of remainder)	$ 992	$ 992	$ 1,655	$ 1,319
Less: Tax Credit for Investment in Equipment	70	700	700	700
Income Tax Expense	$ 922		$ 955	
Income Tax Currently Payable		$ 292		$ 619
Deferred Investment Tax Credit ($700 – $70).	$ 630			
[b] Income Taxes Deferred by Timing Difference for Depreciation (.48 × $700)			$ 336	

Officers' Bonuses. Conservative Company reports expense of $120,000 for the cash bonuses it pays while High Flyer Company reports no expense for the stock options granted. Under generally accepted accounting principles, the fair market value of qualified stock options granted to employees is not shown as an expense. (When the options are exercised, there will be an accounting transaction but the entry will record merely the cash received at the time of exercise.)

Investment Tax Credit. Since both companies purchased long-term assets costing $7,000,000, each is entitled to a reduction, or "tax credit," of $700,000 (= .10 × $7,000,000) in its tax bill for the year.[2] On its financial statements to stockholders, Conservative Company chooses to report the benefits of that tax reduction over the ten-year life of the equipment that gave rise to the tax reduction *(deferral method,* explained in the Glossary). On its financial statements to stockholders, High Flyer reports the entire benefit of the tax reduction in the first year *(flow-through method,* explained in the Glossary).

Income Tax Calculation. Because Conservative Company reports the same revenues and expenses on both its financial statements and income tax return, its taxable income is the same as reported income before taxes. High Flyer Company shows larger deductions from revenues on the income tax return than it reports to stockholders and one of these differences—for depreciation of equipment—is viewed as a timing difference. That is, in subsequent years, High Flyer Company may report smaller deductions on its tax return than it reports to stockholders. Consequently, High Flyer Company reports a deferred tax expense on its income statement and will show a deferred tax liability on its balance sheet.

Published Income Statements

The income statements for both companies are shown on the previous page. As a result of its conservative treatment of accounting alternatives, Conservative Company reports net income and earnings per share less than half of what High Flyer Company reports. Both companies used generally accepted accounting principles and each would receive a "clean" opinion from its auditor.

Comparisons of Fund Flows

Until the time when the two companies paid their respective executive bonuses and income taxes, they were exactly alike in all economically significant respects. Because of the difference in executives' bonuses—Conservative Company paid cash, while High Flyer granted stock options with the same value—Conservative Company paid out $120,000 more cash than did High Flyer for this item. High Flyer Company, in order to report higher net income, had to pay income taxes $327,000 (= $619,000 – $292,000) larger than did Conservative Company. Thus, after tax payments, Conservative Company, in a real sense, is considerably better off than is High Flyer. Overall, then, Conservative Company ends the year with $207,000 (= $327,000 – $120,000) more cash, or other liquid net assets, than does High Flyer.

You might find it instructive to construct statements of changes in financial position for each of the two companies. If you use cash as the definition of funds, you will find that Conservative Company generates $207,000 more cash than does High Flyer. If you use working capital (= current assets – current liabilities) as the definition of funds, you will find that High Flyer generates $353,000 more funds than does Conservative Company. The difference between these two amounts, $560,000, arises from the different cost flow assumptions for inventory. High Flyer uses FIFO; its ending inventory is valued at $68 per unit. Conservative Company uses LIFO; its ending inventory is valued at $60 per unit. The difference in inventory valuation is $8 per unit. Since there are 70,000 more units in ending inventory than in beginning inventory, the difference in the increase in working capital over the increase in cash is $560,000 (= $8 × 70,000). Again, we see the major impact of the inventory flow assumption in times of changing prices on published financial statements.

---

[2]As this book goes to press, the percentage for the investment tax credit is 10 percent, but it changes from time to time. A larger rate will increase the difference between reported earnings of the two companies; a smaller rate will reduce the difference.

Other Choices Not Illustrated

The simple illustration for Conservative Company and High Flyer Company by no means exhausts the set of choices between alternative generally accepted accounting principles. Some of the other economic events that can be alternatively reported are briefly described next.

Revenue Recognition on Long-Term Projects. If a company engages in long-term projects, such as constructing buildings or machinery for others, it can report all income on the contract either at the time the contract is completed, which may be several years after work on the project commences (conservative), or it can report for each year during construction a portion of the expected income equal to the portion of the project that has been completed during the year.

Revenue Recognition on Marketable Securities. Suppose that a company bought marketable securities at the beginning of the year that have increased substantially in market price during the year. The company that wants to report higher income can sell the securities at year end and reinvest the proceeds in other securities. Such a transaction will allow the gain to be reported currently. The conservative company would continue to hold the original marketable securities and to report them as a balance sheet asset at original cost.

Treatment of Past and Prior Service Pension Costs. Suppose that a company enacts a pension plan at the start of the year, or "sweetens" an already-existing plan, granting retroactive benefits to current employees. The company thus incurs *past service costs* under the new plan or *prior service costs* under the "sweetened" plan. Assume that the interest rate used for these purposes is six percent per year and that the present value of the past (or prior) service cost is $3,000,000. The conservative treatment of these costs for tax purposes, under the Pension Reform Act of 1974, would be to amortize and fund them over ten years, while charging income each year with the interest on the unamortized portion of the past (or prior) service costs. In the first year, the conservative treatment would show pension costs under the new law of $462,000 (= $1/10 \times$ $3,000,000 + .06 \times 9/10 \times 3,000,000 = 300,000 + 162,000$). The less conservative treatment would amortize and fund the past (or prior) service costs over thirty years, while charging income each year with the interest on the unamortized portion of the costs. The less conservative treatment would show pension costs in the first year of $274,000 (= $1/30 \times 3,000,000 + .06 \times 29/30 \times$ $3,000,000 = 100,000 + 174,000$). The more conservative company would show pension costs almost 70 percent larger than the less conservative company.

GENERAL ⊛ ELECTRIC

1974 Annual Report

Authors' Introduction

This is an excerpt from GE's Annual Report. GE's annual reports are consistently among the best we see. GE provides copious explanations and discloses helpful items beyond those that are currently required. The first 29 pages of the Annual Report consist of general information about the company, illustrations, and highlights of the year's operations. We have commented on various aspects of the financial statements, which follow the general information (GE calls this section the "1974 Financial Summary"), in numbered footnotes keyed to the GE annual report. None of our criticisms is major. The page numbers of the original, 30 through 43, are left intact and references, both in the report and our notes, use these numbers. The Report of Independent Certified Public Accountants on page 30 attests only to those pages of financial statements reproduced here. The "1974 Financial Highlights" shown on the next page is taken from page 3 of GE's annual report. It is reproduced here to provide additional information for assessing GE's operating performance during 1974.

Our footnotes are numbered "*," "**," and from 1 to 84. Generally, they are shown on a page facing the page of the annual report being commented on. Our notes begin at the bottom of this page. The bold face numbers shown in the margins of the annual report do not, of course, appear in the original. All accounting terms used in our supplementary footnotes are explained in the Glossary.

We think there is no better way to learn financial accounting than to try to understand all that appears in GE's statements. (The GE corporate signature, as it appears above is a trademark of General Electric Company. It is, perhaps, the single most valuable asset of the Company. In accord with generally accepted accounting principles, this asset does not appear anywhere in the financial statements.)

Authors' notes for page 3 of GE Annual Report

* This is the style of our commentary footnotes. The report shown here appears on page 3 of the GE annual report. It is called a "line of business" or "segment" report.
** The major difficulty in constructing meaningful and useful segment reports is the allocation of these "corporate items." They are truly common or joint costs of running the entire corporation but which have to be allocated to the various segments in order to present subtotals for segment earnings that add up to total earnings. The "Sales" columns tend to show meaningful information, but the "Net earnings" columns are arbitrary to the extent that the allocation of "corporate expenses" is arbitrary.

1974 Financial highlights
(Dollar amounts in millions; per-share amounts in dollars)

Summary of operating results	1974	1973
Sales of products and services	$13,413	$11,575
Operating costs		
Employee compensation, including benefits	5,223	4,710
Materials, supplies, services and all other operating costs	7,195	5,910
	12,418	10,620
Operating margin	995	955
Other income	186	184
Interest and other financial charges	(180)	(127)
Earnings before income taxes and minority interest	1,001	1,012
Provision for income taxes	(383)	(419)
Minority interest	(10)	(8)
Net earnings	$ 608	$ 585
Earnings per common share	$3.34	$3.21
Dividends declared per common share	$1.60	$1.50
Operating margin as a percentage of sales	7.4%	8.2%
Earned on share owners' equity	17.2%	18.1%

	Sales		Net earnings		Earnings as a percentage of sales		
Operating results by major categories	1974	1973	1974	1973(a)	1974	1973(a)	*
Industrial Power Equipment	$ 2,787	$ 2,477	$101	$129	3.6%	5.2%	
Consumer	3,214	3,097	86	148	2.7	4.8	
Industrial Components and Systems	4,529	3,728	254	181	5.6	4.9	
Aerospace	1,916	1,611	75	44	3.9	2.7	
International	3,218	2,318	174	139	5.4	6.0	
General Electric Credit Corporation	—	—	43	42	—	—	
Corporate eliminations	(2,251)	(1,656)	(125)	(98)	—	—	
Total Company	$13,413	$11,575	$608	$585	4.5	5.1	

(a) Amounts for 1973 and prior years have been reclassified, consistent with refinements of corporate interest allocation procedures implemented in 1974. This reclassification's principal effect on previously reported earnings was to increase the Industrial Power Equipment and decrease the International categories.

Sales and net earnings by major category throughout this Report include intercategory transactions. To the extent that sales and earnings are recognized in more than one category, appropriate elimination is made at corporate level. Net earnings for each major category are after allocation of corporate items such as expenses of headquarters personnel, ** corporate research and development, interest and other financial charges and income as well as income taxes. Unless otherwise indicated by the context, the terms "General Electric" and "Company" are used on the basis of consolidation described on page 30.

Report of Independent Certified Public Accountants

To the Share Owners and Board of Directors of General Electric Company

We have examined the statement of financial position of General Electric Company and consolidated affiliates as of December 31, 1974 and 1973, and the related statements of current and retained earnings and changes in financial position for the years then ended. Our examination was made in accordance with generally accepted auditing standards, and accordingly included such tests of the accounting records and such other auditing procedures as we considered necessary in the circumstances.

In our opinion, the aforementioned financial statements
1 present fairly the financial position of General Electric Company and consolidated affiliates at December 31, 1974 and 1973, and the results of their operations and the changes in their financial position for the years then ended, in conformity with generally accepted accounting principles applied on a consistent basis.

Peat, Marwick, Mitchell & Co.

Peat, Marwick, Mitchell & Co.
345 Park Avenue, New York, N.Y. 10022
February 14, 1975

1974 Financial Summary

This summary comments on significant items in the consolidated financial statements on pages 31, 32 and 33, generally in the same order as they appear in those statements.

The information contained in this summary, in the opinion of management, substantially conforms with or exceeds the information required in the annual financial statements constituting part of the report (commonly called the "10-K Report") submitted to the Securities and Exchange Commission. The few exceptions, considered non-substantive, are noted as appropriate in the following text. A reproduction of the following statements and summary is filed with that agency.

As an aid in evaluating the data in this Financial Summary, significant accounting and reporting principles and policies followed by General Electric are printed in 2 blue.

Consolidated financial statements and accompanying schedules in this Report include a consolidation of the accounts of the Parent—General Electric Company— and those of all majority-owned affiliates (except finance affiliates since their operations are not similar to those of 3 the consolidated group). All significant items relating to transactions between Parent and affiliated companies 4 are eliminated from consolidated statements. Sales and net earnings attributable to each of the Company's major categories are summarized on page 3. 5

Except for plant and equipment and accumulated depreciation, assets and liabilities of foreign affiliates are translated into U.S. dollars at year-end exchange rates, and income and expense items are translated at average rates prevailing during the year. Plant and equipment and accumulated depreciation are translated at rates in effect at dates of acquisition of the assets. The net effect of translation gains and losses is included as other costs in current year operations. Translation losses for 1974 6 and 1973 were $17.5 million and $3.5 million respectively.

Net earnings include the net income of finance affiliates 7 and the consolidated group's share of earnings of associated companies which are not consolidated but in which the group owns 20% or more of the voting stock.

During 1974, net earnings amounted to $608.1 million compared with prior year earnings of $585.1 million. Earnings per common share were $3.34 in 1974 compared with $3.21 in 1973. Fully diluted earnings per common share, which would result from the potential exercise or conversion of such items as stock options and convertible debt outstanding, were $3.31 in 1974 8 and $3.18 in 1973.

(Continued on page 34)

AUTHORS' SUPPLEMENTARY FOOTNOTES

1. A "clean" opinion on an excellent annual report.
2. APB Opinion No. 22 requires that financial reports include a "summary of significant accounting and reporting principles and policies." Most companies devote a page or so to showing this summary. GE provides much more detail than most other companies and intermixes the summary with the report, printing the summary in blue ink. We cannot reproduce the blue ink but we think our readers are adequately served by the footnote explanations.
3. If these finance affiliates were consolidated, there would be a significant change in the composition of consolidated assets and equities as shown on page 32. The separate financial statements of General Electric Credit Corporation are shown on page 37. As can be seen there, most (94 percent) of GE Credit Corporation's assets are receivables and most (89 percent) of its financing is debt, rather than owners' equity. In this sense, the operations of the finance affiliates "are not similar to those of the consolidated group." See note 65.
4. Consolidated financial statements present information about a group of affiliated companies essentially as if the group were one company. Consequently, any gains or losses on sales of assets between companies in the consolidated group must be eliminated. The recognition of such gains or losses is postponed until the assets are sold by one company of the consolidated group to a buyer outside of the consolidated group.
5. Excerpts from page 3 of the GE report are shown on the page preceding this one. The information shown from page 3 is GE's line of business (or segment) report, which is the same as the data reported to the SEC.
6. The first Statement of Financial Standards of the FASB, issued in 1973, requires separate disclosure of these translation gains or losses caused by fluctuating rates of exchange between the dollar and other currencies. During 1974, GE owed substantial amounts denominated in foreign currencies while the value of the dollar declined relative to the value of those foreign currencies. Hence, GE experienced foreign exchange losses. Early in 1975, the FASB circulated an Exposure Draft of a proposed Statement of Financial Accounting Standards which gives details of how these calculations should be made in the future. This book went to press before a final statement was issued. Under the terms of the Exposure Draft, inventories as well as "plant and equipment and accumulated depreciation" generally would be translated at rates in effect at the time the assets were acquired. It is likely that this change would reduce GE's reported foreign exchange loss and, hence, increase reported income.
7. GE is saying that it uses, as it must, the equity method of accounting for its investment in affiliated and associated companies (unconsolidated subsidiaries) where more than 20 percent of the stock is held. Under the equity method, GE's net earnings include its share of the earnings, not just the dividends, of these companies. See notes 26 and 66.
8. Fully diluted earnings per share, in addition to being shown here, would be shown on the face of the income statement if the dilution were more than three percent. See notes 15 and 75.

Statement of Current and Retained Earnings

General Electric Company and consolidated affiliates *(In millions)*

For the year	**1974**	**1973**
Sales of products and services to customers	$13,413.1	$11,575.3
9 **Operating costs**		
Employee compensation, including benefits	5,223.0	4,709.7
10 Materials, supplies, services and other costs	6,966.7	5,690.5
Depreciation	376.2	334.0
Taxes, except those on income	123.0	113.5
10 Increase in inventories during the year	(270.8)	(227.2)
	12,418.1	10,620.5
Operating margin	995.0	954.8
11 Other income	185.8	183.7
Interest and other financial charges	(180.1)	(126.9)
Earnings before income taxes & minority interest ..	1,000.7	1,011.6
12 Provision for income taxes	(382.4)	(418.7)
Minority interest in earnings of		
13 consolidated affiliates	(10.2)	(7.8)
Net earnings applicable to common stock	608.1	585.1
14 Dividends declared	(291.2)	(272.9)
Amount added to retained earnings	316.9	312.2
Retained earnings at January 1	2,683.6	2,371.4
Retained earnings at December 31	$ 3,000.5	$ 2,683.6
15 **Earnings per common share** *(In dollars)*	$3.34	$3.21
Dividends declared per common share *(In dollars)*	$1.60	$1.50

The 1974 Financial Summary beginning on page 30 and ending on page 41 is an integral part of this statement.

9. *Operating Costs* is a poor term. The title should be *Operating Expenses*. See note 73.
10. If "purchases" are defined to mean purchases of manufacturing materials, labor, and overhead, then,
Cost of Goods Sold = Beginning Inventory + Purchases − Ending Inventory. Rearranging terms,
Cost of Goods Sold = Purchases − (Ending Inventory − Beginning Inventory), or
Cost of Goods Sold = Purchases − Increase in Inventory.
If all purchases for manufacturing are shown as "operating expenses," the increase in inventories must be subtracted from purchases for proper computation of cost of goods sold.
11. The components of "Other income" are given on page 35 of the annual report.
12. "Provision" means "estimated expense" in this country; see Glossary.
13. Notice the subtraction for the minority's share of earnings is properly shown. See note 30.
14. Notice that "dividends declared," not dividends paid, is the title shown; see note 18. Dividends are *not* expenses. They are distributions of earnings and are properly excluded from the determination of "net earnings."
15. This is primary earnings per share; see note 8. Because fully diluted earnings per share is greater than 97 percent of earnings divided by the average of shares outstanding, it need not be shown here. That is, potential dilution is not considered "material."

16 Statement of Financial Position

General Electric Company and consolidated affiliates *(In millions)*

December 31	1974	1973
Assets		
Cash	$ 314.5	$ 296.8 M(16)
Marketable securities	57.3	25.3
Current receivables	2,593.8	2,177.1 M
Inventories	2,257.0	1,986.2
Current assets	5,222.6	4,485.4
17 Investments	1,004.8	869.7
Plant and equipment	2,615.6	2,360.5
18 Other assets	526.1	608.6
Total assets	$9,369.1	$8,324.2
Liabilities and equity		
Short-term borrowings	$ 644.9	$ 665.2
Accounts payable	696.0	673.5
19 Progress collections and price adjustments accrued	1,000.5	718.4
20 Dividends payable	72.8	72.7
Taxes accrued	337.2	310.0
21 Other costs and expenses accrued	1,128.1	1,052.6
Current liabilities	3,879.5	3,492.4 M
Long-term borrowings	1,195.2	917.2 M
Other liabilities	518.9	492.1
Total liabilities	5,593.6	4,901.7
22 Minority interest in equity of consolidated affiliates	71.2	50.1
Preferred stock	—	—
Common stock	465.2	463.8
Amounts received for stock in excess of par value	414.5	409.5
Retained earnings	3,000.5	2,683.6
	3,880.2	3,556.9
23 Deduct common stock held in treasury	(175.9)	(184.5)
Total share owners' equity	3,704.3	3,372.4
Total liabilities and equity	$9,369.1	$8,324.2

The 1974 Financial Summary beginning on page 30 and ending on page 41 is an integral part of this statement.

16. The most common title for this statement is the Balance Sheet. The items marked "M" in the right-hand margin are monetary. Identifying monetary items is required for constructing general price level adjusted financial statements; see the explanation in the next section of this book.
17. The components of "Investments" and the ones which are monetary are given in a supplementary table on page 37 of the annual report.
18. The components of "Other assets" and the ones which are monetary are given in a supplementary table on page 38 of the annual report.
19. See note 72.
20. See note 14. Dividends actually paid during 1974 must have been $291.1 [= $291.2 – ($72.8 – $72.7)] million. That is, the amount paid is the amount declared minus the increase in the amount payable.
21. See note 73 for criticism; the word *costs* is inappropriate in this context.
22. Here classified neither as a liability nor as stockholders' equity. We prefer to classify it as an indeterminate-term liability.
23. See note 79.

Statement of Changes in Financial Position

General Electric Company and consolidated affiliates *(In millions)*

	For the year	1974	1973
24 Source of funds			
From operations:			
25	Net earnings	$ 608.1	$ 585.1
26	Less earnings retained by the Credit Corporation ...	(8.7)	(10.7)
27	Depreciation	376.2	334.0
28	Income tax timing differences	26.0	—
		1,001.6	908.4
29	Major domestic long-term borrowings	300.0	—
29	Overseas Capital Corporation long-term borrowings	8.1	17.1
	Increases in other long-term borrowings—net	13.9	2.0
	Newly-issued common stock	24.6	11.7
	Total source of funds	1,348.2	939.2
	Application of funds		
	Plant and equipment additions	671.8	598.6
	Dividends declared	291.2	272.9
	Investments	135.1	114.8
29	Reduction in major domestic long-term borrowings	17.0	31.5
29	Reduction in Overseas Capital Corporation		
	long-term borrowings	27.0	17.7
30	Other—net	(144.0)	20.3
	Total application of funds	998.1	1,055.8
31 Net increase (decrease) in working capital		$ 350.1	$ (116.6)
	Analysis of changes in working capital		
	Cash and marketable securities	$ 49.7	$ 27.8
	Current receivables	416.7	251.1
	Inventories	270.8	227.2
	Short-term borrowings	20.3	(225.8)
	Other payables	(407.4)	(396.9)
31 Net increase (decrease) in working capital		$ 350.1	$ (116.6)

The 1974 Financial Summary beginning on page 30 and ending on page 41 is an integral part of this statement.

24. *Funds = Working Capital = Current Assets - Current Liabilities.*

25. This statement, as is customary, starts with net income as shown on page 31. The next few lines show subtractions for revenues which produce no funds, and additions for expenses which did not use funds, to derive the total of $1,001.6 of funds provided by operations. An acceptable alternative statement format, but one seldom used, shows only those revenues that produce funds and subtracts only those expenses that use funds.

26. Because all Credit Company earnings ($42.7 million in 1974) are included in income under the equity method (see "Other Income" on page 35 and note 66) but only $34 million of dividends were declared by the Credit Company in 1974, the difference of $8.7 million provided no funds to GE and must be subtracted to derive funds provided by operations. That is, the entire $42.7 million is included in the $608.1 million shown by GE as net earnings but dividends provided funds of only $34 million.

27. Depreciation is *not* a source of funds. Rather, it is an expense reducing net income that did not use funds. The arithmetic is correct but the caption is misleading.

28. 1974 income tax expense deducted in computing net income exceeded the actual tax payments by $26.0 million because of timing differences. The timing differences in 1973, by unusual coincidence, net out exactly to zero. This item, also, is not a source of funds, but an adjustment of an expense for the portion of it that did not use funds. See notes 47-54.

29. As is preferable, GE shows new borrowings and reductions in old borrowings separately—the borrowings as sources of funds and the reductions as applications (uses). Some companies show only the net effects as either a source or an application and thus provide no information about the extent of actual borrowing during the period.

30. Included here is the effect of adding back minority interest ($10.2 million in 1974, $7.8 million in 1973) in earnings of consolidated subsidiaries (see note 13) and the deferral of the investment credit (see note 54). We would prefer that these items be added back to funds from operations at the top of this statement because they are deductions to derive net earnings that do not use funds. Then, the articulated relationship of this statement and the income statement would be clearer.

31. Notice the self-balancing nature of this statement. Some companies do not show the Analysis of Changes in Working Capital here so that the elegance of the statement is lost. One apparent paradox of the modern corporation is that working capital may well decline when there are positive earnings and increase in spite of losses. This phenomenon did not occur during 1974, but GE's 1973 change in working capital (see page 33 of the report) illustrates it. 1973 was GE's best year until that time. GE used working capital to expand plant, to declare dividends, to acquire investments, and to retire substantial portions of long-term debt. All these actions used working capital and the sum of uses exceeded the amount of working capital provided by operations and other sources during 1973.

(continued from page 30)

Sales of products and services to customers are reported in operating results only as title to products

32 passes to the customer and as services are performed as contracted. Sales in 1974 totaled $13,413.1 million, an increase of 16% over the 1973 level. Approximately one seventh of sales in 1974 and 1973 were to agencies of the U.S. government, which is the Company's largest single customer.

33 Operating costs are classified in the statement of current earnings according to the principal types of costs incurred. Operating costs reclassified as required by the

34 Securities and Exchange Commission and pertinent supplemental details are shown in the table below.

Operating costs:		*(In millions)*
	1974	**1973**
35 Cost of goods sold	$10,137.6	$8,515.2
Selling, general and administrative expenses	2,280.5	2,105.3
Supplemental Details:		
36 Company funded research and development	351.9	330.7
Maintenance and repairs	318.7	319.6
Social security taxes	254.6	225.8
Advertising	161.0	170.5
Rent	100.4	86.6

Employee compensation, including the cost of employee benefits, amounted to $5,223.0 million in 1974.

General Electric Company and its affiliates have a number of pension plans, the total cost of which was $167.8 million in 1974 and $135.5 million in 1973. The most significant of these plans is the General Electric Pension Plan in which substantially all employees in the United States who have completed one year of service with the Company are participating and the obligations of which are funded through the General Electric Pension Trust. Financial statements of the General Electric Pension Trust appear at right.

Investments of the Pension Trust are carried at amortized cost plus programmed appreciation in the common stock portfolio, the recognition of which is limited by a maximum ratio, calculated on a moving basis, of book to market values over a multiyear period. The limit was not exceeded at year-end 1974 or 1973. This accounting recognizes both the long-term nature of pension obligations and long-term market trends.

37 The funding program uses 6% as the estimated rate of future income which includes provision for the systematic recognition of appreciation in the common stock portfolio without giving undue weight to short-term market fluctuations.

Earnings of the Trust, including the programmed rec-

ognition of appreciation, as a percentage of book value of the portfolio were 6.7% for 1974 and 6.5% for 1973.

Unfunded liabilities of the Trust are being amortized **38** over a 20-year period and are estimated to be $458 million at December 31, 1974 based on book value of Trust assets compared with $474 million at the end of 1973. These amounts included unfunded vested liability of $345 million at December 31, 1974 and $377 million at December 31, 1973. It is estimated that amendments to the Plan which became effective January 1, 1975 will result in an increase in the unfunded liability of approximately **39** $150 million. The Pension Plan substantially conforms with the Employee Retirement Income Security Act of **40** 1974. The estimated market value of Trust assets was $2,347 million at December 31, 1974 and $2,805 million at December 31, 1973.

A supplementary pension plan was approved by the Board of Directors effective July 1, 1973. The purpose is to ensure that pension benefits for long-service professional and managerial employees, when combined with their social security benefits, bear a reasonable relationship to their final average earnings. Obli- **41** gations of this pension supplement are not funded. Current service costs and amortization of past service costs

General Electric Pension Trust		*(In millions)*
Operating statement	**1974**	**1973**
Total assets at January 1	$2,496.0	$2,267.1
Company contributions	148.6	125.9
Employee contributions	44.4	38.6
	193.0	164.5
Dividends, interest and sundry income	119.9	111.4
Common stock appreciation: Realized	(7.0)	34.2
Accrued	86.2	34.4
Total programmed	79.2	68.6
Pensions paid	(126.1)	(115.6)
Total assets at December 31	$2,762.0	$2,496.0
Financial position—December 31		
U.S. Government obligations and guarantees	$ 49.8	$ 56.0
Corporate bonds, notes and mineral interests	263.6	344.8
Real estate and mortgages	448.3	410.7
Common stocks and convertibles	1,797.0	1,530.6
	2,558.7	2,342.1
Cash and short-term investments	108.9	55.8
Other assets—net	94.4	98.1
Total assets	$2,762.0	$2,496.0
Funded liabilities: Liability to pensioners	$ 975.3	$ 874.9
Liability for pensions to participants not yet retired	1,786.7	1,621.1
Total funded liabilities	$2,762.0	$2,496.0

32. GE uses the completed contract method of recognizing revenue on long-term projects. See note 72.
33. *Expenses* would be a better term than *costs;* see notes 9 and 73.
34. That is, a natural, rather than a functional, classification is used in the income statement. The SEC requires that the results of a functional classification be reported in notes, as is done here, if a natural classification is used in the income statement.
35. Cost of goods sold includes depreciation. Most of GE's depreciation charges are product costs, included in the cost of inventory; see the Glossary at *flow of costs.*
36. FASB Statement No. 2 requires the expensing of all R & D costs and the disclosure of the amounts expensed. See note 70.
37. That is, in computing future values of pension fund investments and interest on unfunded obligations for prior service costs, a six-percent rate is used.
38. Since these items are not shown on the balance sheet, we prefer to call them *obligations,* not *liabilities.*
39. That is, prior service costs will increase because the plan was "sweetened" as of January 1, 1975.
40. The new pension reform legislation will require drastic changes in the practices of many corporate pension plans, but GE's, however, is already in substantial conformity with the new law.
41. This practice of not funding pension plans was acceptable and widespread prior the new pension law of 1974. By 1976, however, GE and other companies will begin funding these pension obligations in an orderly fashion over not more than 40 (or, in some cases, 30) years. Ordinarily, GE funds pension liabilities as they are recognized. Thus the ordinary pension-related entries are, first, to debit pension expense and to credit pension liability:

> Pension Expense X
>   Pension Liability X

and, then, to fund the liability with a debit to pension liability and a credit to cash:

> Pension Liability X
>   Cash X
> The actual funding need not be, but usually is, exactly equal to the amount of expense recognized in the entry above.

For this new plan, the past service costs are being recognized with amortization over 20 years, but the liability is not being funded. Only the first of the two entries is made. Therefore an explicit pension liability, to be shown on the balance sheet, arises. This liability is so small now, however, that it is shown as part of "Other liabilities." See note 77.

over a period of 20 years are being charged to operations currently. Cost of this plan was $4.2 million for 1974 and $2.0 million for the partial year 1973. Unamortized past service costs for the supplementary pension plan were $36 million and $34 million at the end of 1974 and 1973 respectively.

Depreciation amounted to $376.2 million in 1974 and $334.0 million in 1973.

An accelerated depreciation method, based principally on a sum-of-the-years digits formula, is used to depreciate plant and equipment in the United States purchased in 1961 and subsequently. Assets purchased 42 prior to 1961, and most assets outside the United States, are depreciated on a straight-line basis. Special depreciation is provided where equipment may be subject to abnormal economic conditions or obsolescence.

Taxes, except those on income, totaled $123.0 million in 1974 and $113.5 million in 1973. These were mainly franchise and property taxes. They exclude social security taxes which are included with employee benefits.

Other income amounted to $185.8 million in 1974, an increase of $2.1 million from 1973. Significant items included in other income are shown below.

Other income		(In millions)
	1974	**1973**
43 Net earnings of the Credit Corporation	$ 42.7	$ 41.7
Income from:		
Customer financing	40.2	32.4
Royalty and technical agreements	42.8	36.9
44 Marketable securities and bank deposits	17.3	17.7
Other investments	29.5	31.6
Sale of Honeywell stock	0.4	7.8
Other sundry income	12.9	15.6
	$185.8	$183.7

Net earnings of General Electric Credit Corporation were $42.7 million in 1974, about the same as in 1973. Condensed financial statements for the Credit Corporation appear on page 37.

The Company sold 174,716 shares of Honeywell common stock in 1974 and 168,000 shares in 1973. Cap-45 ital gains (using average cost) from these sales were $0.4 million and $7.8 million respectively ($0.3 million and $5.5 million after taxes).

Interest and other financial charges increased to $180.1 million in 1974 from $126.9 million in 1973 primarily because of higher short-term borrowing rates and a higher level of borrowings in support of sales growth. Amounts applicable to principal items of long-term borrowings were $74.1 million in 1974 and $58.3 million in 1973.

Provision for income taxes amounted to $382.4 million in 1974. Details of this amount are shown below.

Provision for income taxes is based on the income and costs included in the Statement of Current and Retained Earnings on page 31.

Provision for income taxes		(In millions) 46
	1974	**1973**
U.S. Federal income taxes:		
Estimated amount payable	$262.1	$321.2
Effect of timing differences	30.2	0.4 47
Investment credit deferred—net	11.1	13.0 48
	303.4	334.6
Foreign income taxes:		
Estimated amount payable	74.5	71.4
Effect of timing differences	(4.2)	(0.4) 47
	70.3	71.0
Other (principally state and local income taxes)	8.7	13.1
	$382.4	$418.7

Amounts of income taxes shown as payable are determined by applicable statutes and government regulations. Timing differences result from the fact that under applicable statutes and regulations some items of income and cost are not recognized in the same time period as good accounting practice requires them to be recorded. The cumulative net effect of such items is that earnings on which tax payments were required have been higher than earnings reported in the Company's Annual Reports. Accordingly, a deferred-tax asset has been established to record the reduction of future tax 49 payments. This asset is shown under Other assets in the table on page 38. Details of the effect of timing differences on the provision for U.S. Federal income taxes are shown below. Individual timing differences reflected in foreign income taxes were not significant.

Provision has been made for Federal income taxes to be paid on that portion of the undistributed earnings of

Effect of timing differences on U.S. Federal income taxes (In millions)		
Increase (decrease) in provision for income taxes		
	1974	**1973**
Tax over book depreciation	$16.7	$12.1 50
Undistributed earnings of affiliates	10.5	6.7 51
Margin on installment sales	3.6	1.1 52
Provision for:		
Warranties	(6.6)	(7.7) 53
Other costs and expenses	15.0	(2.4)
Other—net	(9.0)	(9.4)
	$30.2	$ 0.4

42. Many foreign countries do not allow accelerated depreciation for tax purposes. Most of GE's depreciation charges are product costs; see note 35.
43. GE uses the equity method in accounting for its 100 percent ownership of the Credit Corporation. Hence it shows 100 percent of the earnings of the Credit Corporation as revenues. See note 26.
44. That is, dividends and interest revenue on securities and bank deposits.
45. GE holds shares of Honeywell acquired at different times for different prices. When some shares are sold, a flow assumption, much like an inventory flow assumption, must be made. GE uses the average-cost flow assumption. In similar circumstances, other companies use FIFO or specific identification of shares sold.
46. This schedule shows the details of income tax expense; it starts with the amounts payable, U.S. and foreign, then adds or subtracts the effects of timing differences and the investment tax credit to arrive at estimated income tax expense, called a "provision."
47. Timing differences in the U.S. resulted in U.S. income tax expense being larger than U.S. taxes payable; foreign income tax expense was less than foreign taxes payable because of timing differences.
48. The company follows the deferral method of accounting for the investment (tax) credit; see note 54. On the statement of changes in financial position, the $11.1 million deferral ($13.0 million in 1973) might better have been combined with the income tax timing differences on the fourth line instead of being included in "Other—net" (see note 30).
49. The cumulative effect of income tax timing differences is such that GE has prepaid income taxes; cumulative taxes payable have exceeded cumulative tax expense.
50. Depreciation on the tax return exceeded the amount included in the cost of goods sold. For most companies, tax depreciation exceeds book depreciation because an accelerated method is used for taxes and straight-line for the books. GE, however, uses accelerated depreciation for both; see note 42. The excess of tax over book depreciation for GE arises from its using shorter lives for tax than for book calculations. See Glossary at *asset depreciation range.*
51. Revenue from subsidiaries ("affiliates") shown on the financial statements under the equity method exceeded taxable revenue from subsidiaries which is based primarily on dividends.
52. The installment basis of revenue recognition used for tax returns showed smaller amounts of revenue in both 1973 and 1974 than did the completed sales method used for financial reports.
53. Estimated warranty expense recognized by the "allowance" method does not qualify as a tax deduction. The cost of providing warranty services becomes a tax deduction only in the period when the repairs are made. The following statement is true for both 1973 and 1974: Since the provision for warranties results in a decrease in deferred taxes, it can be determined that the estimated expense of rendering warranty service in future years for sales in the current year is greater than the warranty expenditures made in the current year, most of which related to sales of earlier years.

affiliates and associated companies expected to be remitted to the Parent. Undistributed earnings intended to be reinvested indefinitely in these companies totaled $423 million at the end of 1974 and $328 million at the end of 1973.

During 1974, U.S. Federal income tax returns of the Parent were settled for the years 1965 through 1968.

The Company follows the practice of amortizing the **54** investment credit to income over the life of the underlying facilities rather than in the year in which facilities are placed in service. Investment credit amounted to $23.9 million in 1974 compared with $23.6 million in the prior year. In 1974 $12.8 million was added to net earnings compared with $10.6 million in 1973. At the end of 1974, the amount still deferred and to be included in net earnings in future years was $83.9 million. If the Company had "flowed through" the investment credit, this amount would have been included in earnings during 1974 and prior years.

Provision for income taxes amounted to 38.2% of income before taxes in 1974 compared with 41.4% in 1973.A reconciliation of these effective tax rates to the U.S. Federal statutory rate of 48.0% is shown below.

55 Reconciliation of statutory and effective income tax rates

	1974	1973
U.S. Federal statutory rate	48.0%	48.0%
Reduction in taxes resulting from:		
56 Consolidated affiliate earnings (including DISC) subject to aggregate effective tax rates generally less than 48%	(6.4)	(2.5)
Inclusion of earnings of the Credit Corporation in before-tax income on an "after-tax" basis	(2.0)	(2.0)
Investment credit	(1.3)	(1.0)
Income taxed at capital gains rates	(0.3)	(0.3)
Other—net	0.2	(0.8)
Effective tax rate	38.2%	41.4%

Minority interest in earnings of consolidated affiliates represents the interest which other share owners have in net earnings and losses of consolidated affiliates not wholly owned by the Company.

Cash and marketable securities totaled $371.8 million at the end of 1974, an increase of $49.7 million from the end of 1973. Time deposits and certificates of deposit aggregated $85.4 million at December 31, 1974 and $134.4 million at December 31, 1973. Deposits restricted as to **57** usage and withdrawal or used as partial compensation for short-term borrowing arrangements were not material.

Marketable securities are carried at the lower of amortized cost or market value. Carrying value was substantially the same as market value.

Current receivables, less allowance for losses, totaled **58** $2,593.8 million at December 31, 1974 as shown in the table below. The increase of $416.7 million, or 19%, during the year was due principally to the increase in sales **59** in 1974. Other current receivables include the current portion of advances to suppliers and similar items not directly arising from sales of goods and services. Long-term receivables, less allowance for losses, are reported under Other assets. Supplemental information on sources of charges and credits to allowance for losses is included in the Form 10-K Report.

Current receivables		(In millions)
December 31	1974	1973
Customers' accounts and notes	$2,288.9	$1,996.4
Nonconsolidated affiliates	0.8	0.5
Other	361.3	238.7
	2,651.0	2,235.6
Less allowance for losses	(57.2)	(58.5)
	$2,593.8	$2,177.1

Inventories are summarized below, and at the end of 1974 were $2,257.0 million compared with $1,986.2 million at December 31, 1973 and $1,759.0 million at January 1, 1973. About 80% of total inventories are in the United States and substantially all of these are valued on a last-in, first-out (LIFO) basis. Substantially all of those outside the United States are valued on a first-in, first-out **60** (FIFO) basis. Such valuations are not in excess of market and are based on cost, exclusive of certain indirect manufacturing expenses and profits on sales between the Parent and affiliated companies. If the FIFO method of inventory accounting had been used by the Company, inventories would have been $783.7 million and $429.7 **61** million higher than reported at December 31, 1974, and December 31, 1973, respectively.

Inventories		(In millions)
December 31	1974	1973
Raw materials and work in process	$1,483.1	$1,276.1
Finished goods	658.5	604.6
Unbilled shipments	115.4	105.5
	$2,257.0	$1,986.2

Working capital (current assets less current liabilities) totaled $1,343.1 million, an increase of $350.1 million during 1974. The statement on page 33 provides a sum- **62** mary of major sources and applications of funds as well as an analysis of changes in working capital.

54. GE uses the deferral method of accounting for the investment (tax) credit rather than the less conservative flow-through method. (The great majority of U.S. corporations use the flow-through method.) GE earned $23.9 million of tax credits during 1974. A portion (which cannot be determined from the published data) of this $23.9 reduced reported tax expense in 1974; the remainder is shown as a deferred investment credit. A portion of previous years' investment credits, which had been deferred, also served to reduce 1974 reported tax expense. The total of these two reductions of reported tax expense in 1974 was $12.8 million. If GE had used the less conservative flow-through method, income tax expense would have been reduced by an additional $11.1 (= $23.9 − $12.8) million and 1974 net income would have been $11.1 million, or about 2 percent, larger. Cumulative net income, including 1974, would have been $83.9 million larger. Total deferred investment credit ($83.9 million) appears as part of "Other liabilities" on the balance sheet (see note 77) and the net increase in the deferred credit during 1974 ($11.1 million) appears as part of "Other—net" on the statement of changes in financial position (see note 30). See also the income tax computation for Conservative Company in the *Accounting Magic* section of this book.

55. Ordinarily, corporate income is taxed at a rate of 48 percent. GE is showing why its effective rate of income tax expense differs from 48 percent of pre-tax income. 85 percent of dividends received from other companies are exempt from tax. Long-term capital gains are taxed to corporations at a rate of 25 or 30 percent, depending on the circumstances.

56. See the Glossary for an explanation of *DISC*.

57. See *compensating balance* in the Glossary. Since compensating balances increase the stated cost of borrowing, the SEC requires disclosure of such amounts, if they are significant. GE is saying that its compensating balances are not significant.

58. "Allowances for losses" might better be called an "allowance for uncollectible accounts receivable."

59. We can check for ourselves that this is a valid explanation by examining the *receivables turnover;* see *ratio* in Glossary. The current receivables turnover in 1974 is $13,413.1/[.5 × ($2,593.8 + $2,177.1)] = 5.64 times, assuming all sales were on current account. (The assumption is only approximately correct.) The comparable receivables turnover in 1973 was 5.62 times, which indicates only slightly more rapid collections during 1973. Thus we conclude that the increase in receivables is not caused primarily by debtors paying significantly less promptly.

60. Few foreign governments allow LIFO for tax purposes.

61. GE provides information that allows us to calculate what income would have been if a FIFO cost flow assumption had been used. (See Glossary at *LIFO* and *Accounting Magic* for an explanation of why LIFO leads to lower reported net income in periods of rising prices.) The IRS does not allow companies using LIFO for tax purposes to disclose directly what income would have been under FIFO, but the SEC requires (and the IRS allows) the disclosure of beginning and ending inventories as they would have been under FIFO, if these amounts are significantly different from the LIFO amounts. See note 10 for an explanation of why an increase in ending inventory implies a reduction in cost of goods sold and hence an increase in income. As of December 31, 1974, cumulative pre-tax income is $783.7 million less than it would have been under FIFO. As of January 1, 1974, cumulative pre-tax income is $429.7 million less than it would have been under FIFO. This difference increased by $354.0 (= $783.7 − $429.7) million during the year 1974. Hence 1974 pre-tax income would have been $354.0 million, or about 35 percent, larger if FIFO had been used.

62. See note 31.

Investments amounted to $1,004.8 million at the end of 1974 as shown in the following table.

Investments		(In millions)	
December 31		1974	1973
Nonconsolidated finance affiliates		$ 456.5	$327.4
Honeywell Inc. and Honeywell Information Systems Inc.		141.3	154.6
Associated companies		48.3	68.1
Miscellaneous investments:			
M Government and government guaranteed securities		210.7	181.2
AEG (Germany)—stock and convertibles		39.2	39.2
Toshiba (Japan)—stock		34.1	33.9
Other		87.2	77.4
		371.2	331.7
Less allowance for losses		(12.5)	(12.1)
		$1,004.8	$869.7

63 Investments in nonconsolidated finance affiliates are carried at equity plus advances. Advances to these fi- **M** nance affiliates aggregated $0.7 million at the end of 1974 and 1973.

Investment in General Electric Credit Corporation, a wholly-owned nonconsolidated finance affiliate, amounted to $449.2 million at the end of 1974 and $321.4 million at the end of 1973. Condensed financial statements for the General Electric Credit Corporation and its consolidated affiliates are shown at right. Copies of its 1974 Annual Report may be obtained by writing to General Electric Credit Corporation, P.O. Box 8300, Stamford, Conn. 06904.

Investments in the common stock of Honeywell Inc. and Honeywell Information Systems Inc. (HIS), a subsidiary of Honeywell, are recorded at appraised fair value as of date of acquisition, October 1, 1970, when the information systems equipment business was transferred to HIS. The appraised fair value recognized such factors as the size of the holdings, the various requirements and restrictions on the timing of the sale or other disposition of the securities, as well as the uncertainty of future events. The recorded value at December 31, 1974 was substantially less than tax cost.

At December 31 1974 General Electric held 1,437,716 shares of Honeywell common stock compared with 1,612,432 shares at December 31, 1973. As commented upon under Other income, on page 35, General **64** Electric sold 174,716 shares of Honeywell common stock in 1974 and 168,000 in 1973. Cumulative sales through the end of 1974 were 1,087 716 shares.

In addition, General Electric continues to hold its 18½% ownership in HIS. In 1974 the Agreement between General Electric and Honeywell concerning the disposition of this interest was revised. Under the terms of the revised Agreement, General Electric can require Honeywell to purchase its interest at any time during 1976 for 1,500,000 shares of Honeywell stock, at any time during 1977 for 1,800,000 shares of Honeywell stock and at any time during 1978 for 2,200,000 shares of Honeywell stock. In addition, under certain circumstances Honeywell has the right during the 1976-1977 period to require General Electric to sell its HIS interest to Honeywell in return for 2,200,000 shares of Honeywell stock. During 1978 Honeywell has an unlimited right to purchase General Electric's HIS interest for 2,200,000 shares of Honeywell stock. The December 31, 1974 investment in Honeywell Inc. and HIS, expressing the investment in HIS in terms of the 2,200,000 option shares, would have

General Electric Credit Corporation (In millions)
Financial position

December 31	1974	1973	
Cash and marketable securities	$ 161.8	$ 141.4	
Receivables	4,668.4	3,835.0	
Deferred income	(525.6)	(396.7)	
Allowance for losses	(92.7)	(76.7)	
Net receivables	4,050.1	3,361.6	
Other assets	98.0	27.0	
Total assets	$4,309.9	$3,530.0	**65**
Notes payable:			
Due within one year	$2,111.1	$1,756.2	
Long-term—senior	959.6	760.8	
—subordinated	250.3	254.8	
Other liabilities	240.8	220.6	
Total liabilities	3,561.8	2,992.4	**65**
Deferred credits	299.7	216.9	**65**
Capital stock	267.5	160.0	
Additional paid-in capital	11.5	—	
Retained earnings	169.4	160.7	
Equity	448.4	320.7	
Total liabilities, deferred credits and equity	$4,309.9	$3,530.0	

Current and retained earnings

For the year	1974	1973	
Earned income	$ 561.3	$ 406.4	
Expenses:			
Operating and administrative	163.3	117.0	
Interest and discount	283.7	190.3	
Provision for receivable losses	45.9	28.1	
Provision for income taxes	25.7	29.3	
	518.6	364.7	
Net earnings	42.7	41.7	**66**
Less dividends	(34.0)	(31.0)	
Retained earnings at January 1	160.7	150.0	
Retained earnings at December 31	$ 169.4	$ 160.7	

M. See note 16.
63. The equity method is used for finance affiliates.
64. These sales resulted in gains reported in the "Other Income" schedule shown on page 35.
65. If the Credit Corporation were consolidated, rather than accounted for on the equity method, all these assets, liabilities, and deferred credits would be shown on GE's balance sheet, page 32. GE's consolidated retained earnings would be no different, however, since the equity method records income of unconsolidated subsidiaries as earned. The $448.4 (= $4,309.9 – $3,561.8 – $299.7) million of net assets added to GE's balance sheet would be offset with the elimination of $448.4 million from "Nonconsolidated finance affiliates," one component of "Investments," shown on the balance sheet and detailed in the schedule in the left-hand column of page 37. Test your understanding by convincing yourself that GE's investment in "Nonconsolidated finance affiliates" *other* than the Credit Corporation increased by $1.4 million during 1974.
66. Observe the effect of the equity method on page 35 in the "Other income" Schedule. GE reports $42.7 million in 1974 from GE Credit, not just the $34 million of dividends. See also note 26.

been $76 million using the closing market price of Honeywell Inc. common stock.

General Electric's commitment to the U.S. Department of Justice concerning the disposition of the Honeywell stock was also revised during 1974. General Electric is now committed to dispose of its current holding of Honeywell common stock in an orderly manner by June 30, 1978 and all other shares of Honeywell common stock that General Electric receives for its interest in HIS by December 31, 1980.

A voting trust has been established in which General Electric must deposit all shares of Honeywell common stock received as part of these transactions.

Investments in associated companies which are not consolidated but in which the Company owns 20% or more of the voting stock are valued by the equity method.

Miscellaneous investments are valued at cost. On December 31, 1974, the estimated realizable value of these **67** investments was approximately $402 million, a decrease of $3 million during the year.

Plant and equipment represents the original cost of land, buildings and equipment less estimated cost consumed **68** by wear and obsolescence. Details of plant and equipment and accumulated depreciation are shown in the table below. Additions, dispositions, provisions for depreciation and other changes in plant and equipment, analyzed by major classes, are included in the 10-K Report. Expenditures for maintenance and repairs are charged to operations as incurred.

Plant and equipment		(In millions)
	1974	1973
Major classes at December 31:		
Land and improvements	$ 112.5	$ 104.4
Buildings, structures and related equipment	1,617.6	1,445.9
Machinery and equipment	3,500.6	3,138.5
Leasehold costs and plant under construction	216.4	231.0
	$5,447.1	$4,919.8
Cost at January 1	$4,919.8	$4,449.2
Additions	671.8	598.6
Dispositions	(144.5)	(128.0)
Cost at December 31	$5,447.1	$4,919.8
Accumulated depreciation		
Balance at January 1	$2,559.3	$2,312.6
Current year provision	376.2	334.0
Dispositions	(121.1)	(95.8)
Other changes	17.1	8.5
Balance at December 31	$2,831.5	$2,559.3
Plant and equipment less depreciation at December 31	$2,615.6	$2,360.5

Other assets, less allowance for losses of $9.6 million ($15.1 million at December 31, 1973), totaled $526.1 million at December 31, 1974. Details of Other assets are shown below.

Other assets			(In millions)
December 31		1974	1973
Long-term receivables		$178.0	$173.4 M
Customer financing		78.1	141.2 M
Deferred income taxes		104.8	131.0
Recoverable engineering costs on Government contracts		54.7	61.3 M
Deferred charges		41.1	32.4
Licenses and other intangibles—net		30.5	30.9
Other		38.9	38.4
		$526.1	$608.6

The reduction in Customer financing in 1974 was due principally to the granting by the Company to General Electric Credit Corporation of a 100% participation in approximately $67 million of these assets, as well as approximately $18 million of receivables, in exchange for additional equity.

Deferred income taxes applicable to current assets **69** and liabilities were $95.9 million and $97.8 million at the end of 1974 and 1973 respectively.

Research and development expenditures, except those specified as recoverable engineering costs on Government contracts, are charged to operations as incurred. Expenditures of Company funds for research and **70** development are shown under Supplemental Details in the table on page 34.

Licenses and other intangibles acquired after October 1970 are being amortized over appropriate periods of **71** time.

Short-term borrowings, those due within one year, totaled $644.9 million at the end of 1974, compared with $665.2 million at the end of the previous year. A summary of these borrowings at year-end 1974 and 1973, and the applicable average interest rates at December 31 are shown in the tabulation at upper right.

The average balance of short-term borrowings, excluding the current portion of long-term borrowings, during 1974 was $858.2 million (calculated by averaging all month-end balances for the year) compared with an average balance of $594.7 million in 1973. The maximum balance included in these calculations was $1,089.0 million and $775.1 million at the end of April 1974 and November 1973, respectively. The average interest rate for the year 1974 was 11.7%, and for 1973 was 9.9%. These average rates represent total short-term interest expense divided by the average balance outstanding.

67. Compare with book value shown in the "Investments" schedule on page 37. There is a substantial unrealized holding gain since the time these "Miscellaneous investments" were acquired. The unrealized holding gain declined, however, by more than 50 percent during 1974. At January 1, 1974, the unrealized holding gain was $73.3 (= $402.0 + $3.0 − $331.7) million. By December 31, 1974, the unrealized holding gain had declined to $30.8 (= $402.0 − $371.2) million. Thus there was an unrealized holding loss during 1974 of $42.5 (=$73.3 − $30.8) million. That is, if GE were allowed to use current market prices for valuing these securities and did so, it would have recognized income of $73.3 million from the securities during the time prior to January 1, 1974, but would have recognized a loss of $42.5 million during 1974.

68. That is, less accumulated depreciation caused by wear and obsolescence.

M. See note 16.

69. See note 49 for explanation.

70. FASB Statement No. 2 issued in 1974 requires expensing of R & D costs in the year incurred; GE had been expensing them all along. As a result of expensing R & D costs, GE's total assets on the Balance Sheet are less than they would be if these costs were capitalized and subsequently amortized.

71. APB Opinion No. 17 requires such amortization of intangibles.

Short-term borrowings				*(In millions)*
December 31	**1974**		**1973**	
	Amount	Average rate at Dec. 31	Amount	Average rate at Dec. 31
Parent				
Banks	$ —	— %	$ 99.0	9.68%
Notes with Trust Departments	225.8	8.74	215.8	7.93
Commercial paper	45.1	9.75	124.3	9.71
Consolidated affiliates				
Banks	279.4	15.37	168.9	12.12
Commercial paper	31.3	12.81	—	—
Other, including current portion of long-term borrowings	63.3	—	57.2	—
	$644.9		$665.2	

Parent borrowings are from U.S. sources. Borrowings of affiliated companies, most of which are foreign, are primarily from sources outside the U.S.

Although the total unused credit available to the Company through banks and commercial credit markets is not readily quantifiable, informal credit lines in excess of $850 million had been extended by approximately 135 U.S. banks at.year-end 1974.

Accounts payable at December 31, 1974 and 1973 are shown below.

Accounts payable		*(In millions)*
December 31	**1974**	**1973**
Trade	$607.5	$583.4
Collected for the account of others	87.7	67.0
Nonconsolidated affiliates	0.8	23.1
	$696.0	$673.5

72 Progress collections and price adjustments accrued represents primarily collections from customers on contracts in progress as well as anticipated price adjustments on contracts.

Taxes accrued include estimated amounts payable for current and prior year U.S. Federal income taxes, current and prior year foreign income taxes and social security taxes.

73 Other costs and expenses accrued at the end of 1974 included compensation and benefit costs accrued of $452.1 million and interest expense accrued of $27.6 million. At the end of 1973, compensation and benefit costs accrued were $385.6 million and interest expense accrued was $22.6 million. The remaining costs and expenses accrued included liabilities for such items as product claims, allowances to customers, advertising costs, utility charges and employee-related expenses.

Long-term borrowings amounted to $1,195.2 million at **74** December 31, 1974, compared with $917.2 million at the end of 1973 as summarized below.

During 1974, the Company issued $300 million of 8½% Debentures due in 2004. The net proceeds of this offering were added to the general funds of the Company and were used to reduce short-term borrowings.

Borrowings of General Electric Overseas Capital Corporation (a wholly-owned consolidated affiliate) are unconditionally guaranteed by General Electric as to payment of principal, premium, if any, and interest. This Corporation primarily assists in financing capital requirements of foreign companies in which General Electric has an equity interest as well as financing certain customer purchases. The borrowings include the Corporation's 4¼% Guaranteed Bonds due in 1985 which are convertible through November 1975 into General Electric com- **75** mon stock at $65.50 a share, the Corporation's 4¼% Guaranteed Debentures due in 1987 which are convertible until June 15, 1987 into General Electric common stock at $80.75 a share and 5½% Sterling/Dollar Guaranteed Loan Stock due in 1993 in the amount of £3.6 million ($8.4 million), convertible from October 1976 into General Electric common stock at $73.50 a share.

Other long-term borrowings were largely by foreign affiliates with various interest rates and maturities.

Long-term borrowing maturities during the next five years, including the portion classified as current, are $53 0 million in 1975, $144.0 million in 1976, $28.6 million in 1977, $34.5 million in 1978 and $163.2 million in 1979. These amounts are after deducting reacquired debentures held in the treasury for sinking fund requirements.

Long-term borrowings			*(In millions)*
Outstanding December 31	**1974**	**1973**	Sinking fund/ pre-payment period
General Electric Company:			
3½% Debentures due in 1976	$ 84.3	$ 84.3	1961-75
6¼% Debentures due in 1979	125.0	125.0	None
5¾% Notes due in 1991	100.0	106.2	1972-90
5.30% Debentures due in 1992	150.0	160.8	1973-91
7½% Debentures due in 1996	200.0	200.0	1977-95
8½% Debentures due in 2004	300.0	—	1985-03
General Electric Overseas Capital Corporation:			
4¼% Bonds due in 1985	48.8	50.0	1976-84
4¼% Debentures due in 1987	50.0	50.0	None
5½% Sterling/Dollar Guaranteed Loan Stock due in 1993	8.4	8.3	None
Other	55.3	73.1	
Other	73.4	59.5	
	$1,195.2	$917.2	

72. Since GE uses the completed contract method of reporting revenues from long-term construction projects, the credit when cash is received prior to completion of such contracts is to a liability, frequently labeled "advances from customers" but called "progress collections" by GE.
73. The word *costs* here is inappropriate; see note 9. Here GE is showing accrued liabilities.
74. The inference is that all these bonds were issued at par because neither discounts nor premiums are shown. This inference is probably incorrect.
75. See note 8. Fully diluted earnings per share is less than primary earnings per share probably because some of these convertible bonds are not common stock equivalents (for primary earnings per share) but are dilutive for fully diluted earnings per share. The total dilution is immaterial, so that GE's fully diluted earnings per share need not be separately disclosed.

Sinking fund transactions for 1974 are shown below.

76

1974 Sinking fund transactions			(In millions)
	Retirements		Face value in
	Face value	Re-acquired cost value	treasury December 31, 1974
General Electric Company:			
3½% Debentures	$14.7	$13.0	$14.1
5.30% Debentures	10.0	7.9	30.0
General Electric Overseas Capital Corporation:			
4¼% Bonds due in 1985	—	—	1.2

General Electric Company 5¾% Notes having a value of $6.2 million were retired during 1974 in accordance with pre-payment requirements.

Additional miscellaneous details pertaining to long-term borrowings are available in the 10-K Report.

Other liabilities were $518.9 million at December 31, 1974 compared with $492.1 million at December 31, 1973 and included such items as the deferred invest-ment tax credit, the noncurrent portion of the allowance **77** for replacements under guarantees, deferred incentive compensation, and other miscellaneous employee plans costs.

Preferred stock, $1.00 par value, to a total of 2,000,000 **78** shares, has been authorized by the share owners. No preferred shares have been issued.

Common stock, $2.50 par value, a total of 210,000,000 shares, has been authorized by the share owners. Shares issued and outstanding at the end of the last two years are shown below.

Common stock issued and outstanding	1974	1973
Shares issued at January 1	185,518,257	185,243,848
New shares issued:		
Stock option plans	49,091	274,409
Savings and Security Program	500,000	—
Shares issued at December 31	186,067,348	185,518,257
Less shares held in treasury	(3,416,316)	(3,370,759)
Shares outstanding at December 31	182,651,032	182,147,498

Common stock held in treasury for various corporate purposes totaled $175.9 million at the close of 1974. The comparable amount at the end of 1973 was $184.5 mil-lion. Purchases during 1974 totaled 1,256,896 shares in-cluding 249,557 at current market prices from employees who acquired them through employee plans other than stock option plans. Other purchases were primarily through regular transactions in the security markets. Dispositions are shown at upper right.

Included in common stock held in treasury for the de-

Dispositions of treasury shares	1974	1973
Employee savings plans	1,066,158	1,011,101
Incentive compensation plans	129,405	107,216
Business combinations	15,776	105,000
Other	—	49
	1,211,339	1,223,366

ferred compensation provisions of incentive compensa-tion plans were 1,297,576 shares at December 31, 1974 and 1,222,422 shares at December 31, 1973. These shares are carried at market value at the time of allotment which amounted to $61.4 million and $56.8 million at December 31, 1974 and 1973 respectively. The liabil-ity is recorded under other liabilities.

The remaining common stock held in treasury is car-ried at cost, $114.5 million at the end of 1974 and $127.7 **79** million at the end of 1973. These shares are held for future corporate requirements including 1,483,374 shares for possible conversion of General Electric Over-seas Capital Corporation convertible indebtedness de-scribed under long-term borrowings, for distributions under employee savings plans and for incentive com-pensation awards.

Amounts in excess of par value received for stock in-creased $5.0 million during 1974, resulting principally from amounts received for newly-issued shares in ex-cess of par value of $20.0 million, partially offset by net losses from treasury stock transactions of $15.0 million. **80** During 1973, there was an increase of $12.9 million which resulted from amounts received for newly-issued shares in excess of par value of $11.1 million and net gains from treasury stock transactions of $1.8 million.

Incentive compensation plans provide incentive for outstanding performance to over 3,000 key employees. Allotments made in 1974 for services performed in 1973 aggregated $30.7 million. Allotments made in 1973 for services performed in 1972 totaled $27.8 million.

Retained earnings at year-end 1974 totaled $3,000.5 million and included approximately $178.3 million repre- **81** senting the excess of earnings of General Electric Credit Corporation over dividends received from this affiliate since its formation. In addition, retained earnings have been reduced by $1.3 million, which represents the change in equity in associated companies since acquisi-tion. At the end of 1973, these amounts were $169.6 million and $0.6 million respectively.

The Stock Option and Stock Appreciation Rights Plan approved by the share owners in 1973, and previous plans under which options remain outstanding, provide continuing incentive for more than 500 employees. Op-tion price under these plans is the full market value of

76. These transactions, acquiring bonds in the market and retiring them, result in gains shown as part of "Other sundry income" in the "Other income" schedule on page 35. Under the terms of FASB Statement No. 4, future gains like these will be classified as extraordinary.

77. Included here are the recognized, but unfunded, liabilities under the new "supplementary pension plan" referred to at note 41. Also included are the deferred investment credits which result from using the deferral method; see note 54.

78. Since no preferred shares have been issued, there is no preferred stock amount shown in the stockholders' equity portion of the Balance Sheet.

79. Treasury stock, at cost, is properly shown as contra to all of stockholders' equity as an unallocated reduction in stockholders' equity. GE uses the *cost method for treasury stock;* see the Glossary.

80. Neither gain nor loss can be recognized on transaction in treasury shares. GE improperly uses the terms *losses* and *gains* here. When GE reissues previously-acquired shares at a price different from its acquisition cost, the balancing plug is not to a gain or loss account, but to Amounts Received for Stock in Excess of Par Value. If treasury stock acquired at a cost of $1,000 is reissued for $1,200, the entry would be:

Cash	1,200	
Common Stock Held in Treasury		1,000
Amounts Received for Stock in Excess of Par Value(Not Gain).		200

81. The $178.3 million represents the cumulative excess of equity method revenues over cost method revenues since GE organized the Credit Corporation.

General Electric common stock on date of grant. Therefore, participants in the plans do not benefit unless the stock's market price rises, thus benefiting all share own-
82 ers. Also, an employee can only exercise his option to the extent that annual installments have matured, normally over a period of nine years. Thus the plans encourage managers and professional employees to have the long-term entrepreneurial interest that will benefit all share owners.

At the end of 1974, there were 2,500,000 shares reserved for the 1973 Plan, and 1,899,392 shares covered by outstanding options granted under prior plans, for a total of 4,399,392 shares. Of this total amount, 970,541 shares were subject to exercisable options, 2,199,941 shares were under options not yet exercisable and 1,228,910 shares were available for granting options in the future. The number of shares available for granting options at the end of 1973 was 1,945,035. A summary of stock option transactions during the last two years is shown below. Further details on stock options are available in the 10-K Report.

Stock Options		Average per share	
	Shares subject to option	Option price	Market price
Balance at Dec. 31, 1972	2,476,911	$50.27	$72.88
Options granted	554,965	64.75	64.75
Options exercised	(273,569)	42.84	63.69
Options terminated	(80,076)	52.50	—
Balance at Dec. 31, 1973	2,678,231	53.96	63.00
Options granted	734,537	39.39	39.39
Options exercised	(48,689)	44.55	53.49
Options terminated	(193,597)	50.52	—
Balance at Dec. 31, 1974	3,170,482	50.94	33.38

83 Lease commitments and contingent liabilities, consisting of guarantees, pending litigation, taxes and other claims, in the opinion of management, are not considered to be material in relation to the financial position of the Company.

Audit and Finance Committee **84**

During 1974 this committee continued to serve share owners' interests by monitoring and counseling management in the utilization of the Company's financial resources.

At our February joint meeting with the Operations Committee we reviewed the 1973 Annual Report and the 1974 Proxy Statement and, with no employee members of the Board present, met with the responsible executives of the independent public accountants with respect to their audit of the financial statements contained in the Annual Report. The committee determined to its satisfaction that the accountants had received the full cooperation of management and had no qualifications to make in their report.

In our other 1974 meetings, the committee conducted reviews of the Company's financial condition, including short- and long-term borrowings, changes in cash and marketable securities, receivable and inventory balances, holdings of Honeywell stock, plant and equipment expenditures, and total debt and equity relationships.

Aware of the unusually severe impact that external forces are having on the Company's financial structure, we maintained a dialogue with management on public positions to be taken, especially those regarding financial matters.

John E. Lawrence, *Chairman*
Reginald H. Jones, *Vice Chairman*
Silas S. Cathcart
Thomas S. Gates
Henry H. Henley, Jr.
Dean A. McGee
Samuel R. Pierce, Jr.
Gilbert H. Scribner, Jr.
Herman L. Weiss
Walter B. Wriston

Ex officio members
Walter D. Dance
Jack S. Parker

82. The unwary reader might mistakenly infer that these options do not dilute the equity of other stockholders. Options will not be exercised unless the market price at time of exercise exceeds the exercise price. If the option exercise price exceeds the market price, then the holder of the option can obtain a share more cheaply by merely purchasing it on the stock market. At the time options are exercised, shares are issued at a price less than would be realized if the shares were issued to the general investing public. Notice, for example, that as of the end of *1973* if the 2.7 million options were exercised, the average share would be issued for about $9 less than the market price and the dilution of owners' equity would be about $24.3 million (or about .72 percent) of stockholders' equity as of that time. This phenomenon is not as easy to demonstrate as of the end of 1974 when, because of stock market declines in GE share prices, the *average* option exercise price exceeded market price.

83. The SEC requires disclosure of material commitments under long-term, noncancelable leases. GE has no such material commitments. In general, the disclosures must include the effects on both the income statement and the balance sheet of capitalizing such leases.

84. Including the report of the audit committee (see Glossary) is one of GE's innovative actions in reporting. Many companies have audit committees; both the New York Stock Exchange and the SEC encourage the practice. Only a few companies include the audit committee's report in the statements distributed to stockholders.

Historical review

The historical data summarized at right is presented as a supplement to the information provided in this Annual Report.

For a discussion and analysis of results of operations, and the Company's financial position and changes affecting it for the year 1974 compared with 1973, see the Financial Summary on pages 30 to 41. In addition, the Review of Operations on pages 8 to 21 reports on significant factors, including inflation and the cost-price squeeze, that affected operating results for major categories of the Company's business for the same two years. The summary of operations at right provides a longer time frame for analyzing results and other data frequently of interest to share owners.

For additional perspective on the most recent five years, it should be recalled that many domestic operations were affected by a strike which began in 1969 and extended into February 1970. Also, in October 1970, computer operations, which had been operating at a loss, were transferred to Honeywell Inc. Thus, direct comparisons of subsequent years' results with those of 1970 may be distorted. Sales in 1972 increased 9 percent from 1971 and sales in 1973 increased 13 percent from 1972. Operating costs increased in each of these years generally in line with increased sales volume. The sharp increases in Other income in 1971 and 1972 resulted in large part from gains on sales of Honeywell Inc. stock and improved earnings by General Electric Credit Corporation. The increase in interest expense in 1973 resulted primarily from higher short-term borrowing rates. Provision for income taxes as a percent of pre-tax income, while increasing from 40.0 in 1971 to 41.4 in 1973, was relatively stable, although specific elements entering into tax calculations for each period have varied. The tabular data on pages 8 through 21 show the operating results as reported by major categories for 1970 through 1974 and should be referred to for a better understanding of their differing impacts on total Company results for any particular year.

Supplemental market price data for General Electric common stock showing high and low prices on the New York Stock Exchange by quarter for each of the last two years are as follows:

	1974		1973	
First Quarter	$65	$50¾	$75⅞	$62¼
Second Quarter	56	46¾	64⅞	55
Third Quarter	49¾	30	65⅝	55¾
Fourth Quarter	40½	30½	68⅝	57

Dividends declared during the first two quarters of 1973 were 35 cents per share and were increased to the present rate of 40 cents per share in the third quarter of that year.

Ten year financial highlights	1974
Summary of operations	
Sales of products and services	$13,413.1
Materials, engineering & production costs	10,137.6
Selling, general & administrative expenses	2,280.5
Operating costs	12,418.1
Operating margin	995.0
Other income	185.8
Interest and other financial charges	(180.1)
Earnings before income taxes & minority interest	1,000.7
Provision for income taxes	(382.4)
Minority interest	(10.2)
Net earnings	$ 608.1
Earnings per common share *(a)*	$ 3.34
Dividends declared per common share *(a)*	$ 1.60
Earnings as a percentage of sales	4.5%
Earned on share owners' equity	17.2%
Cash dividends declared	$ 291.2
Shares outstanding–average *(In thousands) (a)*	182,120
Share owner accounts–average	547,000
Market price range per share *(a) (b)*	65-30
Price / earnings ratio range	19-9
Current assets	$ 5,222.6
Current liabilities	3,879.5
Total assets	9,369.1
Share owners' equity	3,704.3
Plant and equipment additions	$ 671.8
Depreciation	376.2
Employees–average worldwide	404,000
–average U.S.	307,000

(a) Amounts have been adjusted for the two-for-one stock split in April 1971.

(b) Represents high and low market price on New York Stock Exchange for each year.

(Dollar amounts in millions; per-share amounts in dollars)

1973	1972	1971	1970	1969	1968	1967	1966	1965
$11,575.3	$10,239.5	$9,425.3	$8,726.7	$8,448.0	$8,381.6	$7,741.2	$7,177.3	$6,213.6
8,515.2	7,509.6	6,962.1	6,423.6	6,346.1	6,251.7	5,779.4	5,311.0	4,449.2
2,105.3	1,915.2	1,726.2	1,754.2	1,615.3	1,482.1	1,320.9	1,234.3	1,118.9
10,620.5	9,424.8	8,688.3	8,177.8	7,961.4	7,733.8	7,100.3	6,545.3	5,568.1
954.8	814.7	737.0	548.9	486.6	647.8	640.9	632.0	645.5
183.7	189.2	152.0	106.8	98.7	86.3	91.4	72.4	72.1
(126.9)	(106.7)	(96.9)	(101.4)	(78.1)	(70.5)	(62.9)	(39.9)	(27.4)
1,011.6	897.2	792.1	554.3	507.2	663.6	669.4	664.5	690.2
(418.7)	(364.1)	(317.1)	(220.6)	(231.5)	(312.3)	(320.5)	(347.4)	(352.2)
(7.8)	(3.1)	(3.2)	(5.2)	2.3	5.8	12.5	21.8	17.1
$ 585.1	$ 530.0	$ 471.8	$ 328.5	$ 278.0	$ 357.1	$ 361.4	$ 338.9	$ 355.1
$ 3.21	$ 2.91	$ 2.60	$ 1.81	$ 1.54	$ 1.98	$ 2.00	$ 1.88	$ 1.97
$ 1.50	$ 1.40	$ 1.38	$ 1.30	$ 1.30	$ 1.30	$ 1.30	$ 1.30	$ 1.20
5.1%	5.2%	5.0%	3.8%	3.3%	4.3%	4.7%	4.7%	5.7%
18.1%	18.0%	17.6%	13.2%	11.5%	15.4%	16.5%	16.2%	18.0%
$ 272.9	$ 254.8	$ 249.7	$ 235.4	$ 235.2	$ 234.8	$ 234.2	$ 234.6	$ 216.7
182,051	182,112	181,684	181,114	180,965	180,651	180,266	180,609	180,634
537,000	536,000	523,000	529,000	520,000	530,000	529,000	530,000	521,000
75⅞-55	73-58¼	66½-46½	47¼-30⅛	49⅛-37	50¼-40⅛	58-41¼	60-40	60⅛-45½
24-17	25-20	26-18	26-17	32-24	25-20	29-21	32-21	31-23
$ 4,485.4	$ 3,979.3	$3,639.0	$3,334.8	$3,287.8	$3,311.1	$3,207.6	$3,013.0	$2,842.4
3,492.4	2,869.7	2,840.4	2,650.3	2,366.7	2,104.3	1,977.4	1,883.2	1,566.8
8,324.2	7,401.8	6,887.8	6,198.5	5,894.0	5,652.5	5,250.3	4,768.1	4,241.5
3,372.4	3,084.6	2,801.8	2,553.6	2,426.5	2,402.1	2,245.3	2,128.1	2,048.1
$ 598.6	$ 435.9	$ 553.1	$ 581.4	$ 530.6	$ 514.7	$ 561.7	$ 484.9	$ 332.9
334.0	314.3	273.6	334.7	351.3	300.1	280.4	233.6	188.4
388,000	369,000	363,000	397,000	410,000	396,000	385,000	376,000	333,000
304,000	292,000	291,000	310,000	318,000	305,000	296,000	291,000	258,000

Additional information, including financial statements of the General Electric Pension Trust and the Company's Form 10-K Report, is available to share owners. Requests should be sent to: Investor Relations, General Electric Company, Fairfield, Connecticut 06431

The 1974 Annual Report is one of four quarterly issues of *The General Electric Investor,* published to inform share owners and investors about activities of the General Electric Company Others may receive the *Investor* on request.

EDITOR: Frederick N. Robinson
ASSOCIATE EDITORS: Devere E. Logan; Edna Vercini
FINANCIAL EDITOR: Sidney D. Spencer
EDITORIAL BOARD: David W. Burke; *Manager, Public Relations Programs;* J. Hervie Haufler, *Manager, Corporate Editorial Communications;* John L. Ingersoll, *Manager, Investor Relations Operation.*

ART DIRECTION: Page, Arbitrio & Resen

NOTE: *The corporate signature as it appears on the front cover is a trademark of General Electric Company.* ® *and* ⓣ *indicate registered and unregistered trade and service marks of General Electric Company.*

Inflation Accounting

The most significant and persistent complaint about published financial statements in recent years is that they do not recognize the economic facts of life. Inflation is a reality throughout the world, yet its effects are not explicitly reported in conventional financial statements. To attempt to cope with this problem, the Financial Accounting Standards Board in 1975 circulated a Proposed Statement of Financial Accounting Standards (Exposure Draft) which, if adopted, would require all firms to present excerpts from general price level adjusted financial statements as supplementary disclosures in their annual reports.[1] This section explains the rudiments of general price level adjusted accounting and shows an estimated general price level adjusted income statement for the General Electric Company's operations during 1974 as well as estimates of 1974 general price level adjusted income for several other companies.

General Price Level Adjusted Accounting

General price level accounting adjusts the recorded historical cost amount of each item disclosed in the conventional financial statements for changes in the general purchasing power of the dollar since the item was first recorded in the accounts. The adjustments rely on an index of the general price level and attempt to show all financial statement items in terms of the purchasing power of the dollar at the end of the year being reported. The Gross National Product (GNP) Implicit Price Deflator is the index used in the United States to restate all items to end-of-year dollars. General price level adjusted statements are not based on market values. Rather, they are based on historical costs adjusted to end-of-year purchasing power by the use of a *general* price index, not specific price indexes. Many critics, including us, question the usefulness of much of the information in general price level adjusted statements. (See the Glossary at "PuPu.")

General price level adjusted income statements differ in essentially five important respects from conventional income statements. These differences, illustrated in Exhibit 1 with data estimated from the General Electric Company's annual report, are explained next.[2]

1. *Revenues and expenses occuring fairly evenly throughout the year.* Sales and expenses, other than cost of goods sold and depreciation, usually occur fairly evenly through the year. To restate them in terms of dollars of end-of-year general purchasing power, they are adjusted for half a year of general price change. Since the price increase in 1974 (as measured by the GNP deflator) was about 11.8 percent, the price change for half a year was about 5.7 percent.[3] Sales and other income (except revenue recognized on the equity method—see next item) as well as expenses (except cost of goods sold and depreciation) are increased by about 5.7 percent in the adjustment process. See our notes 11, 33, and 43 to the GE report for identification of these items.

2. *Revenue recognized under the equity method.* In the conventional income statement, the investor company recognizes its share of the income of the investee company (in GE's case, "unconsolidated finance subsidiaries;" see GE report at note 66.) In general price level adjusted income statements, the investor recognizes its share of the adjusted income of the investee. The

---

[1] The FASB designates such statements as "reporting in units of general purchasing power."

[2] The techniques for making these estimates are described in detail in Sidney Davidson and Roman L. Weil, "Inflation Accounting: What Will General Price Level Adjusted Income Statements Show?" *Financial Analyst Journal,* January/February, 1975, 27-31, 70-84, and in our book *Inflation Accounting,* New York: McGraw-Hill Book Co., 1976.

[3] The correct method of finding an average of a series of price changes is to use a geometric, rather than an arithmetic, average. The geometric average price change for one-half a year when prices increased by 11.8 percent for the entire year is $\sqrt{1+.118}$ 1, which is approximately equal to 5.7 percent. The arithmetic average price change for one-half a year when prices increased by 11.8 percent for the entire year is 5.9 (= 11.8/2) percent. Using one-half the year's price change, 5.9 percent, rather than the price change for one-half a year, 5.7 percent, biases the adjustments somewhat by assuming, in effect, that prices increased more rapidly in the second half of the year than in the first. Such a bias results in slight *over*adjustments.

EXHIBIT 1

General Electric Company
Income Statement for 1974

(Dollar Amounts Shown in Millions)

		Historical Dollars (Shown In Annual Report)	In 12/31/74 Dollars (As Estimated)	Percentage Change
Revenues				
(1)[1]	Sales and Other Income	$13,556	$14,335	+ 5.7%
(2)	Equity Method Revenue......................	43	–24	–155.8
	Total.....................................	$13,599	$14,311	+ 5.2
Expenses and Deductions				
(3)	Cost of Goods Sold[2]	$ 9,762	$10,357	+ 6.1
(4)	Depreciation (SYD)[3]	376	545	+ 44.9
(1)	Other Expenses and Deductions..............	2,853	3,017	+ 5.7
	Total.....................................	$12,991	$13,919	+ 7.2
	Income before Gain on Monetary Items.......	$ 608	$ 392	– 36.5
(5)	Gain on Monetary Items[4]...................	—	177	—
	Net Income	$ 608	$ 569	– 6.4

[1]Adjustment number, keyed to description in text.
[2]Inventories are 80 percent LIFO; 20 percent FIFO.
[3]Average life of depreciable assets is estimated to be 6.3 years; price index increased by 44.9 percent during the 6.3 years preceding December 31, 1974.
[4]Monetary items are all marked "M" in GE's balance sheet (see page 32 of GE annual report and our footnote 16) and in the notes to the balance sheet (pages 36-39 of the annual report). The net monetary liabilities for GE are computed as follows:

	(Historical Dollars in Millions)	
	12/31/74	**12/31/73**
Monetary Liabilities		
Current Liabilities and Long-term (Domestic) Borrowings	$5,068.3	$4,401.3
Monetary Assets		
Cash, Receivables (both long- and short-term), Customer Financing, Recoverable Costs, Government Securities, and Advances to Affiliates	–3,430.5	–3,031.7
Net Monetary Liabilities	$1,637.8	$1,369.6

The average of net monetary liabilities for the year 1974 was $1,503.7 [= .5 × ($1,637.8 + $1,369.6)] million. The price change for the year was 11.8 percent. GE's gain from being a net debtor during 1974 when prices increased by 11.8 percent was, then, about .118 × $1,503.7 = $177 million.

100-percent owned GE Credit Corporation reported income of $42.7 million on a conventional basis; restated on a general price level adjusted basis, this would have been a *loss* of about $23.9 million. (For simplicity, the estimated restatement of the Credit Company is not presented here.) The large difference between conventional income and adjusted income for GE Credit is caused almost entirely by its loss on holding net monetary assets during the period of general price increase—see adjustment 5 below.

3. *Cost of goods sold.* With rising prices, cost of goods sold on a price level adjusted basis will be higher than that reported in conventional financial statements. How much higher depends in large part on the cost flow assumption—FIFO, LIFO, etc.—used. During periods of rising prices and increasing inventory quantities, the inflation adjustment will be greatest for firms using a FIFO assumption. GE uses a LIFO flow assumption for 80 percent of its inventory and a FIFO flow assumption for 20 percent (see GE report at note 60). Our analysis indicates that this results in an average increase of a little over 6 percent in cost of goods sold in the adjusted income statement.[4] (We subtract depreciation from cost of goods sold reported at our note 35 and adjust depreciation expense separately; see next item.)

4. *Depreciation.* General price level adjusted depreciation is almost always much larger than depreciation as conventionally reported. For most firms, depreciable assets typically are acquired many years before the period being reported on and price levels have increased substantially since acquisition. The depreciation adjustment reflects a portion (equal to the depreciation rate) of the cumulative change in prices since the depreciable assets were acquired. (For example, if the depreciation rate for an asset is 10 percent and general price levels have increased by 60 percent since that asset was acquired, then the depreciation adjustment will be 6 percent (= .10 × .60) of the asset's acquisition cost.) Our analysis indicates that GE's depreciable assets were acquired, on average, a little over six years before December 31, 1974. The cumulative price increase over that time has been about 45 percent; the depreciation expense is correspondingly increased.

5. *Gain or loss on monetary items.* Price level adjusted income statements explicitly show the gain for the period in purchasing power captured by a debtor (or the loss suffered by a creditor) during a period of rising general price levels. Since most industrial companies are typically net debtors, they will usually show purchasing power gains from this debt. (The liabilities will be paid off, or discharged, with dollars of smaller general purchasing power than was originally borrowed. The difference between the purchasing power borrowed and that repaid is the gain on a monetary liability during the term of the loan.) The gain from being in a net monetary liability position, although real in an economic sense, does not produce a current inflow of cash.

The gain or loss from holding monetary items is in many ways the most meaningful of the general price level adjustments. The interest expense reported in the conventional income statements is the actual cost of borrowing. It depends upon the interest rate negotiated at the time of the loan. That interest rate, in turn, depends in part on the leader's and borrower's anticipations about the rate of inflation during the term of the loan. (Interest rates are increased when the lender expects inflation during the term of the loan. The borrower accepts the higher rate because he or she expects to repay "cheaper" dollars.) Thus, the borrower's conventional income statement shows an interest expense that reflects the inflation expected by both the borrower and the lender. The gain from being in a net monetary liability position in a time of rising prices is, in a real sense, an offset to reported interest expense. It reflects a gain from being a debtor during a period of inflation that both parties to the loan expected. After the fact, who benefited, the borrower or the lender, depends on whether the actual rate of price increase during the term of the loan differed from the rate anticipated by both parties to the loan at the time the loan was made. If the actual rate of price increase turns out to be less than the anticipated rate, then the lender benefits. If the actual rate turns out to be greater than the anticipated rate, then the borrower benefits.

Summary

The difference between income as conventionally reported and income adjusted for general price level changes is equal to the sum of basically five adjustments. We estimated adjustments for the 1974 annual reports of 64 companies similar to those illustrated for General Electric in Exhibit 1. We used reports for the other 29 companies in the Dow Jones Industrial Index and for 35 other large companies. The results are summarized in Exhibits 2 and 3. Column (1) shows adjusted

---

[4] Many of the companies reported on in Exhibit 2 and 3 below use a FIFO assumption for all their inventories. Adjustments for some of these companies result in increases of the reported cost of goods sold by more than 10 percent.

income before gain or loss on monetary items as a percentage of (conventionally) reported net income. Column (2) shows adjusted net income (which includes gain or loss on monetary items) as a percentage of reported net income. Column (3) shows adjusted earnings per common share—that is, Column (2), per share, less the effects of preferred dividends plus the effects of "monetary" gain on preferred stock—as a percentage of reported earnings per share. (Preferred stock, for purposes of computing earnings per share, is treated much like a monetary liability for some companies.)

The results of our estimates of general price level adjusted income can be summarized as follows. Income before gain on net money items is decreased for virtually all companies.[5] This reduction is caused by the substantial increase in depreciation charges and, except for LIFO companies, a more than half-year adjustment in cost of goods sold.[6] The median for adjusted income before gain on net money items as a percentage of reported income of the Dow companies is 63 to 64 percent and for the 35 others is 69 percent. The difference, while not large, suggests that the Dow companies have somewhat older plant on average.

When gain or loss on money items is added to obtain adjusted net income, the percentage of adjusted net income to reported income goes up in almost all cases. This is another way of saying that almost all corporations are net debtors, or borrowers. The exceptions are companies with relatively conservative financial policies, such as Eastman Kodak and Sears. The median of adjusted income as a percentage of reported income for the Dow companies is 88 percent and is 96 percent for the other 35. These percentages are surprisingly (to us and to most other observers, we believe) high. Eight of the Dow companies and fifteen of the other 35 showed adjusted incomes greater than reported income. Recognizing inflation effects, including gains from net debtor position, has little effect on adjusted net income, on the average, but in a substantial minority of the cases, income is increased by making the inflation adjustments.

Differences between Columns (2) and (3) in Exhibits 2 and 3 arise if the corporation has preferred stock outstanding. Common stockholders secure a monetary gain at the expense of preferred stockholders in a period of rising prices. This does not affect adjusted net income, but it does increase adjusted earnings per common share. Even where a firm has preferred stock outstanding, the difference between Columns (3) and (2) is relatively small in most cases reported here. For a few Dow companies, such as American Brands, AT&T, and Westinghouse, the differences between Columns (3) and (2) are significant, but the median of the Dow companies adjusted earnings per share as a percentage of reported earnings per share does not change from the percentage shown in Column (2). There are a few more significant changes among the other 35 and the median rises to 97 percent of reported earnings per share. In a way, it is ironic that after going through the complex adjustment procedures, earnings per share for this group is, on the average almost unaffected. But analysts are interested in individual companies, not averages. Perhaps the most significant fact to be derived from the exhibits is the wide range of effects on individual corporations. Clearly adjusting net incomes for increases in general price levels produces dramatically different results among companies.

Additional Inflation Accounting Information (Shell Oil)

Shell Oil Company published supplementary general price level adjusted financial information during 1975. This information is reproduced below on pages 104 and 105. Several items in the supplementary disclosure are worthy of note. First, this information is somewhat more than the FASB proposes to require. Second, Shell shows comparisons of financial ratios based on both conventional and price level adjusted financial statements. Except for the debt-equity ratio, which Shell calls the *debt: total capital* ratio, the ratios based on price level adjustments are different from those based on conventional statements in a way that analysts and investors generally consider less favorable. Third, Shell classifies deferred federal income taxes as monetary. The auditors concur (as do we) with this classification, although contrary to the FASB proposal. Classifying deferred federal income taxes as monetary increases price level adjusted net income.

[5] The one exception among the 65 companies we illustrate is Coca Cola; for it, there is a small increase. This is caused by its relatively small depreciation expense (less than 3 percent of revenues) and its use of LIFO. Although Chrysler shows 602 percent in Column (1), this means that its adjusted *loss* is more than 6 times its reported loss.

[6] Since revenues are increased by an adjustment factor reflecting one-half year of price increase = 5.7 percent for 1974), the cost of goods sold adjustment, if it is to reduce adjusted income, must be for more than one-half year. GE uses FIFO for 20 percent of its inventories and has a 6.1 percent adjustment of cost of goods sold which represents about 6 1 3 months of price change (Exhibit 1).

EXHIBIT 2. THE THIRTY COMPANIES IN THE DOW JONES INDUSTRIAL INDEX

Estimates of General Price Level Adjusted Income Statements
Amounts for 1974

Company	Adjusted Income before Gain on Monetary Items, as a Percentage of Reported Net Income (1)	Adjusted Net Income, Including Gain on Monetary Items, as a Percentage of Reported Net Income* (2)	Adjusted Earnings Per Share as a Percentage of Reported Earnings Per Share** (3)
Allied Chemical	60	90	90
Alcoa	69	127	132
American Brands	56	110	117
American Can	63	105	110
AT&T	76	189	208
Anaconda	94	110	110
Bethlehem Steel	64	83	83
Chrysler	602†	302†	302†
Du Pont	43	46	52
Eastman Kodak	85	74	74
Esmark	7	60	66
Exxon	85	88	88
General Electric	64	94	94
General Foods	20	67	67
General Motors	-34††	-43††	-42††
Goodyear	1	90	90
International Harvester	-45††	43	43
International Nickel	83	95	95
International Paper	64	81	81
Johns-Manville	84	105	105
Owens-Illinois	68	137	142
Procter & Gamble	83	98	98
Sears	3	-4††	-4††
Standard Oil of California	65	87	87
Texaco	96	104	104
Union Carbide	86	93	93
U.S. Steel	63	79	79
United Technologies (Aircraft)	-4††	25	41
Westinghouse Electric	-334††	-166††	-165††
Woolworth	-68††	68	63
Median	63-64	87	87

*Monetary items are those classified as monetary in FASB Exposure Draft dated December 31, 1974. Deferred taxes and deferred investment tax credits are not included although we believe they should be.

**Strictly speaking, this column shows adjusted net income to common as a percentage of reported net income. For companies with dilutive securities outstanding, percentages below (above) 106 would be slightly increased (decreased) in comparing earnings per share amounts. (106 represents the adjustment factor for one-half year of 1974's price change one plus .057.) A number in this column is equal to the corresponding number in Column 2 when the company has no preferred stock outstanding or when the purchasing power gain for the year on preferred stock outstanding just equals, and offsets, the price level adjusted amount of preferred dividends declared. A number in this column is less than the corresponding number in Column 2 when the price level adjusted amount of preferred dividends is greater than the purchasing power gain on preferred stock.

†Estimated loss as a percentage of reported loss.

††Loss equal to indicated percentage of positive net income.

EXHIBIT 3. THIRTY-FIVE OTHER LARGE COMPANIES

Estimates of General Price Level Adjusted Income Statements
Amounts for 1974

Company	Adjusted Income before Gain on Monetary Items, as a Percentage of Reported Net Income (1)	Adjusted Net Income, Including Gain on Monetary Items, as a Percentage of Reported Net Income* (2)	Adjusted Earnings Per Share as a Percentage of Reported Earnings Per Share** (3)
Anheuser-Busch	69	92	92
Avon	96	94	94
Baxter Labs	42	101	101
Brunswick	12	66	66
Caterpillar	85	122	122
Chemetron	70	91	91
Coca-Cola	101	94	94
Dow Chemical	97	118	118
Ford Motor Company	−108†	7	7
Gould	40	78	80
Gulf Oil	78	83	83
Hilton Hotels	50	165	165
Holiday Inns	78	166	167
Inland Steel	68	96	96
ITT	73	120	123
Koppers	84	108	112
Lehigh Portland Cement	27	29	29
Liggett & Myers	21	88	97
Martin Marietta	71	103	103
Merck	83	83	83
Minnesota Mining and Manufacturing (3M)	67	74	74
Northwest Industries	84	102	110
Pfizer	98	108	108
Philip Morris	39	110	111
Rockwell International	28	92	111
Safeway Stores	48	121	121
Shell Oil	86††	97††	97††
Texas Instruments	79	69	69
Time Inc.	70	79	79
Trans Union	20	207	207
United Airlines (UAL)	25	106	106
Walgreen	66	225	225
Weyerhaeuser	85	118	118
Xerox	78	90	90
Zenith	53	86	86
Median	70	96	97

*See footnote * to Exhibit 2.
**See footnote ** to Exhibit 2.
†Loss equal to 108 percent of positive net income.
††Shell published GPLA Statements in 1975. The numbers shown in this row are calculated from Shell's statements. Shell, however, includes deferred taxes among monetary liabilities. We approve of this treatment, but the FASB does not, at least in its exposure draft. Columns (2) and (3) show 100 percent when deferred taxes are included in monetary items, as was done by Shell in its annual report.

Pronouncements
Governing Generally Accepted Accounting Principles, 1962–1975

Accounting Principles Board Opinions

FASB Statements of Financial Accounting Standards

Note: This list shows pronouncements issued through June 1, 1976.

An Annual Report
for a Company
Approaching Bankruptcy

On June 21, 1970, the Penn Central Company filed a bankruptcy petition for its major subsidiary, the Penn Central Transportation Company. On March 12, 1970, only three months before, the 1969 financial statements of the Penn Central Transportation Company had been issued. The income statement and balance sheet from those statements are shown here. They indicate one important point: analysis of the stockholders' equity section of a balance sheet need not give any indication of impending insolvency or bankruptcy.

Notice that at the end of 1969, Penn Central Transportation Company had retained earnings of almost half a billion dollars which was a part of stockholders' equity of over $1.8 billion. Much of this equity, however, was invested in track and roadbed, assets for which there is no ready market. Penn Central could not dispose of these assets to raise working capital. You can compute that at the end of 1968 and 1969, the Transportation Company had negative working capital; that is, current liabilities (as shown, plus debt due within one year) exceeded current assets. Working capital increased by about $18 million during 1969, but net quick assets—cash and receivables less current liabilities—decreased. The Company was in a less liquid position at the end of the year than at the start.

At the end of 1969, the Transportation Company had over $100 million of debt to repay in the following year. Although the Transportation Company had sufficient "net worth" to show almost half a billion dollars of retained earnings and almost two billion dollars of stockholders' equity, it did not have the funds to meet "only" a few hundred million dollars in current obligations. The company was approaching insolvency by the end of 1969, as can be discerned from these statements. (The declaration of $43 million in dividends during the first three quarters of 1969 under these circumstances seems a questionable step.)

Like Penn Central Transportation Company, many bankrupt firms have positive net assets, or stockholders' equity, on the books at the time of bankruptcy.

Statement of Earnings and Retained Earnings

Current Earnings	*Year ended December 31*	1969	1968
Income	Railway operating revenues...............	**$1,651,978,000**	$1,514,071,000
	Income from rental of properties, net........	**33,772,000**	27,131,000
	Dividends and interest—consolidated subsidiaries..	**66,324,000**	40,155,000
	Dividends and interest—other.............	**2,661,000**	15,451,000
	Net gain on sales of properties and investments....	**12,587,000**	35,437,000
	Income under tax allocation agreements (note 5)...	**21,543,000**	19,038,000
	Total Income	**1,788,865,000**	1,651,283,000
Costs and Expenses	Railway operating expenses, excluding items listed below..	**1,296,397,000**	1,173,761,000
	Depreciation, including depreciation on leased lines (note 3)	**91,279,000**	94,135,000
	Taxes, except Federal income..	**144,059,000**	125,602,000
	Equipment and other rents, net (note 13)....	**183,802,000**	169,292,000
	Interest on debt.	**96,764,000**	68,787,000
	Guaranteed dividends and interest— leased lines.	**26,173,000**	26,315,000
	Miscellaneous, net . ..	**6,719,000**	(1,454,000)
	Total Costs and Expenses	**1,845,193,000**	1,656,438,000
Earnings (Loss)	From ordinary operations (note 13)........	**(56,328,000)**	(5,155,000)
	Extraordinary item (loss on investment in long-haul passenger service facilities) (note 12)..	**(126,000,000)**	—
Net Earnings (Loss)	For the year notes 12 and 13	**(182,328,000)**	(5,155,000)
Retained Earnings	From prior years:		
	As previously reported.	**730,047,000**	788,220,000
	Adjustment note 13	**(8,818,000)**	(6,436,000)
	As adjusted........	**721,229,000**	781,784,000
		538,901,000	776,629,000
	Cash dividends........................	**43,396,000**	55,400,000
	Balance at end of year.....	**$ 495,505,000**	$ 721,229,000

Balance Sheet

Assets	December 31	1969	1968
Current Assets	Cash and temporary cash investments.......	$ 80,331,000	$ 46,915,000
	Accounts receivable and unbilled revenue....	293,181,000	240,211,000
	Material and supplies, etc., at cost.........	104,303,000	88,692,000
	Total Current Assets	477,815,000	375,818,000
Noncurrent Assets	Investments and advances, at cost or less (notes 2 and 7)......................	1,139,038,000	1,217,796,000
	New Haven—net assets acquired, at cost (note 1).............................	—	127,544,000
	Properties (notes 3, 6, 7 and 12)		
	Road, structures, etc....................	2,066,769,000	1,904,536,000
	Revenue equipment (rolling stock).......	1,662,759,000	1,745,448,000
	Other...........	96,051,000	90,541,000
		3,825,579,000	3,740,525,000
	Less accumulated depreciation and losses upon merger.................	902,731,000	992,036,000
	Total Properties—Net	2,922,848,000	2,748,489,000
	Deferred charges and sundry assets....... ...	56,939,000	43,703,000
	Total Assets	$4,596,640,000	$4,513,350,000

Liabilities and Shareholder's Equity

		1969	1968
Current Liabilities*	Notes payable (none to subsidiaries in 1969; $19,420,000 in 1968)...	$ 102,048,000	$ 87,420,000
	Accounts payable and accrued expenses.....	396,407,000	356,519,000
	Total Current Liabilities (excluding debt due within one year)*	498,455,000	443,939,000
Long-Term Debt	Due within one year.........	106,058,000	76,716,000
	Due after one year......................	1,585,585,000	1,407,610,000
	Total Long-Term Debt (note 7)	1,691,643,000	1,484,326,000
Other	Estimated liabilities incurred upon merger (note 6)............................	101,935,000	119,346,000
	Casualty and other claims	90,667,000	81,803,000
	Amounts payable to subsidiary companies...	167,711,000	122,582,000
	Other................................	240,857,000	231,015,000
	Total Other	601,170,000	554,746,000
Shareholder's Equity	Capital stock—$10 par value. Authorized 27,000,000 shares; issued 24,113,703 shares (1968—24,085,329) (note 8).......	241,137,000	240,853,000
	Additional paid-in capital (note 8)..........	1,068,730,000	1,068,257,000
	Retained earnings (note 13)...............	495,505,000	721,229,000
	Total Shareholder's Equity	1,805,372,000	2,030,339,000
	Total Liabilities and Shareholder's Equity	$4,596,640,000	$4,513,350,000

An Annual Report for the U.S. Government

On the following pages we show a set of financial statements for the U.S. Government. The statements are developed from ones presented in *Fortune* magazine, and, as will become apparent, they are based upon *Fortune's* estimates for many items.[1] Estimation is necessary because for the most part the federal government keeps its books on a cash, rather than on an accrual, basis. Even the cash basis data are never presented by the government in the form of articulated, or linked, balance sheet and income statements. Thus, the *Fortune* article is a significant move toward presenting the financial story of this most important institution in the same form that we are accustomed to seeing for corporate annual reports.

In constructing these financial statements, *Fortune* took some needed liberties with generally accepted accounting principles, as they apply to corporations, in order to make the results more meaningful. For example, GAAP generally require that all assets be shown at original acquisition cost. The government owns millions of acres of land that were either secured from the Indians by treaty or conquest, or were acquired many years ago at what now seem to be bargain prices. *Fortune* has decided to show such land, and gold, at estimated current value rather than at a now-meaningless acquisition cost. Consequently, increases in market values of these assets for a year are shown on the income statement as special revenues for the year. These revenues have not been realized in market transactions and, of course, they provide no inflows of funds.

Virtually all the numbers shown in the financial statements are taken, as reported, from the *Fortune* article. We have used slightly different captions for some items and slightly modified the statements for what we feel is a more meaningful presentation. In addition, we comment on certain items in the statements and extract comments from the *Fortune* article that accompanied the statements. The notes are cross-numbered with the items commented on.

Income Statement

1. Revenues are reported on an accrual basis. Thus, for example, tax collections in 1972 relating to collectibles from earlier years are not counted as part of 1972 revenues in the income statement. The government, however, reports receipts as revenues in the year the cash is received.
2. This item represents "Social Security" taxes paid by both employees and employers.
3. The reduction in excise tax revenues in 1972 is caused mainly by the elimination of the excise tax on automobiles.
4. "Other" revenues include items such as fees for passports, patents, copyrights, and stock registrations.
5. Employees of the federal government are given life insurance policies and are promised retirement annuities in addition to their Social Security benefits. Unlike many private corporations, the government does not purchase policies from an insurance company to provide these benefits but, instead, self-insures (see Glossary). *Fortune* counts the estimated liability to current employees for benefits earned during the year as expenses of the year. The debit to expense is matched with a credit to an estimated liability; see note 19.
6. *Fortune* amortized plant assets over varying lives. For example, aircraft are depreciated over eleven years and dams are depreciated over sixty years in these computations. The government's accounting expenses plant assets as funds are disbursed for their acquisition.

[1]"An Annual Report for the Federal Government," *Fortune*, May 1973, pp. 193-99 and pp. 322-23. The article was conceived and written by Carol J. Loomis.

for fiscal years ended June 30, 1972 and 1971	1972	1971
	($ amounts in millions)	
Revenues (1)		
Income taxes		
Individual	$ 94,737	$ 86,230
Corporate	30,250	28,967
Social insurance taxes and contributions (2)	53,914	48,578
Excise taxes (3)	15,477	16,614
Estate and gift taxes, customs duties	8,723	6,326
Sale of timber, power, and other products	885	672
Rents, royalties, and sales of leases	514	1,294
Other (4)	1,117	1,105
Total revenues	$205,617	$189,786
Expenses		
Social security and welfare	$ 64,876	$ 55,712
National defense	60,524	56,478
Health	17,112	14,383
Veterans' benefits and services	11,431	10,340
Commerce and transportation	10,901	11,124
Education and manpower	9,451	8,418
Agriculture and rural development	5,363	5,735
Employee benefits (5)	2,900	2,723
Other operating expenses	7,691	6,619
Depreciation (6)	11,749	11,013
Interest	20,835	19,925
Total expenses	$222,833	$202,470
Operating deficit	$ 17,216	$ 12,684
Less special revenues		
Earnings of Federal Reserve System (7)	$ 3,252	$ 3,533
Seigniorage (8)	581	378
Revaluation of assets (9)		
Gold and monetary items (10)	1,038	—
Land	3,235	3,011
Total special revenues	$ 8,106	$ 6,922
Deficit for year (11)	$ 9,110	$ 5,762

7. The Federal Reserve System holds substantial amounts of government securities. This item represents mainly interest the Fed earns on those securities. It is the net amount after deducting the statutory dividends the Fed must pay to its member banks.
8. The market value of metals in a coin is less than the face value of the coin. When the government mints a coin, the excess of the face amount of the coin over the cost of minting is called *seigniorage*. This excess is a form of revenue to the government.
9. As mentioned above, *Fortune* revalues assets so it must show revenues for the increase in those values during the year.
10. See note 13. The gain is the difference between the "official" government price of $38 an ounce at June 30, 1972, and $35 an ounce at June 30, 1971, times the number of ounces held.
11. The government, using a cash basis, reported a deficit of more than $24.3 billion for 1972. The accrual basis shows a smaller deficit.

June 30, 1972 and 1971	1972	1971
	($ amounts in millions)	
Assets		
Cash	$ 15,473	$ 12,726
Corporate taxes receivable	16,170	17,048
Accounts receivable	4,866	5,260
Materials and supplies	1,538	1,465
Other current assets (12)	3,772	3,700
Total current assets	$ 41,819	$ 40,199
Gold (at official value) (13)	10,410	10,332
Mortgages receivable	9,410	9,513
Loans receivable		
Domestic	38,163	36,418
Foreign	13,602	12,259
Commodities		
Strategic materials	6,657	6,689
Agricultural and other	2,068	2,094
Land (at estimated market value) (14)	94,147	90,912
Plant and equipment		
Military (net of accumulated depreciation of $99,575,000,000 and $89,752,000,000)	132,672	124,248
Nonmilitary (net of accumulated depreciation of $47,026,000,000 and $45,100,000,000)	68,075	65,189
Other (15)	4,536	5,104
Total	$421,559	$402,957

12. "Other current assets" consists mainly of items related to holdings of international currencies—Special Drawing Rights and currency credits with the International Monetary Fund.

13. The prices used to value gold are the "official" government prices, $35 an ounce in 1971 and $38 an ounce in 1972. On June 30, 1972, the free market price of gold was about $90 an ounce so that the amounts shown are conservative. Valued at the $90 price, the June 30, 1972, amount would be over $24 billion, or more than twice the amount shown. (In early 1974, the market price of gold was in excess of $170 an ounce.)

14. The current values attributed to land are *Fortune's* estimates and, according to *Fortune,* are surely conservative. For example, *Fortune* valued off-shore "land" (the continental shelf) at only $32 billion although the revenues produced by this "land" were about $4 billion in 1972. (The oil alone that is known to exist is worth more than $65 billion when valued at 1974 prices.)

15. "Other" noncurrent assets include many things but not the value of items donated to the government, such as Nixon's vice-presidential papers, the Hope Diamond, and Lindbergh's airplane, *The Spirit of St. Louis.*

16. Deposit funds are items such as liabilities to state and local governments for nonfederal income taxes withheld from federal government employees' wages and salaries.

17. Technically, the government has an obligation to redeem coins and currency if presented by the holder to the government. (What one is supposed to get has never been specified; we remember reading of a man who mailed in a ten dollar bill for redemption and was mailed a check for $10.)

18. These represent notes payable to the Federal Reserve System for money received from it. The Fed is authorized to "lend" money to the government in amounts up to the official value of the government's land.

June 30, 1972 and 1971	1972	1971
	($ amounts in millions)	
Liabilities and Net Worth		
Accounts payable	$ 2,834	$ 3,861
Interest payable	2,642	2,389
Deposit funds *(16)*	7,030	5,627
Treasury currency and coin *(17)*	6,508	6,573
Other current liabilities	10,993	6,250
Total current liabilities	$ 30,007	$ 24,700
Gold certificates *(18)*	$ 10,303	$ 10,223
Debt		
Nonmarketable securities		
Savings bonds	$ 55,921	$ 53,003
Other	22,485	14,814
Marketable securities		
Due within one year		
Held by Federal Reserve	40,085	35,117
Held by public	79,509	74,803
Due after one year		
Held by Federal Reserve	31,271	30,401
Held by public	86,470	87,061
Agency issues	8,794	9,911
Total debt	$324,535	$305,110
Estimated liabilities for		
government employee benefits *(19)*		
Life insurance	$ 7,556	$ 7,375
Retirement fund	31,710	28,991
Total liabilities *(20)*	$404,111	$376,399
Net worth *(21)*	17,448	26,558
Total	$421,559	$402,957

19. See note 5. These accounts represent the cumulative, estimated obligations to government employees for life insurance and retirement benefits.

20. One obligation of the government is to pay Social Security benefits to nearly all people (or their survivors) employed in the country when they retire, become disabled, or die. To the extent this obligation has not been funded, one might reasonably judge that it is the government's equivalent of prior service costs in corporate pension accounting. Generally accepted accounting principles do not require that the amount of such obligations be classified as a liability on the balance sheet, but merely that the amount of the obligation be disclosed in the notes. The amount of the unfunded obligation for prior service costs is calculated each year by actuaries in the Department of Health, Education, and Welfare. The amounts were $1,865 billion and $435 billion at the end of fiscal years 1972 and 1971, respectively. (The large increase was caused by a "sweetening" of Social Security benefits authorized by the Congress. At the end of fiscal 1975, the unfunded obligations had present value of about $2.5 trillion.

Generally accepted accounting principles also require that the interest on the unfunded obligations for prior service costs be included in expenses of the period. Under this principle, the government's expenses and deficit for 1972 would be about $100 billion larger than shown on *Fortune's* income statement.

21. Net worth is the equivalent of stockholders' equity. We all are the "stockholders." In this statement, net worth is derived as the plug to equate assets and equities. Ordinarily, of course, stockholders' equity is not only a plug, but the sum of contributed capital and retained earnings accounts.

STATEMENT OF CHANGES IN FINANCIAL POSITION   U.S. GOVERNMENT

for fiscal years ended June 30, 1972 and 1971	1972	1971
	($ amounts in millions)	
Sources of Working Capital		
Deficit for year	$(9,110)	$(5,762)
Add back expenses not using working capital:		
Depreciation	11,749	11,013
Estimated expense for employee benefits *(22)*.	2,900	2,723
Subtract gains not producing working capital:		
Increase in value of assets *(23)*:		
Gold	822	—
Land	3,235	3,011
Total from operations and special revenues	$ 1,482	$ 4,963
Sales of assets, including gold	1,370	432
Addition to debt (net) *(24)*:		
Provided by foreign lenders	17,300	17,900
Provided by domestic lenders	2,205	1,648
Total sources	$22,357	$24,943
Uses of Working Capital		
Loans and mortgages	$ 2,985	$ 2,039
Expenditures for capital assets:		
Plant		
Military.......................................	1,195	811
Nonmilitary	3,482	2,975
Equipment		
Military.......................................	17,282	19,037
Nonmilitary	1,100	1,083
Total uses	$26,044	$25,945
Decrease in working capital for year	$ 3,687	$ 1,002
Analysis of Changes in Working Capital		
Increases (decreases) in current assets:		
Cash	$ 2,747	
Corporate taxes receivable	(878)	
Accounts receivable	(394)	
Materials and supplies	73	
Other current assets	72	
Total increases in current assets	$ 1,620	
Less increases (decreases) in current liabilities:		
Accounts payable	$(1,027)	
Interest payable	253	
Deposit funds	1,403	
Treasury currency and coin	(65)	
Other current liabilities	4,743	
Total increases in current liabilities	$ 5,307	
Decrease in working capital for year	$ 3,687	

22. See notes 5 and 19. The expense for estimated employee benefits used no funds so the amount of the expense must be added back to working capital produced by operations.
23. The special revenues recognized from increases in assets during the year produced no working capital so the amount of these increases must be subtracted from the other sources.
24. Under generally accepted accounting principles, the net amount would not be shown. Rather, the gross amount of proceeds from new debt issues would be shown as a source and the gross disbursements for retiring outstanding issues would be shown as a use. Gain (or loss) on retirement of outstanding issues would be shown as a subtraction (or addition) to working capital from operations as a transaction involving no additional working capital.

AMERICAN ACCOUNTING ASSOCIATION
(Until 1936, The American Association of University Instructors in Accounting)

YEAR	PRESIDENT	DIRECTOR(S) OF RESEARCH
1917	John R. Wildman	
1918	Fayette H. Elwell	
1919	Henry R. Hatfield	
1920	Hiram T. Scovill	
1921	John T. Madden	
1922	William A. Paton	
1923	Charles F. Rittenhouse	
1924	James O. McKinsey	
1925	Roy B. Kester	
1926	Edward J. Filbey	
1927	William S. Krebs	
1928	J. Hugh Jackson	
1929	David Himmelblau	
1930	Arthur H. Rosenkampff	
1931	Russell A. Stevenson	
1932	Howard C. Greer	
1933	George H. Newlove	
1934	James L. Dohr	
1935	Howard S. Noble	
1936	Eric L. Kohler	William A. Paton, A. C. Littleton
1937	Jacob B. Taylor	William A. Paton, A. C. Littleton
1938	Ernest A. Heilman	William A. Paton, A. C. Littleton
1939	Sidney G. Winter	William A. Paton, A. C. Littleton
1940	George A. MacFarland	A. C. Littleton, Herbert F. Taggart
1941	Henry T. Chamberlain	A. C. Littleton, Herbert F. Taggart
1942	Herbert F. Taggart	A. C. Littleton, Frank P. Smith
1943	A. C. Littleton	Frank P. Smith
1944	Carman G. Blough	Robert L. Dixon
1945	Harvey G. Meyer	Robert L. Dixon
1946	Eric L. Kohler	Robert L. Dixon
1947	Hermann C. Miller	Thomas W. Leland
1948	Thomas W. Leland	Paul J. Graber
1949	Robert L. Dixon	Paul J. Graber
1950	Perry Mason	Ralph C. Jones
1951	S. Paul Garner	Ralph C. Jones
1952	George R. Husband	Ralph C. Jones
1953	Russell H. Hassler	Ralph C. Jones
1954	Frank P. Smith	John Arch White
1955	Willard J. Graham	John Arch White
1956	John Arch White	Sidney Davidson
1957	C. A. Moyer	Ralph L. Boyd
1958	C. Rollin Niswonger	Ralph L. Boyd
1959	Martin L. Black, Jr.	A. B. Carson
1960	Charles J. Gaa	Raymond C. Dein
1961	A. B. Carson	Samuel R. Hepworth
1962	Raymond C. Dein	Samuel R. Hepworth
1963	Walter G. Kell	John H. Myers
1964	Glenn A. Welsch	John H. Myers
1965	Robert K. Mautz	Charles T. Horngren
1966*	Herbert E. Miller	Charles T. Horngren
1967	Lawrence L. Vance	Robert K. Jaedicke
1968	Frank S. Kaulback	Robert K. Jaedicke
1969	Sidney Davidson	David Solomons
1970	Norton M. Bedford	David Solomons
1971	James Don Edwards	Hector R. Anton
1972	Charles T. Zlatkovich	Hector R. Anton
1973	Robert T. Sprouse	Robert R. Sterling
1974	Robert N. Anthony	Robert R. Sterling
1975	R. Lee Brummet	K. Fred Skousen
1976	Wilton T. Anderson	K. Fred Skousen

*Starting in September, 1965, terms of office coincide with academic years. For example, Herbert E. Miller's term in office was from September, 1965, through August, 1966.

Shell Oil Company

Supplementary Price Level Adjusted Financial Information

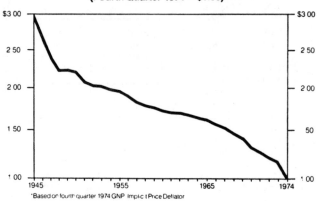

Purchasing Power of the Dollar
(Fourth Quarter 1974 = $1.00)*

*Based on fourth quarter 1974 GNP Implicit Price Deflator

The accelerating decline in the value of the U.S. dollar has focused attention on the inadequacies of traditional measurements of income and wealth. Financial statements prepared under generally accepted accounting principles report the actual number of dollars received or expended without regard to changes in the purchasing power of the currency. Investments made over extended periods of time are added together as though the dollars involved were common units of measurement. Amortization of these prior period costs is deducted from current period revenues in calculations of net income. As shown in the chart above, the dollar's value has changed materially and this change should be considered for a proper assessment of economic progress.

Individual business enterprises are affected differently by inflation. Holders of monetary assets, such as cash or receivables, lose purchasing power during inflationary periods since these assets will purchase fewer goods and services in time. Conversely, holders of liabilities benefit during such periods because less purchasing power will be required to satisfy their obligations. Rates of return and other financial ratios are also influenced greatly by the age of the investments and subsequent changes in the value of the dollar. For example, a capital asset acquired in 1965 for $1 is restated to $1.60 in terms of 1974 dollars in the 1974, 1973 and 1972 supplementary information and depreciation is similarly restated. Such historical financial information adjusted for changes in the purchasing power of the dollar is believed to provide a useful measure of financial performance.

Explanatory Note

The accompanying supplementary price level adjusted financial information, expressed in terms of December 31, 1974 dollars, is based on the historical dollar financial information which is also presented in adjoining columns for comparative purposes. Both the supplementary and historical financial information presented here should be read in conjunction with the notes and other financial statement information in the Annual Report. The supplementary price level information reflects adjustments only for changes that have occurred in the general purchasing power of the dollar as measured by the Gross National Product Implicit Price Deflator. The amounts shown, therefore, do not purport to represent appraised value, replacement cost, or any other measure of the current value of assets. The Accounting Principles Board Statement No. 3 and a Proposed Statement of Financial Accounting Standards, which give general guidance on how to prepare and present price level financial statements, reflect deferred income taxes as nonmonetary items. For purposes of Shell's general price level restatement, such balances were classified as monetary items because Shell believes that when reversals of such tax differences take place, they give rise immediately to taxable income and to additional taxes payable in current dollars at that time. Had Shell followed the nonmonetary treatment for deferred income taxes, restated net income would have been $23.5, $12.5, and $1.2 million less in 1974, 1973 and 1972 and restated shareholders' equity would have been $102.1, $78.6 and $66.1 million less for these years.

See page 91 for authors' comments on this information.

(Millions of dollars except per share amounts)	CURRENT DOLLARS*			HISTORICAL DOLLARS		
	1974	1973	1972	1974	1973	1972
Summary Statement of Income						
Revenues	$8,866.7	$6,614.4	$5,876.1	$8,493.0	$5,749.6	$4,849.8
Costs and expenses:						
Depreciation, depletion, etc.	654.2	626.5	585.4	502.9	441.7	396.8
Income, operating and consumer taxes	1,320.2	1,236.2	1,163.6	1,264.5	1,074.6	960.4
Interest & discount amortization on						
indebtedness	63.5	69.9	72.0	60.8	60.8	59.4
Other costs & expenses	6,317.3	4,426.2	3,866.1	6,044.3	3,839.8	3,172.7
Income before purchasing power gain						
or loss on monetary items	$ 511.5	$ 255.6	$ 189.0	$ 620.5	$ 332.7	$ 260.5
Purchasing power gain (loss) on:						
Long term debt	117.0	82.9	36.4	—	—	—
Other monetary items	(5.1)	(4.8)	2.2	—	—	—
Net income	$ 623.4	$ 333.7	$ 227.6	$ 620.5	$ 332.7	$ 260.5
Summary Balance Sheet						
Current assets	$2,161.7	$1,953.4	$1,925.2	$2,072.2	$1,713.1	$1,596.1
Investments & long term receivables	129.5	110.3	106.1	116.0	91.7	84.1
Properties, plant & equipment (net)	5,146.6	4,906.7	4,923.3	3,905.3	3,526.9	3,438.9
Deferred charges	42.3	61.4	67.5	35.4	49.5	52.5
Current liabilities	1,272.6	1,097.4	1,113.4	1,272.6	981.6	928.2
Long term debt	976.6	1,119.0	1,230.3	976.6	1,000.9	1,025.6
Deferred credits—federal income taxes	320.0	339.5	351.4	320.0	303.6	292.8
Shareholders' equity	$4,910.9	$4,475.9	$4,327.0	$3,559.7	$3,095.1	$2.925.0
Per Share Data†						
Net income	$ 9.25	$ 4.95	$ 3.38	$ 9.21	$ 4.94	$ 3.86
Cash dividends	$ 2.56	$ 2.76	$ 2.91	$ 2.45	$ 2.40	$ 2.40
Ratios						
Return on shareholders' equity	13.9%	7.7%	5.3%	20.0%	11.4%	9.2%
Return on total capital	11.7%	6.6%	5.0%	16.0%	9.2%	8.0%
Net income: revenues**	7.7°∘	5.9°∘	4.6°∘	8.1%	6.7°∘	6.3°∘
Dividends: net income	27.7%	55.7%	86.1°∘	26.6%	48.6%	62.1°∘
Debt: total capital	16.6%	20.0°∘	22.1°∘	21.5%	24.4%	26.0°∘

*Based on purchasing power dollars at December 31, 1974.
†Per weighted average share outstanding each year.
**Excluding consumer excise and sales taxes.

REPORT OF INDEPENDENT ACCOUNTANTS

To the Board of Directors and Shareholders of Shell Oil Company:

We have examined the financial statements of Shell Oil Company appearing in the Annual Reports to Shareholders for the years 1974, 1973 and 1972, which are covered by our reports dated February 4, 1975 and February 4, 1974. Those financial statements do not reflect the changes in the general purchasing power of the U.S. dollar from the time transactions took place. We have also examined the supplementary information for the years 1974, 1973 and 1972 restated for effects of changes in the general price level as described in the Explanatory Note on page 4. In our opinion, the supplementary Summary Statement of Income, Summary Balance Sheet and Per Share Data shown above present fairly the historical financial information restated in terms of the general purchasing power of the U.S. dollar at December 31, 1974 in accordance with guidelines, consistently applied, recommended in Accounting Principles Board Statement No. 3 and a Proposed Statement of Financial Accounting Standards, except for the treatment, with which we concur, of deferred income taxes as monetary items.

1200 Milam Street
Houston, Texas 77002
February 4, 1975

Price Waterhouse & Co.

1974
Annual Report

(Excerpts)

Statement of Income

$ in thousands	Year Ended January 31	
	1975	1974*
Net sales (including finance charge revenues—note 8)............	$13,101,210	$12,306,229
Cost of sales, buying and occupancy expenses..................	8,293,810	7,664,123
Selling and administrative expenses...........................	3,733,549	3,401,594
	12,027,359	11,065,717
Operating income from sales and services.....................	1,073,851	1,240,512
Equity in income of (note 1)		
Allstate Group		
Insurance companies		
In the absence of operating or investment reasons compelling liquidation, it is inappropriate to reflect in income temporary fluctuations in market values of long-term equity investments. Consequently, investment results exclude unrealized market decreases in equity investments of $422,125 and $258,667.		
Underwriting and investment income......................	156,024	172,723
Realized capital gains...................................	10,830	26,146
Allstate Enterprises, Inc....................................	536	4,421
	167,390	203,290
Other unconsolidated subsidiaries and affiliates................	21,503	41,533
Other companies (dividends)................................	1,977	1,869
	190,870	246,692
Operating income and equity in income of unconsolidated companies	1,264,721	1,487,204
General expenses		
Interest (less capitalization of $19,570 and $23,113)..............	361,347	253,587
Contribution to Employes' Profit Sharing Fund	87,783	119,891
Income taxes (note 2).....................................	304,200	433,500
	753,330	806,978
Net income..	$ 511,391	$ 680,226
Per share (average shares 157,473 and 157,151)	$3.25	$4.33

* **Authors' Comments.** Allstate and Sears, in accord with generally accepted accounting principles, do not recognize in income unrealized holding gains or losses in Allstate's investment portfolio. Note that if Allstate's investments were shown at market value, rather than at cost, net income for 1974 would have been about $422 (= $469 − $47) million smaller, ignoring income tax effects. Note, too, the large amount, $782 million, of "current liability" for deferred income taxes. This current liability for deferred taxes and the $108 million of noncurrent liability for deferred income taxes will, in all likelihood, never become payable. (Sears' management believes that these taxes will not become payable "in the forseeable future;" see Sears' note 2 on the next page.) If generally accepted accounting principles did not require comprehensive income tax allocation, then Sears' 1974 reported income would be almost $100 million larger (see note 2) and shareholders' equity would be about $890 (= $782 + $108) million larger. If we were analyzing Sears' financial statements, we would not count the current year's portion of deferred taxes ($98 million) in expenses and we would reclassify the deferred tax items on the balance sheet ($890 million) as shareholders' equity. The Statement of Financial Position (balance sheet) below is remarkable in that no indication of balance is shown. It would be customary to add together the Total Liabilities ($6.1 billion) and the Shareholders' Equity ($5.2 billion) to show the equality with Total Assets ($11.3 billion).

Statement of Financial Position

$ in thousands	January 31	
	1975	1974*
Assets		
Current Assets		
Cash..........	$ 192,015	$ 198,085
Receivables...............	4,979,355	4,615,245
Inventories.............	1,979,280	1,879,101
Prepaid advertising and other charges........	97,827	79,277
Total Current Assets	7,248,477	6,771,708
Investments (note 1)		
Allstate Insurance Company (cost $54,600; carrying value excludes		
* unrealized decreases of $469,455 and $47,330 between cost and		
market of equity investments)	1,308,416	1,141,562
Other investments and advances	542,898	531,544
	1,851,314	1,673,106
Property, Plant and Equipment	2,223,930	1,978,194
Deferred Charges	15,689	7,625
Total Assets	$11,339,410	$10,430,633
Liabilities		
Current Liabilities		
Short-term borrowings (note 9)		
Commercial paper.........	$ 2,300,742	$ 1,909,041
Banks	227,181	170,991
Agreements with bank trust departments	539,615	429,795
Accounts payable and accrued expenses........	843,216	959,339
Unearned maintenance agreement income........	203,240	192,822
* Deferred income taxes........	781,620	731,137
Total Current Liabilities.........	4,895,614	4,393,125
* Deferred Income Taxes	107,570	60,471
Long-Term Debt	1,095,120	980,496
Total Liabilities	$ 6,098,304	$ 5,434,092
Shareholders' Equity........	$ 5,241,106	$ 4,996,541

Notes
(Excerpts)

1. Financial information of principal unconsolidated subsidiaries and affiliates

The financial statements of Allstate Insurance Company and consolidated subsidiaries and condensed financial statements of Allstate Enterprises, Inc., Homart Development Co. and Simpsons-Sears Limited are included in this annual report.

Common and preferred stock investments of Allstate are carried in its Statement of Financial Position at quoted market values, a generally accepted accounting practice in the insurance industry. In the absence of operating or investment reasons compelling liquidation, it is inappropriate to reflect in income temporary fluctuations in market values of long-term equity investments. Consequently, investment results exclude such market increases and decreases in the Statement of Income of Allstate as well as the Consolidated Statements of Financial Position and Income of Sears.

The excess of cost over market of these equity investments of $469 million at December 31, 1974, decreased to approximately $291 million at March 28, 1975. During this period there has been a net decrease of investments in equity securities amounting to approximately $130 million with no significant effect on income.

Six of the unconsolidated manufacturing subsidiaries and affiliates of Sears changed in 1974 to the LIFO inventory method, decreasing Sears equity in their net income by $7.6 million.

2. Income taxes

Federal and state income taxes consist of:

(millions)	Year Ended January 31	
	1975	1974
Current portion (before investment tax credit)...	$218	$346
Investment tax credit (flow-through method)	(12)	(13)
Deferred tax expense—		
Current		
Installment sales.....	58	83
Receivable reserves..	(1)	(12)
Maintenance agreement income......	(5)	(11)
Other	(1)	(9)
Long-term		
Depreciation	32	30
Carrying costs of property	12	14
Other..............	3	5
Total deferred......	98	100
Financial statement income tax provision ...	$304	$433

Because of expected future income tax deferrals, it is not expected that tax payments will exceed the tax expense shown in the financial statements in the foreseeable future. The financial statement tax expense for 1974 and 1973 includes state income tax expense of $30 million ($13 million deferred) and $50 million ($16 million deferred), respectively. A reconciliation of effective rates, based upon income before taxes and equity in income of unconsolidated subsidiaries, with the statutory federal tax rate is:

	Year Ended January 31	
	1975	1974
Statutory federal income tax rate.....................	48.0%	48.0%
State income taxes, net of federal income taxes......	2.5	3.0
Investment tax credit (flow-through method).....	(1.9)	(1.5)
Miscellaneous items........	.1	.5
Effective income tax rate....	48.7%	50.0%

3. Acquisition

On March 18, 1974, Sears issued 64,485 shares of common stock for the assets and business of Chico Savings and Loan Association. This business subsequently became a subsidiary of Allstate Enterprises, Inc. The acquisition has been accounted for as a pooling of interests, and the financial statements of Sears and its wholly owned financial services subsidiary, Allstate Enterprises, Inc., have been restated to reflect this acquisition.

Accordingly, the investment in Allstate Enterprises, Inc. and shareholders' equity at February 1, 1973, have been increased $2,878,000 and net income for the year ended January 31, 1974, has been increased $324,000.

4. Long-term debt

The indentures provide that the company cannot take certain actions, including the declaration of cash dividends, which would cause its unencumbered assets to drop below 150 per cent of liabilities. The excess unencumbered assets at January 31, 1975, were $491 million.

Aggregate long-term debt maturities, including minimum sinking fund payments (excludes $338 million of 7.46% notes which have no specified maturity) through January 31, 1980 are:

Year Ended January 31

1977.................................	$145
1978.................................	49
1979.................................	24
1980.................................	25

In March 1975, Sears issued $250 million in principal amount of 7¾% debentures due 1985.

5. Supplemental pension plan

This noncontributory plan provides pension benefits to salaried employes based upon length of service and remuneration over $15,000 per year. For fiscal years 1974 and 1973, the company provided $22,994,000 and $18,917,000, respectively, for this plan.

At December 31, 1974, the actuarially computed value of vested benefits was $115,000,000 in excess of the market value of the plan's assets.

Effective October 1, 1974, the plan was changed to provide full vesting after 10 years' employment. Although this change did not have a significant effect on the plan's annual cost, it increased the amount of vested benefits. The decline in the market value of plan investments was also a contributing factor in the change from the prior year's position.

The actuarially computed unfunded past service costs of $48,733,000 are being amortized over 40 years.

6. Employe stock options

Options under Sears plans are granted at the fair market value on the date of the grant. Generally options become exercisable in four annual and cumulative installments beginning one year after the date of grant and expire 10 years after the date of grant.

In October 1974, options for 3,077,288 shares, at a price range of $85.94 to $89.82 per share, were cancelled at the election of the optionees.

On January 22, 1975, options for 3,489,070 shares were granted to 15,727 employes at $52.19 per share.

Outstanding options at year end ranged in price from $52.19 to $116.44 per share, aggregating $187,820,000. At January 31, 1975, 51,392 shares were exercisable and 1,522,572 shares were available for future grants under the 1967 and 1972 Employe Stock Plans.

A summary of option shares outstanding is:

(thousands of shares)	Year Ended January 31	
	1975	1974
Beginning balance.........	3,211	3,076
Cancelled.................	(3,147)	(2,489)
Granted...................	3,489	2,629
Exercised.................	—	(5)
Ending balance.	3,553	3,211

7. Leases

Rental payments are based upon contractual minimum rates and, for certain retail stores, amounts in excess of these minimum rates are payable based upon specified percentages of sales. Certain of the leases include renewal or purchase provisions at the company's option. Minimum fixed rentals exclusive of taxes, insurance and other expenses payable directly by the company under leases (over one year)

in effect as of January 31, 1975 are:

(millions)

1975—$76*	1980–1984—$200
1976—$70*	1985–1989—$142
1977—$57*	1990–1994—$ 94
1978—$50*	after 1994—$102
1979—$46	

*Includes computer rentals of $16, $12, $2 and $1 million, respectively

The present value (interest rates range from 3.4% to 8.5% with a 6.3% weighted average interest rate) of all future contractual minimum rental payments on the above leases (all presented on a net lease basis) as of January 31, 1975, is $426 million.

If financing leases, as defined by the Securities and Exchange Commission, had been recorded as long-term debt and the related property rights depreciated under the straight-line method, net income for the year ended January 31, 1975, would have been decreased by $1.9 million. The present value of these financing leases (5.8% weighted average interest rate) at January 31, 1975, is $352 million.

Authors' Comments on Notes.

Note 1. See our comments on page 107.
Note 2. See our comments on page 107. $58 million of the current deferred income tax expense in 1974 arises because Sears uses the sales basis of revenue recognition for credit sales on financial statements, but the cash collection (installment) basis for tax returns. So long as Sears' credit sales continue to grow, income taxes payable will probably not exceed income tax expense.
Note 3. During March 1974, the market price of Sears' stock was more than $80 per share. Thus Sears gave up consideration of over $5 million (= $80 per share × 64,485 shares) for Chico Savings and Loan. Under pooling-of-interests accounting, Sears' books reflect this acquisition at a cost of less than $3 million. If the acquisition had been accounted for as a purchase, as we think nearly all corporate acquisitions should be, then the full $5 million of cost would be reflected in Sears' accounts.
Note 4. Long-term debt due within one year is a part of current liabilities. This note, showing maturities of debt during the next 4 years, is designed to help analysts appraise intermediate-term liquidity.
Note 5. See the Glossary for definitions of *noncontributory*, *vested*, *unfunded*, and *past service costs*.
Note 6. This disclosure parallels General Electric's. See the GE report at our note 82, page 85 of this book.
Note 7. The disclosure in the first two paragraphs conforms to the requirements of APB Opinion No. 31 and in the last paragraph, to SEC requirements. The SEC requires disclosure of the effect on net income of capitalizing financing leases if the effect is material. Sears tells us that net income would decline by $1.9 million in 1974 if financing leases were capitalized. This reduction is probably not material, so the disclosure is probably not required.

Consolidated Financial Position at December 31
(Millions of dollars)

	1974	1973
Current assets:		
Stated on basis of realizable values:		
Cash	$ 75.4	$ 43.0
Short-term investments	4.9	4.1
Receivable from customers and others (note 6)	488.8	343.6
Prepaid expenses and income taxes allocable to the following year	86.6	53.5
	655.7	444.2
Stated on basis of cost using principally "last-in, first-out" method:		
Inventories (note 1C)	1,061.8	818.3
	1,717.5	1,262.5
Deduct: Current liabilities:		
Notes payable	203.8	161.7
Payable to material suppliers and others	532.0	356.2
Taxes based on income	57.3	73.2
Long-term debt due within one year	21.5	.8
	814.6	591.9
Net current assets (statement 3)	902.9	670.6
Buildings, machinery and equipment—net (note 1D)	1,076.5	859.3
Land—at original cost	33.8	28.8
Investments in affiliated companies (notes 1A and 3)	53.7	49.3
Investments in and advances to subsidiary credit companies (note 1A)	23.7	23.0
Deferred taxes based on income	9.3	6.1
Other assets	19.5	9.9
Total assets less current liabilities	2,119.4	1,647.0
Deduct: Long-term debt due after one year (note 7)	655.9	320.2
Net assets	$1,463.5	$1,326.8
Ownership (statement 4):		
Preferred stock of no par value (note 8):		
Authorized shares: 5,000,000		
Outstanding shares: none		
Common stock of no par value (note 9):		
Authorized shares: 70,000,000		
Outstanding shares: 1974—57,207,039; 1973—57,173,306	$ 150.1	$ 148.3
Profit employed in the business (note 7)	1,313.4	1,178.5
	$1,463.5	$1,326.8

Authors' Comments. Caterpillar's balance sheet is slightly unusual. Not many companies (U.S. Steel is another) show current assets less current liabilities as working capital directly on the balance sheet. Then come the noncurrent assets less long-term debt. The total of working capital plus noncurrent assets less long-term debt is shown as net assets. The balance sheet shows the equality of these net assets and the total ownership, or stockholders' equity. Caterpillar, unique among major U.S. corporations we know of, discloses the causes of all changes in ownership amounts since the company was incorporated more than 50 years ago. These changes are shown in Statement 4, Source of Consolidated Net Assets, which is reproduced next. This statement makes clear the fact that ownership is always independently derived in double-entry record keeping and is not merely a residual or plug.